Volume A

FUNDAMENTALS OF
ENGLISH
GRAMMAR
Second Edition

Volume A

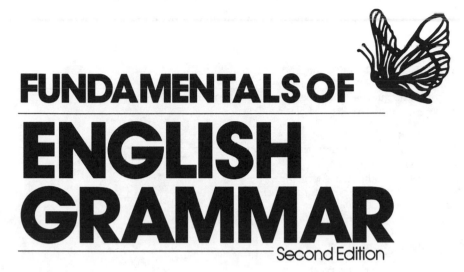

FUNDAMENTALS OF
ENGLISH
GRAMMAR
Second Edition

Betty Schrampfer Azar

Longman

Library of Congress Cataloging-in-Publication Data

Azar, Betty Schrampfer, 1941–
    Fundamentals of English grammar / Betty Schrampfer Azar. — 2nd
ed.
      p. cm.
    Includes index.
    ISBN 0-13-327552-3 (v. A : pbk.)
    ISBN 0-13-347139-X (v. B : pbk.)
    1. English language—Textbooks for foreign speakers. 2. English
language—Grammar—1950– I. Title.
PE1128.A965 1992b   92-7657
428.2′4—dc20   CIP

Publisher: *Tina B. Carver*
Managing editor, production: *Sylvia Moore*
Editorial/production supervision: *Janet Johnston*
Prepress buyer: *Ray Keating*
Manufacturing buyer: *Lori Bulwin*
Scheduler: *Leslie Coward*
Illustrations: *Don Martinetti*
Cover supervisor: *Karen Salzbach*
Cover designer: *Joel Mitnick Design*
Interior designer: *Ros Herion Freese*
Page makeup: *Mary Fitzgerald*

© **1992 by Prentice Hall Regents**
A Pearson Education Company
Pearson Education, 10 Bank Street, White Plains, NY 10606

Printed in the United States of America

20 19 18 17 16 15 14

ISBN 0-13-338278-8

ISBN 0-13-327552-3 {VOL.A}

ISBN 0-13-347139-X {VOL.B}

To my sister,
JO

Contents

Preface to the Second Edition

Fundamentals of English Grammar remains a developmental skills text for mid-level students of English as a second or foreign language. It focuses on key structures and provides ample opportunities for practice through extensive and varied exercises. While focusing on grammar, it promotes the development of all language skills.

The chief difference in the second edition of *Fundamentals of English Grammar* is the inclusion of additional grammar areas that are important at the intermediate level. The principal additions deal with personal pronouns; forms of *other*; connecting ideas with coordinating and subordinating conjunctions, including the use of commas and periods; and comparisons. Other short units have also been included: for example, the use of *must* to make logical conclusions; expressing immediate future with *be about to*; nonspecific vs. specific pronouns (e.g., *May I have one* vs. *May I have it*); uncompleted infinitives; and using a gerund after a preposition. This edition seeks to fill in gaps in an intermediate grammar syllabus. Not every class will cover every unit, but the second edition makes a broad table of contents available. Other changes in the second edition are directed toward clarifying the structure presentations in the charts and improving the exercises.

Another significant difference in the second edition lies in the support material: a workbook and a teacher's guide.

The workbook provides independent study opportunities in the form of Selfstudy Practices (with the answers given). It also provides Guided Study Practices (no answers given) for additional classwork, homework, and individualized instruction as the teacher sees the need.

The teacher's guide contains presentation suggestions; specific techniques for handling the varied types of exercises; background grammar notes; item notes on cultural content, vocabulary, and structure usage; problems to anticipate; suggestions for oral and written student-centered activities; and answers to the exercises.

Acknowledgments

Many people have parts in the work I do as a writer. They make my work possible and enjoyable.

I wish especially to thank Donald Azar, Tina Carver, Barbara Matthies, and Janet Johnston.

In addition, I wish to thank Joy Edwards, R. T. Steltz, Susan Abbott, Jonni Reed, Ralph Hastings, Gordon Adams, Frank Sullivan, Sylvia Moore, Andy Martin, Efrain Rojas, Gil Muller, Noel Carter, Dennis Hogan, Anne Riddick, Mary Vaughn, Don Martinetti, Gordon Johnson, Rick Spencer, Eric Bredenberg, Ed Stanford, Rick Essig, Jack Ross, David Haines, Sally Howard, Ray Keating, Ed Perez, Roger Olsen, Judy Winn-Bell Olsen, Martin Tenney, Wayne Spohr, Norman Harris, Terry Jennings, Jerry Smith, Bruce Kennan, Connie Hernandez, Amelia Azar, and Chelsea Parker.

Special appreciation is due the seven reviewers who marked up copies of the first edition to guide the revisions: Gari Browning, Arline Burgmeier, Linda Misja, Larry Robinson, Luis Sanchez, Grace Tanaka, and Cheryl Youtsey. Their insights were invaluable.

Last, I want to thank my amazing parents. Both are retired educators in their late 80s. My father wrote reams of ideas for exercise entries, for this revision and for the workbook. My mother input the entire text of the first edition so that I had it available for revision on disk. How can I thank them enough? Maybe by saying it in print—Thanks, Mom and Dad. Thank you very, very much.

Volume A

FUNDAMENTALS OF
ENGLISH
GRAMMAR

Second Edition

CHAPTER *1*
Present Time

☐ **EXERCISE 1—ORAL:** Pair up with another student in the class. Interview each other. Then introduce each other to the rest of the class. In your conversation with the other person, find out this person's *name, native country, residence, field of study or place of work, and free-time activities or hobbies.* Take notes during the interview.

   1. Below is an example of a possible conversation.

   A. Hi. My name is Kunio.

   B: Hi. My name is Maria. I'm glad to meet you.

   KUNIO: I'm glad to meet you, too. Where are you from?

   MARIA: I'm from Mexico. Where are you from?

   KUNIO: I'm from Japan.

   MARIA: Where are you living now?

   KUNIO: On Fifth Avenue in an apartment. And you?

   MARIA: I'm living in a dorm.

   KUNIO: What is your field of study?

   MARIA: Business. After I study English, I'm going to attend the School of Business Administration. How about you? What's your major?

   KUNIO: Chemistry.

   MARIA: What do you like to do in your free time? Do you have any hobbies?

   KUNIO: I like to swim. How about you?

   MARIA: I read a lot, and I collect stamps from all over the world.

   KUNIO: Really? Would you like some stamps from Japan?

   MARIA: Sure! That would be great. Thanks.

KUNIO: I have to write your full name on the board when I introduce you to the class. How do you spell your name?

MARIA: My first name is Maria; M-A-R-I-A. My last name is Lopez.

KUNIO: My first name is Kunio: K-U-N-I-O. My family name is Akiwa.

MARIA: Kunio Akiwa. Is that right?

KUNIO: Yes, it is. It's been nice talking with you.

MARIA: I enjoyed it, too.

2. Later Kunio stands up, writes Maria's full name on the board, and says:

I would like to introduce you to Maria Lopez. Maria, would you please stand up? Thank you. Maria is from Mexico. She's living in a dorm. Her field of study is business administration. She likes to read a lot, and her hobby is collecting stamps from all over the world.

3. Next, Maria introduces Kunio to the class. What is Maria going to say?

I would like to introduce you to Kunio Akiwa. Kunio, would you please stand up? Thank you. Kunio is from Japan. She's living on fifth Avenue in an apartment. Her field of study is chemistry. She likes to swim. (Her hobby is swimming)

4. Write the names of your classmates in your book as they are introduced in class.

1-1 THE SIMPLE PRESENT AND THE PRESENT PROGRESSIVE

THE SIMPLE PRESENT	(a) Ann **takes** a shower every day. (b) I usually **eat** lunch at the cafeteria. (c) Babies **cry**. (d) The earth **revolves** around the sun. (e) A square **has** four equal sides. (f) The sky **is** blue.	The simple present expresses *daily habits* or *usual activities*, as in (a) and (b). The simple present expresses *general statements of fact*, as in (c) and (d). In sum, the simple present is used for events or situations that exist always, usually, or habitually in the past, present, and future.
THE PRESENT PROGRESSIVE	(g) Ann can't come to the phone right now because she **is taking** a shower. (h) It's noon. I **am eating** lunch at the cafeteria right now. (i) Jimmy and Susie are babies. They **are crying**. I can hear them right now. Maybe they are hungry.	The present progressive expresses *an activity that is in progress (is occurring, is happening) right now*. The event is in progress at the time the speaker is saying the sentence. The event began in the past, is in progress now, and will probably continue into the future. FORM: *am, is, are* + *-ing*.

1-2 FORMS OF THE SIMPLE PRESENT AND PRESENT PROGRESSIVE

	SIMPLE PRESENT	PRESENT PROGRESSIVE
STATEMENT:	{I-You-We-They} **work**. {He-She-It} **works**.	I **am working**.* {You-We-They} **are working**. {He-She-It} **is working**.
NEGATIVE:	{I-You-We-They} **do not work**.** {He-She-It} **does not work**.	I **am not working**. {You-We-They} **are not working**.** {He-She-It} **is not working**.
QUESTION:	**Do** {I-you-we-they} **work**? **Does** {he-she-it} **work**?	**Am** I **working**? **Are** {you-we-they} **working**? **Is** {he-she-it} **working**?

* Contractions of pronouns with **be**: *I'm, you're, we're, they're, he's, she's, it's.*

** Contractions of verbs with **not**: *don't, doesn't, aren't, isn't.* (Note: *am* and *not* are not contracted.)

□ **EXERCISE 2:** Complete the sentences by using the words in parentheses. Use the SIMPLE PRESENT or the PRESENT PROGRESSIVE.

1. Shhh. The baby (*sleep*) _____**is sleeping**_____ . The baby
   (*sleep*) _____**sleeps**_____ for ten hours every night.

2. Right now I'm in class. I (*sit*) __*am sitting*__ at my desk. I
   usually (*sit*) __*sit*__ at the same desk in class every day.

3. Ali (*speak*) __*speaks*__ Arabic. Arabic is his native
   language, but right now he (*speak*) __*is speaking*__ English.

4. Our teacher (*stand, not*) __*is not standing*__ up right now. She
   (*sit*) __*sits*__ on the corner of her desk.

5. It's 6:00 P.M. Mary is at home. She (*eat*) __*is eating*__
   dinner. She always (*eat*) __*eats*__ dinner with her
   family around six o'clock.

6. It (*rain, not*) __*isn't raining*__ right now. The sun (*shine*)
   __*shines*__ , and the sky (*be*) __*is*__ blue.

7. (*Rain, it*) __*Does it rain*__ a lot in southern California?

8. Look out the window. (*Rain, it*) __*Is it raining*__ ?
   Should I take my umbrella?

9. It's 7:30 A.M. and the Wilsons are in their kitchen. Mrs. Wilson (*sit*) __*is*__
   __*sitting*__ at the breakfast table. She (*read*) __*is reading*__

the morning paper. She (*read*) ___reads___ the newspaper every morning. Mr. Wilson (*pour*) ___is pouring___ a cup of coffee. He (*drink*) ___drinks___ two cups of coffee every morning before he (*go*) ___goes___ to work. There is a cartoon on TV, but the children (*watch, not*) ___aren't watching___ it. They (*play*) ___are playing___ with their toys instead. They usually (*watch*) ___watch___ cartoons in the morning, but this morning they (*pay, not*) ___are not paying___ any attention to the TV. Mr. and Mrs. Wilson (*watch, not*) ___are not watching___ the TV either. They (*like, not*) ___don't like___ to watch cartoons.

10. Alice (*take, not*) ___doesn't take___ the bus to school every day. She usually (*walk*) ___walks___ instead. (*Take, you*) ___Do you take___ the bus to get to school every day, or (*walk, you*) ___do you walk___ ?

□ **EXERCISE 3—ORAL (BOOKS CLOSED):** STUDENT A: Perform an action.
STUDENT B: Describe the action, using STUDENT A's name and the present progressive.

Example: stand next to your desk
STUDENT A: (Student A stands up.)
TEACHER: Who is standing next to her desk? OR: What is (Maria) doing?
STUDENT B: (Maria) is standing next to her desk.

1. stand up
2. smile
3. whistle
4. open or close the door
5. hum
6. bite your fingernails
7. read your grammar book
8. erase the board
9. look at the ceiling
10. hold your pen in your left hand
11. rub your palms together
12. kick your desk (softly)
13. knock on the door
14. sit on the floor
15. shake hands with someone
16. look at your watch
17. count aloud the number of people in the room
18. shake your head "no"
19. scratch your head
20. Perform any action you choose. Use objects in the classroom if you wish.

□ **EXERCISE 4—ORAL:** Describe *your* daily activities by making sentences with frequency adverbs and the SIMPLE PRESENT. Put the frequency adverb between the subject and the simple present verb.

FREQUENCY ADVERBS: (From 100% of the time to 0% of the time.)*

100% always
usually
often
sometimes
seldom
rarely
0% never

Example: eat breakfast
Response: STUDENT A: I usually eat breakfast.
STUDENT B: I never eat breakfast.
STUDENT C: (Student A) usually eats breakfast. (Student B) never eats breakfast.

1. drink coffee in the morning
2. put sugar in my coffee
3. drink more than two cups of coffee in the morning
4. drink tea in the morning
5. drink orange juice in the morning
6. drink tomato juice in the morning
7. drink milk two times a day
8. have a sandwich for lunch
9. eat dinner around six o'clock
10. come to class
11. get to class on time
12. walk to school
13. take a bus to school
14. take a taxi to school
15. drive to school
16. ride a bike to school
17. watch TV in the evening
18. study in the library
19. do my homework

□ **EXERCISE 5—ORAL (BOOKS CLOSED):** Practice using the SIMPLE PRESENT. Beginning with the time you get up until the time you go to bed, discuss your daily activities. Your teacher will develop and complete a brief conversation with STUDENT A, and then ask STUDENT B to tell the class about STUDENT A. STUDENT B should say each final *-s* loudly and clearly.

Example: from 6:00 A.M. to 9:00 A.M.

TEACHER (to STUDENT A): Tell us about your daily activities from the time you get up until 9:00 A.M. What are some of the things you usually do?

---

* See Chart 7-8, MIDSENTENCE ADVERBS, for more information about frequency adverbs.

STUDENT A: I get up at seven.
T: Always?
A: Usually. I put on my clothes. I eat breakfast.
T: Do you always eat breakfast?
A: Yes.
T: What do you usually have for breakfast?
A: Bread and cheese and coffee. Sometimes I have an egg.
T: Do you ever have cereal for breakfast?
A: No, I don't.
TEACHER (to STUDENT B): Can you tell us about (. . .)? What does he/she usually do in the morning?
STUDENT B: He/She usually gets up at seven. He/She eats breakfast.
T: Always?
B: Yes. He/She always eats breakfast. He/She usually has bread and cheese and coffee for breakfast, but sometimes he/she has an egg. He/She never has cereal for breakfast.

1. from 6:00 A.M. to 9:00 A.M.
2. from 9:00 A.M. to noon
3. from noon to 3:00 P.M.
4. from 3:00 P.M. to 6:00 P.M.
5. from 6:00 P.M. until you go to bed

▽ □ **EXERCISE 6—ORAL (BOOKS CLOSED):** Answer the questions. Use frequency adverbs.

Example: take a bus to school
How often do you take a bus to school?
Response: I usually take the bus. OR: I never take the bus. OR: I always take the bus. (etc.)

PART I: How often do you . . . ?
1. sleep past noon
2. wear a hat to school
3. wash dishes after dinner
4. eat fish for dinner
5. go to (*a particular place in this city*) on weekends
6. drink (*a particular beverage*)
7. speak (*your native language*) instead of English when you're with your friends
8. go swimming before you come to class in the morning
9. watch TV before you come to school in the morning
10. listen to the radio in the evening

PART II: What are some things you always/usually/often/sometimes/seldom/
rarely/never do . . . ?

1. when you eat dinner
2. when you get ready to go to bed at night
3. when you travel abroad
4. when you meet a new person
5. when you're on vacation
6. in this classroom

PART III: What are some things people in your country always/usually/often/
sometimes/seldom/rarely/never do . . . ?

1. at the dinner table
2. at a wedding
3. when a child misbehaves
4. when they have a cold
5. to celebrate their birthdays
6. when they want to have fun

1-3 SPELLING: FINAL -*S* vs. -*ES*

(a) visit → visit**s** answer → answer**s** speak → speak**s** happen → happen**s**	Final -*s*, not -*es*, is added to most verbs. (INCORRECT: *visites, speakes, answeres, happenes*)
(b) hope → hope**s** write → write**s**	Many verbs end in -*e*. Final -*s* is simply added.
(c) catch → catch**es** fix → fix**es** wash → wash**es** buzz → buzz**es** pass → pass**es**	Final -*es* is added if the verb ends in -*ch, -sh, -s, -x*, or -*z*.
(d) do → do**es** go → go**es**	Final -*es* is added to *do* and *go*.
(e) study → stud**ies** try → tr**ies**	If a verb ends in a consonant + -*y*, change the -*y* to -*i* and add -*es*. (INCORRECT: *studys*)
(f) pay → pay**s** buy → buy**s**	If a verb ends in a vowel* + -*y*, simply add -*s* (INCORRECT: *paies* or *payes*)

* Vowels = *a, e, i, o, u.* Consonants = all the other letters in the alphabet.

☐ **EXERCISE 7:** Underline the VERB in each sentence. Add final -*s/-es* to the verb if
necessary. Do not change any other words.

1. A bird <u>sing</u>. → *A bird sings.*

2. Birds <u>sing</u>. → *(no change)*

3. Wood float on water.

4. Rivers flow toward the sea.

5. My mother worry about me.

6. A student buy a lot of books at the beginning of each term.

7. Airplanes fly all around the world.

8. Mr. Wong teach Chinese at the university.

9. The teacher ask us a lot of questions in class every day.

10. Mr. Smith watch game shows on TV every evening.

11. Music consist of pleasant sounds.

12. Pesticides destroy insects.

13. Dust travel through the air.

14. The front page of a newspaper contain the most important news of the day.

15. Water freeze at 32°F (0°C) and boil at 212°F (100°C).

16. Ms. Taylor never cross the street in the middle of a block. She always walk to the corner and use the pedestrian walkway.

17. Many parts of the world enjoy four seasons: spring, summer, autumn, and winter. Each season last three months and bring changes in the weather.

1-4 NONPROGRESSIVE VERBS

(a) I **hear** a bird. It is singing. (b) I'm hungry. I **want** a sandwich. (c) This book **belongs** to Mikhail.	Some verbs are not used in progressive tenses. CORRECT: *I hear a bird (right now).* INCORRECT: *I am hearing a bird (right now).*

NONPROGRESSIVE VERBS

hear	*believe*	*be*	*own*	*need*	*like*	*forget*
see	*think**	*exist*	*have**	*want*	*love*	*remember*
	understand		*possess*	*prefer*	*hate*	
	know		*belong*			

* Sometimes *think* and *have* are used in progressive tenses.
  COMPARE:
  I think that grammar is easy. → When **think** means **believe**, it is nonprogressive.
  I am thinking about grammar right now. → When **think** expresses thoughts that are going through a person's mind, it can be progressive.
  Tom has a car. → When **have** expresses possession, it is not used in the present progressive.
  I'm having a good time. → In certain idiomatic expressions (e.g., *have a good time*), **have** can be used in the present progressive.

□ **EXERCISE 8:** Complete the sentences with the words in parentheses. Use the SIMPLE PRESENT or the PRESENT PROGRESSIVE.

1. Right now Yoko (*read*) _____**is reading**_____ an article in the newspaper, but she (*understand, not*) ____**doesn't understand**____ it. Some of the vocabulary (*be*) _____**is**_____ too difficult for her.

2. Right now I (*look*) _____'m looking_____ at the board. I (*see*) _____'m seeing_____ some words on the board.

3. I (*need*) _____need_____ to call my parents today and tell them about my new apartment. They can't call me because they (*know, not*) _____don't know_____ my new telephone number.

4. This tea is good. I (*like*) _____like_____ it. What kind is it? I (*prefer*) _____prefer_____ tea to coffee. How about you?

5. Right now the children (*be*) _____are_____ at the beach. They (*have*) ____'re having____ a good time. They (*have*) ____have____ a beach ball, and they (*play*) _____are playing_____ catch with it. They (*like*) _____like_____ to play catch. Their parents (*sunbathe*) _____are sunbathing_____. They (*try*) _____are trying_____ to get a tan. They (*listen*) ____'re listening____ to some music on a transistor radio. They also (*hear*) _____are hearing_____ the sound of sea gulls and the sound of the waves.

6. Right now I (*think*) ___'m thinking___ about sea gulls and waves.

7. I (*think*) ___think___ that sea gulls are beautiful birds.

8. A: Who is that man? I (*think*) ___think___ that I (*know*) ___know___ him, but I (*forget*) ___forget___ his name right now.

   B: That's Mr. Martin.

   A: That's right! I (*remember*) ___remember___ him now.

9. Sam is at the library. He (*sit*) ___is sitting___ at a table. He (*write*) ___is writting___ a composition. He (*use*) ___is using___ a dictionary to look up the spelling of some words. The dictionary (*belong, not*) ___doesn't belong___ to him. It (*belong*) ___belongs___ to his roommate. Sam (*look*) ___is looking___ up words in the dictionary because he (*want*) ___wants___ to make sure that he doesn't have any misspelled words in his paper.

10. A: (*Believe, you*) ___Do you believe___ in flying saucers?

    B: What (*talk, you*) ___are you talking___ about?

    A: You know, spaceships from outer space with alien creatures aboard.

    B: In my opinion, flying saucers (*exist*) ___exist___ only in people's imaginations.

11. A: Which color (*prefer, you*) ___do you prefer___, red or blue?

    B: I (*like*) ___like___ blue better than red. Why?

    A: According to this magazine article I (*read*) ___'m reading___ right now, people who (*prefer*) ___prefer___ blue to red (*be*) ___is___ calm and (*value*) ___values___ honesty and loyalty in their friends. A preference for the color red (*mean*) ___means___ that a person (*be*) ___is___ aggressive and (*love*) ___loves___ excitement.

    B: Oh? That (*sound*) ___sounds___ like a bunch of nonsense to me.

Red values honesty & loyalty in their friends.

1-5 SIMPLE PRESENT AND PRESENT PROGRESSIVE: SHORT ANSWERS TO QUESTIONS

	QUESTION	SHORT ANSWER	LONG ANSWER
SIMPLE PRESENT	*Does* Bob *like* tea?	Yes, he **does**. No, he **doesn't**.	Yes, he *likes* tea. No, he *doesn't like* tea.
	Do you *like* tea?	Yes, I **do**. No, I **don't**.	Yes, I *like* tea. No, I *don't like* tea.
PRESENT PRO-GRESSIVE	*Are* you *studying*?	Yes, I **am**.* No, I**'m not**.	Yes, I *am studying*. No, I*'m not studying*.
	Is Yoko *studying*?	Yes, she **is**.* No, she**'s not**. OR: No, she **isn't**.	Yes, she *is studying*. No, she *'s not studying*. OR: No, she *isn't studying*.
	Are they *studying*?	Yes, they **are**.* No, they**'re not**. OR: No, they **aren't**.	Yes, they*'re studying*. No, they*'re not* studying. OR: No, they *aren't studying*.

* *Am*, *is*, and *are* are not contracted with pronouns in short answers.
INCORRECT SHORT ANSWERS: *Yes, I'm. Yes, she's. Yes, they're.*

□ **EXERCISE 9:** Complete the following dialogues by using the words in parentheses. Also give short answers to the questions as necessary. Use the SIMPLE PRESENT and the PRESENT PROGRESSIVE.

1. A: (*Mary, have*) _____**Does Mary have**_____ a bicycle?

   B: Yes, _____**she does**_____ . She (*have*) _____**has**_____ a ten-speed bike.

2. A: (*It, rain*) _____ right now?

   B: No, _____. At least, I (*think, not*) _____

   _____ so.

3. A: (*You, like*) _____ sour oranges?

   B: No, _____. I (*like*) _____ sweet ones.

4. A: (*Your friends, write*) _____ a lot of letters?

   B: Yes, _____. I (*get*) _____ lots of letters all the time.

5. A: (*The students, take*) _____ a test in class right now?

   B: No, _____. They (*do*) _____ an exercise.

6. A: (*You, know*) _____ Tom Adams?

   B: No, _____. I've never met him.

7. A: (*Your desk, have*) _____ any drawers?

   B: Yes, _____. It (*have*) _____ six drawers.

8. A: (*Jean, study*) _____ at the library this evening?

   B: No, _____. She (*be*) _____ at the student union. She (*play*) _____ pool with her friend.

   A: (*Jean, play*) _____ pool every evening?

   B: No, _____. She usually (*study*) _____ at the library.

   A: (*She, be*) _____ a good pool player?

   B: Yes, _____. She (*play*) _____ pool three or four times a week.

   A: (*You, know*) _____ how to play pool?

   B: Yes, _____. But I (*be, not*) _____ very good.

   A: Let's play sometime.

   B: Okay. That sounds like fun.

□ **EXERCISE 10:** Complete the sentences by using the words in parentheses. Use the SIMPLE PRESENT or the PRESENT PROGRESSIVE. Some of the sentences are negative. Some of the sentences are questions. Supply the short answer to a question if necessary.

1. A: Where are the children?

   B: In the living room

   A: What are they doing? (*They, watch*) _____ TV?

   B: No, _____. They (*play*) _____ a game.

2. A: Shhh. I (*hear*) _____ a noise. (*You, hear*) _____

      _____ it, too?

   B: Yes, _____. I wonder what it is.

3. A: My sister (*have*) _____ a new car. She bought it last

      month.

   B: (*You, have*) _____ a car?

   A: No, _____. Do you?

   B: No, but I have a ten-speed bike.

4. A: Shhh.

   B: Why? (*The baby, sleep*) _____?

   A: Uh-huh. She (*take*) _____ her afternoon nap.

   B: Okay, I'll talk softly. I (*want, not*) _____ to

      wake her up.

5. A: Ron, (*be*) _____ this your hat?

   B: No, _____. It (*belong, not*) _____

      to me. Maybe it (*belong*) _____ to Kevin. Why don't

      you ask him about it?

   A: Okay.

6. A: Johnny, (*you, listen*) _____ to me?

   B: Of course I am, Mom. You (*want*) _____ me to take

      out the garbage. Right?

   A: Right! And right now!

7. A: What (*you, think*) _____ about every night
before you fall asleep?

   B: I (*think*) _____ about all of the pleasant things that
happened during the day. I (*think, not*) _____
about my problems.

8. A: A penny for your thoughts.

   B: Huh?

   A: What (*you, think*) _____ about right now?

   B: I (*think*) _____ about English grammar. I (*think,
not*) _____ about anything else right now.

   A: I (*believe, not*) _____ you!

   B: But it's true.

9. A: (*You, see*) _____ that man over there?

   B: Which man? The man in the brown jacket?

   A: No, I (*talk*) _____ about the man who (*wear*)
_____ the blue shirt.

   B: Oh, that man.

   A: (*You, know*) _____ him?

   B: No, I (*think, not*) _____ so.

   A: I (*know, not*) _____ him either.

10. A: (*You, know*) _____ any tongue-twisters?

    B: Yes, _____. Here's one: *She sells sea shells down by the
sea shore.*

    A: That (*be*) _____ hard to say! Can you say this: *Sharon
wears Sue's shoes to zoos to look at cheap sheep?*

    B: That (*make, not*) _____ any sense.

    A: I (*know*) _____.

☐ **EXERCISE 11—ORAL/WRITTEN:** To discuss your classmates' immediate activities, divide into two groups, I and II.

GROUP I: Do anything you each feel like doing (stand up, talk, look out the window, etc.). You may wish to do some interesting or slightly unusual things. All perform these activities at the same time.

GROUP II: Describe the immediate activities of the students in GROUP I (e.g., *Ali is talking to Ricardo. Yoko is scratching her chin. Spyros is leaning against the wall.*). Be sure to use your classmates' names.

Later, GROUP I and GROUP II should reverse roles, with GROUP II acting and GROUP I describing.

☐ **EXERCISE 12—PREPOSITIONS:** Use the following prepositional expressions of place in sentences. Talk about things and people in the classroom. Perform actions to demonstrate the meaning of the expressions if necessary.*

Example: on
Responses: My book is on my desk.
My pen is on my book.
My hand is on my head.

1. on
2. above
3. under/below
4. next to/beside
5. against
6. in front of
7. in back of/behind
8. between
9. among
10. in
11. on (the) top of

12. around
13. across from
14. near/close to
15. (far) away from
16. in the front of
17. in the middle of
18. in the back of
19. at the top of
20. at the bottom of
21. in the corner of
22. on the corner of

☐ **EXERCISE 13—PREPOSITIONS:** Complete the sentences with prepositions. This exercise contains prepositions that follow adjectives. (See Appendix 1 for a list of preposition combinations.)

1. Mr. Porter is nice _____*to*_____ everyone.

2. Kathy was absent _____*from*_____ class yesterday.

---

* See Chart 4-3 for more information about prepositional phrases.

3. Are you ready _____for_____ the test?

4. I'm angry _____with_____ Greg.

5. I'm mad _____at_____ Greg.

6. Are you afraid _____of_____ dogs?

✓ ⑦ Sometimes people aren't kind _____ animals.

8. One inch is equal _____to_____ 2.54 centimeters.

✓ ⑨ I'm thirsty _____ a big glass of ice water.

10. Joe has good manners. He's always polite _____to_____ everyone.

11. I'm not familiar _____with_____ that book. Who wrote it?

12. Jack's thermos bottle is full _____of_____ coffee.

CHAPTER 2
Past Time

☐ **EXERCISE 1—ORAL (BOOKS CLOSED):** Answer the questions. Use the SIMPLE PRESENT or the SIMPLE PAST.

1. What are some things you usually do every morning?
   What are some things you did yesterday (OR: this) morning?

2. What do you usually do in the evening?
   What did you do last night?

3. What do we usually do in this class?
   What did we do in this class yesterday?

4. What do you usually do after this class?
   What did you do after class yesterday?

5. What did you do two days ago? Last week? Last month? Last year?

6. Take out a piece of paper. Write what you did (your activities) yesterday. Write as fast as you can.

2-1 EXPRESSING PAST TIME: THE SIMPLE PAST

(a) Mary **walked** downtown yesterday. (b) I **slept** for eight hours last night.	The simple past is used to talk about activities or situations that began and ended in the past (e.g., *yesterday, last night, two days ago, in 1990*).
(c) Bob **stayed** home yesterday morning. (d) Our plane **arrived** on time.	Most simple past verbs are formed by adding *-ed* to a verb, as in (a), (c), and (d).
(e) I **ate** breakfast this morning. (f) Sue **took** a taxi to the airport.	Some verbs have irregular past forms, as in (b), (e), and (f). See Chart 2-4.

2-2 FORMS OF THE SIMPLE PAST

STATEMENT	I - You - She - He - It - We - They	**worked** yesterday. **ate** breakfast.
NEGATIVE*	I - You - She - He - It - We - They	**did not** (**didn't**) **work** yesterday. **did not** (**didn't**) **eat** breakfast.
QUESTION*	**Did** I - you - she - he - it - we - they	**work** yesterday? **eat** breakfast?
SHORT ANSWER	Yes, I - you - she - he - it - we - they No,	**did**. **didn't**.

* NOTE: *Did* is NOT used with *was* and *were*.
   NEGATIVE: {I - She - He - It}   *was not* (*wasn't*)   busy.
                   {We - You - They}   *were not* (*weren't*) busy.
   QUESTION: *Was*   {I - she - he - it}   right?
                   Were {we - you - they} right?

☐ **EXERCISE 2:** All of the following sentences have inaccurate information. Correct them by:
    (a) writing a negative sentence; and
    (b) writing an affirmative statement with accurate information.

1. Thomas Edison invented the telephone.

    (a)   ***Thomas Edison didn't invent the telephone.***

    (b)   ***Alexander Graham Bell invented the telephone.***

2. Rocks float.

    (a)   ***Rocks don't float.***

    (b)   ***They sink.***

3. Wood sinks.

    (a) _____

    (b) _____

4. You took a taxi to school today.

    (a) _____

    (b) _____

5. You're sitting on a soft, comfortable sofa.

    (a) _____

    (b) _____

6. You stayed home all day yesterday.

   (a) _____

   (b) _____

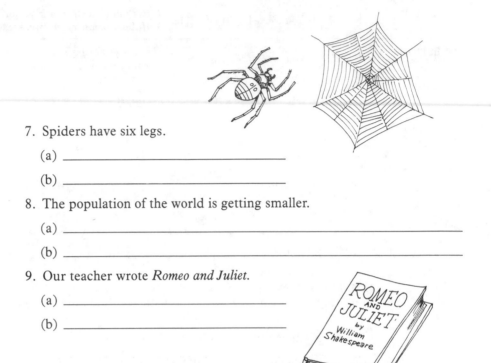

7. Spiders have six legs.

   (a) _____

   (b) _____

8. The population of the world is getting smaller.

   (a) _____

   (b) _____

9. Our teacher wrote *Romeo and Juliet*.

   (a) _____

   (b) _____

☐ **EXERCISE 3—ORAL (BOOKS CLOSED):** Correct the inaccurate statements by using negative then affirmative sentences. Some verbs are past and some are present.

Example:	You drank two cups of tea this morning.
Response:	No, that's not true. I didn't drink two cups of tea this morning. I had coffee with my breakfast.
Example:	(. . .) took a subway to school today. Right?
Response:	That's not possible! I know that (. . .) didn't take a subway to school because there aren't any subways in (*this city*).

1. You got up at 4:30 this morning.
2. (. . .) is standing in the corner of the classroom.
3. (. . .) stands in a corner of the classroom during class each day.
4. (. . .) stood in a corner during class yesterday.
5. This book has 354 pages.

6. Shakespeare wrote novels.

7. A river flows from the bottom of a valley to the top of a mountain.

8. We cook food in a refrigerator.

9. (...) taught this class yesterday.

10. Butterflies have ten legs.

11. This morning, you drove to school in a (*name of a kind of car*).

12. (...) takes a helicopter to get to school every day.

13. You speak (French and Arabic).

14. This room has (*supply an incorrect number*) windows.

15. (...) and you studied together at the library last night.

16. (...) went to (*an impossible place*) yesterday.

2-3 THE PRINCIPAL PARTS OF A VERB

	SIMPLE FORM	SIMPLE PAST	PAST PARTICIPLE	PRESENT PARTICIPLE
REGULAR VERBS	finish stop hope wait play try	finished stopped hoped waited played tried	finished stopped hoped waited played tried	finishing stopping hoping waiting playing trying
IRREGULAR VERBS	see make sing eat put go	saw made sang ate put went	seen made sung eaten put gone	seeing making singing eating putting going
PRINCIPAL PARTS OF A VERB: (1) the simple form	English verbs have four principal forms or "parts." **The simple form** is the form that is found in a dictionary. It is the base form with no endings on it (no final *-s, -ed,* or *-ing*).			
(2) the simple past	**The simple past** form ends in *-ed* for regular verbs. Most verbs are regular, but many common verbs have irregular past forms. See the reference list of irregular verbs that follows in Chart 2-4.			
(3) the past participle	**The past participle** also ends in *-ed* for regular verbs. Some verbs are irregular. It is used in perfect tenses (Chapter 7) and the passive (Chapter 12).			
(4) the present participle	**The present participle** ends in *-ing* (for both regular and irregular verbs). It is used in progressive tenses (e.g., the present progressive and the past progressive).			

SIMPLE FORM	SIMPLE PAST	PAST PARTICIPLE	SIMPLE FORM	SIMPLE PAST	PAST PARTICIPLE
be	was, were	been	lie	lay	lain
become	became	become	light	lit (lighted)	lit (lighted)
begin	began	begun	lose	lost	lost
bend	bent	bent	make	made	made
bite	bit	bitten	mean	meant	meant
blow	blew	blown	meet	met	met
break	broke	broken	pay	paid	paid
bring	brought	brought	put	put	put
broadcast	broadcast	broadcast	quit	quit	quit
build	built	built	read	read	read
buy	bought	bought	ride	rode	ridden
catch	caught	caught	ring	rang	rung
choose	chose	chosen	rise	rose	risen
come	came	come	run	ran	run
cost	cost	cost	say	said	said
cut	cut	cut	see	saw	seen
dig	dug	dug	sell	sold	sold
do	did	done	send	sent	sent
draw	drew	drawn	set	set	set
drink	drank	drunk	shake	shook	shaken
drive	drove	driven	shoot	shot	shot
eat	ate	eaten	shut	shut	shut
fall	fell	fallen	sing	sang	sung
feed	fed	fed	sit	sat	sat
feel	felt	felt	sleep	slept	slept
fight	fought	fought	slide	slid	slid
find	found	found	speak	spoke	spoken
fit	fit	fit	spend	spent	spent
fly	flew	flown	spread	spread	spread
forget	forgot	forgotten	stand	stood	stood
forgive	forgave	forgiven	steal	stole	stolen
freeze	froze	frozen	stick	stuck	stuck
get	got	gotten (got)	strike	struck	struck
give	gave	given	swear	swore	sworn
go	went	gone	sweep	swept	swept
grow	grew	grown	swim	swam	swum
hang	hung	hung	take	took	taken
have	had	had	teach	taught	taught
hear	heard	heard	tear	tore	torn
hide	hid	hidden	tell	told	told
hit	hit	hit	think	thought	thought
hold	held	held	throw	threw	thrown
hurt	hurt	hurt	understand	understood	understood
keep	kept	kept	upset	upset	upset
know	knew	known	wake	woke	waked (woken)
lay	laid	laid	wear	wore	worn
lead	led	led	win	won	won
leave	left	left	withdraw	withdrew	withdrawn
lend	lent	lent	write	wrote	written
let	let	let			

☐ **EXERCISE 4—IRREGULAR VERBS:** Complete the sentences by using the SIMPLE PAST of the given verbs. *Use each verb only one time.* All of the verbs have irregular past forms.

✓ begin	✓ go	✓ read
✓ cut	✓ hold	shake
✓ drink	✓ keep	✓ shut
✓ eat	✓ lose	✓ speak
✓ find	✓ meet	spend

1. Sue _____**drank**_____ a cup of coffee before class this morning.

2. We _____*ate*_____ a delicious dinner at a Mexican restaurant last night.

3. When it _____*began*_____ to rain yesterday afternoon, I _____*shut*_____ all of the windows in the apartment.

4. Chris hurt his finger when he was fixing his dinner last night. He accidentally _____*cut*_____ it with a sharp knife.

5. I don't have any money in my pocket. I _____*spent*_____ my last dime yesterday. I'm flat broke.

6. Jessica didn't throw her old shoes away. She _____*kept*_____ them because they were comfortable.

7. I _____*read*_____ an interesting article in the newspaper yesterday.

8. Jack _____*lost*_____ his pocketknife at the park yesterday. This morning he _____*went*_____ back to the park to look for it. Finally he _____*found*_____ it in the grass. He was glad to have it back.

9. Peter was nervous when he _____*held*_____ his baby in his arms for the first time.

10. I _____*met*_____ Jennifer's parents when they visited her. She introduced me to them.

11. Yesterday I called Jason on the phone. He wasn't home, so I _____*spoke*_____ to his sister.

12. When I introduced Tom to Ryan, they _____*shook*_____ hands and smiled at each other.

□ **EXERCISE 5—IRREGULAR VERBS:** Complete the sentences by using the SIMPLE PAST of the given verbs. *Use each verb only one time.* All of the verbs have irregular past forms.

bite	*feel*	*leave*
draw	*forget*	*lend*
✓ *drive*	*get*	*ride*
fall	*hear*	*steal*
feed	*hurt*	*take*

1. Mary walked to school today. Rebecca _____**drove**_____ her car. Alison _____ her bicycle. Sandy _____ the bus.

2. When Alan slipped on the icy sidewalk yesterday, he _____ down and _____ his back. His back is very painful today.

3. I didn't have any money yesterday, so my roommate _____ me enough so I could pay for my lunch.

4. The children had a good time at the park yesterday. They _____ the ducks small pieces of bread.

5. Alice called the police yesterday because someone _____ her bicycle while she was in the library studying. She's very angry.

6. Dick _____ his apartment in a hurry this morning because he was late for school. That's why he _____ to bring his books to class.

7. The children _____ pictures of themselves in art class yesterday.

8. I have a cold. Yesterday I _____ terrible, but I'm feeling better today.

9. Last night I _____ a strange noise in the house around 2:00 A.M., so I _____ up to investigate.

10. My dog isn't very friendly. Yesterday she _____ my neighbor's leg. Luckily, my dog is very old and doesn't have sharp teeth, so she didn't hurt my neighbor.

☐ **EXERCISE 6—IRREGULAR VERBS:** Complete the sentences by using the SIMPLE PAST of the given verbs. *Use each verb only one time.* All of the verbs have irregular past forms.

break	*dig*	*teach*
bring	*freeze*	*think*
buy	*ring*	*wake*
catch	*rise*	*wear*
come	*sleep*	*write*

1. I dropped my favorite vase. It fell on the floor and _____ into a hundred pieces.

2. When I went shopping yesterday, I _____ some light bulbs and a cooking pot.

3. Alex _____ his book to class with him. He didn't forget it.

4. My brother and his wife _____ to our apartment for dinner last night.

5. Last night around midnight, when I was sound asleep, the telephone _____. It _____ me up.

6. The sun _____ at 6:04 this morning.

7. I _____ a letter to my folks after I finished studying yesterday evening.

8. Ms. Manning _____ chemistry at the local high school last year.

9. The police _____ the bank robbers. They are in jail now.

10. Last night I had a good night's sleep. I _____ nine hours.

11. Today Paul has on slacks and a sports jacket, but yesterday he _____ jeans and a sweatshirt to class.

12. It was really cold yesterday. The temperature was three below zero.* I nearly _____ to death when I walked home!

13. I _____ about going to Florida for my vacation, but I finally decided to go to Puerto Rico.

14. My dog _____ a hole in the yard and buried his bone.

_____
* Note: −3°F (Fahrenheit) equals −20°C (Centigrade or Celsius).

□ **EXERCISE 7:** Complete the following dialogues. Use the words in parentheses. Give short answers to questions where necessary.

1. A: (*you, go*) _____**Did you go**_____ to class yesterday?

   B: No, _____**I didn't**_____ . I (*stay*) _____**stayed**_____ home because I (*feel, not*) _____**didn't feel**_____ good.

2. A: (*you, sleep*) _____ well last night?

   B: Yes, _____. I (*sleep*) _____ very well.

3. A: (*Tom's plane, arrive*) _____ on time yesterday?

   B: Yes, _____. It (*get in*) _____ at 6:05 on the dot.

4. A: (*you, stay*) _____ home and (*study*)

   _____ last night?

   B: No, _____. I (*go*) _____ to a new

   movie, *The Valley of the Vampires.*

   A: (*you, like*) _____ it?

   B: It was okay, I guess, but I don't really like horror movies.

5. A: (*Mary, study*) _____ last night?

   B: No, _____. She (*watch*) _____ TV.

6. A: (*Mark Twain, write*) _____

   _____ Tom Sawyer?

   B: Yes, _____.

   He also (*write*) _____

   Huckleberry Finn.

7. A: (*the children, go*) _____ to the zoo

   yesterday?

   B: Yes, _____. And they (*have*) _____ a

   wonderful time.

8. A: (*you, eat*) _____ breakfast this morning?

   B: No, _____ . I (*have, not*) _____

   enough time. I was late for class because my alarm clock (*ring, not*)

   _____.

□ **EXERCISE 8—ORAL:** Pair up with a classmate. Practice questions, short answers, and irregular verbs.

STUDENT A: Ask questions beginning with "Did you . . . ?" Listen carefully to STUDENT B's answers to make sure he or she is using the irregular verbs correctly. Look at Chart 2-4 if necessary to check the correct form of an irregular verb. Your book is open.

STUDENT B: In order to practice using irregular verbs, answer "*yes*" to all of STUDENT A's questions. Give full answers. Your book is closed.

Example: eat breakfast this morning
STUDENT A: Did you eat breakfast this morning?
STUDENT B: Yes, I did. I ate breakfast at 7:30 this morning.

PART I: (STUDENT A asks the questions.)

1. sleep well last night
2. wake up early this morning
3. eat breakfast this morning
4. take the bus to school
5. drive your car to school
6. ride your bicycle to school
7. bring your books to class
8. lose your grammar book
9. hear about the earthquake
10. say something
11. do your homework last night
12. give your friend a present
13. catch a cold last week
14. feel terrible
15. see a doctor
16. read the newspaper this morning
17. find your grammar book
18. go to a party last night
19. have a good time
20. think about me

PART II: (Switch roles. Now STUDENT B asks the questions.)

21. come to class yesterday
22. buy some books yesterday
23. fly to this city
24. run to class today
25. write your parents a letter
26. send your parents a letter
27. lend (. . .) some money
28. wear a coat yesterday
29. go to the zoo last week
30. feed the birds at the park
31. make your own dinner last night
32. leave home at eight this morning
33. drink a cup of coffee before class
34. fall down yesterday
35. hurt yourself when you fell down
36. break your arm
37. understand the question
38. speak to (. . .) yesterday
39. meet (. . .) the first day of class
40. shake hands with (. . .) when you first met him/her

☐ **EXERCISE 9—ORAL (BOOKS CLOSED):** Perform the action and then describe the action, using the SIMPLE PAST. Most of the verbs are irregular; some are regular.

Example: Give (. . .) your pen. (*The student performs the action.*)
What did you do?
Response: I gave (. . .) my pen.

1. Give (. . .) your dictionary.
2. Open your book.
3. Shut your book.
4. Stand up.
5. Blow on your finger.
6. Put your book in your lap.
7. Bend your elbow.
8. Touch the tip of your nose.
9. Spell the word "happened."
10. Shake hands with (. . .).
11. Bite your finger.
12. Hide your pen.
13. Leave the room.
14. Speak to (. . .).
15. Tear a piece of paper.
16. Tell (. . .) to stand up.
17. Throw your eraser to (. . .).
18. Draw a triangle on the board.
19. Turn to page ten in your book.
20. Hold your book above your head.
21. Choose a pen, this one or that one.
22. Invite (. . .) to have lunch with you.
23. Thank (. . .) for the invitation.
24. Steal (. . .)'s pen.
25. Sell your pen to (. . .) for a (*dime*).
26. Hit your desk with your hand.
27. Stick your pen in your pocket/purse.
28. Read a sentence from your book.
29. Repeat my sentence: This book is black.
30. Hang your (*jacket*) on your chair.
31. Take (. . .)'s grammar book.
32. Write your name on the board.

☐ **EXERCISE 10—ORAL (BOOKS CLOSED):** Practice using irregular verbs by answering the questions.

Example: Where did you sit in class yesterday?
Response: I sat over there.

1. What time did class begin this morning?
2. What time did the sun rise this morning?
3. What time did you get up this morning?
4. What time did you leave home this morning?
5. What did you have for breakfast?
6. What did you drink this morning?
7. Where did you put your books when you came to class this morning?
8. What did you wear yesterday?
9. What time did you wake up this morning?
10. Where did you grow up?
11. What did you buy last week?

12. What did you eat for lunch yesterday? How much did it cost?

13. Where did you sit in class yesterday?

14. When did you meet (. . .)?

15. What cities did you fly to on your way to (*the name of this city*)?

2-5 SPELLING OF *-ING* AND *-ED* FORMS

END OF VERB	DOUBLE THE CONSONANT?	SIMPLE FORM	*-ING*	*-ED*	
-e	NO	(a) smile hope	smiling hoping	smiled hoped	*-ing* form: Drop the *-e*, add *-ing*. *-ed* form: Just add *-d*.
Two Consonants	NO	(b) help learn	helping learning	helped learned	If the verb ends in two consonants, just add *-ing* or *-ed*.
Two Vowels + One Consonant	NO	(c) rain heat	raining heating	rained heated	If the verb ends in two vowels + a consonant, just add *-ing* or *ed*.
One Vowel + One Consonant	YES	**ONE-SYLLABLE VERBS** (d) stop plan	 stopping planning	 stopped planned	If the verb has one syllable and ends in one vowel + one consonant, double the consonant to make the *-ing* or *-ed* form.*
	NO	**TWO-SYLLABLE VERBS** (e) vísit óffer	 visiting offering	 visited offered	If the first syllable of a two-syllable verb is stressed, do not double the consonant.
	YES	(f) prefér admít	preferring admitting	preferred admitted	If the second syllable of a two-syllable verb is stressed, double the consonant.
-y	NO	(g) play enjoy	playing enjoying	played enjoyed	If the verb ends in a vowel + *-y*, keep the *-y*. Do not change it to *-i*.
		(h) worry study	worrying studying	worried studied	If the verb ends in a consonant + *-y*, keep the *-y* for the *-ing* form, but change the *-y* to *-i* to make the *-ed* form.
-ie		(i) die tie	dying tying	died tied	*-ing* form: Change *-ie* to *-y* and add *-ing*. *-ed* form: Just add *-d*.

* Exceptions: Do not double *w* or *x*: *snow, snowing, snowed*
  fix, fixing, fixed

☐ **EXERCISE 11:** Write the -**ING** and -**ED** forms of the following verbs. (The simple past/past participle of irregular verbs is given in parentheses.)

	-ING	-ED
1. start	*starting*	*started*
2. wait		
3. hit		(hit)
4. write		(wrote/written)
5. shout		
6. cut		(cut)
7. meet		(met)
8. hope		
9. hop		
10. help		
11. sleep		(slept)
12. step		
13. tape		
14. tap		
15. rain		
16. run		(ran, run)
17. whine		
18. win		(won)
19. explain		
20. burn		
21. swim		(swam/swum)
22. aim		
23. charm		
24. cram		
25. tame		
26. choose		(chose/chosen)
27. ride		(rode/ridden)
28. remind		

☐ **EXERCISE 12:** Write the **-ING** and **-ED** forms of the following verbs.

	-ING	-ED
1. open	_____	_____
2. begin	_____	(began/begun)
3. occur	_____	_____
4. happen	_____	_____
5. refer	_____	_____
6. offer	_____	_____
7. listen	_____	_____
8. admit	_____	_____
9. visit	_____	_____
10. omit	_____	_____
11. hurry	_____	_____
12. study	_____	_____
13. enjoy	_____	_____
14. reply	_____	_____
15. stay	_____	_____
16. buy	_____	(bought)
17. try	_____	_____
18. tie	_____	_____
19. die	_____	_____
20. lie*	_____	_____

☐ **EXERCISE 13:** Write the **-ING** and **-ED** forms of the following verbs on your own paper.

1. *lift*	6. *map*	11. *drag*	16. *appear*
2. *promise*	7. *mope*	12. *use*	17. *relax*
3. *slap*	8. *smile*	13. *prefer*	18. *borrow*
4. *wave*	9. *fail*	14. *pray*	19. *cry*
5. *carry*	10. *file*	15. *point*	20. *ship*

---

* **Lie** is a regular verb when it means "not tell the truth." **Lie** is an irregular verb when it means "put one's body flat on a bed or another surface": *lie, lay, lain.*

2-6 THE SIMPLE PAST AND THE PAST PROGRESSIVE

THE SIMPLE PAST	(a) Mary **walked** downtown yesterday. (b) I **slept** for eight hours last night.	The simple past is used to talk about activities or situations that **began and ended** at a particular time in the past (e.g., *yesterday, last night, two days ago, in 1990*), as in (a) and (b).
THE PAST PROGRESSIVE	(c) I sat down at the dinner table at 6:00 P.M. yesterday. Tom came to my house at 6:10 P.M. I **was eating** dinner when Tom came. (d) I went to bed at 10:00. The phone rang at 11:00. I **was sleeping** when the phone rang.	The past progressive expresses an activity that **was in progress** (was occurring, was happening) at a point of time in the past (e.g., *at 6:10*) or at the time of another action (e.g., *when Tom came.*) In (c): Eating was in progress at 6:10; eating was in progress when Tom came. FORM: **was, were** + **-ing**.
(e) **When** the phone rang, I was sleeping. (f) The phone rang **while I was sleeping**.		**when** = at that time **while** = during that time (e) and (f) have the same meaning.
(g) **While** I **was doing** my homework, my roommate **was watching** TV.		In (g): When two actions are in progress at the same time, the past progressive can be used in both parts of the sentence.

2-7 FORMS OF THE PAST PROGRESSIVE

STATEMENT	{I-She-He-It} **was working**. {You-We-They} **were working**.
NEGATIVE	{I-She-He-It} **was not (wasn't) working**. {You-We-They} **were not (weren't) working**.
QUESTION	**Was** {I-she-he-it} **working**? **Were** {you-we-they} **working**?
SHORT ANSWER	Yes, {I-she-he-it} **was**. No, {I-she-he-it} **wasn't**. Yes, {you-we-they} **were**. No, {you-we-they} **weren't**.

☐ **EXERCISE 14:** Complete the sentences with the words in parentheses. Use the SIMPLE PAST or the PAST PROGRESSIVE.

1. At 6:00 P.M., Bob sat down at the table and began to eat. At 6:05, Bob

   (eat) _____ dinner.

2. While Bob (eat) _____ dinner, Ann (come)

   _____ through the door.

3. In other words, when Ann (come) _____ through the

   door, Bob (eat) _____ dinner.

4. Bob went to bed at 10:30. At 11:00 Bob (sleep) _____.

5. While Bob (sleep) _____, the phone (ring) _____.

6. In other words, when the phone (ring) _____, Bob (sleep)

   _____.

7. Bob left his house at 8:00 A.M. and (begin)

   _____ to walk to class.

   While he (walk) _____

   to class, he (see) * _____

   Mrs. Smith.

_____

*Some verbs, like *see*, are not used in progressive tenses. See Chart 1-4.

8. When Bob (*see*) _____ Mrs. Smith, she (*stand*)

_____ on her front porch. She (*hold*) _____

_____ a broom. Mrs. Smith (*wave*) _____

at Bob when she (*see*) _____ him.

☐ **EXERCISE 15—ORAL (BOOKS CLOSED):** Perform the actions and answer the
questions.

Example:	A: write on the board B: open the door
To STUDENT A:	Please write on the board. Write anything you wish. (STUDENT A writes on the board.) What are you doing?
Response:	I'm writing on the board.
To STUDENT A:	Good. Please continue.
To STUDENT B:	Open the door. (STUDENT B opens the door.) What did you just do?
Response:	I opened that door.
To STUDENT A:	(STUDENT A), thank you. You may stop now.
To STUDENT C:	Describe the two actions that just occurred, using *when*.
Response:	When (B) opened the door, (A) was writing on the board.
To STUDENT D:	Again, using *while*.
Response:	While (A) was writing on the board, (B) opened the door.

1. A: write a note to (. . .)   B: knock on the door
2. A: walk around the room   B: clap your hands once
3. A: talk to (. . .)   B: come in the room
4. A: read your book   B: tap (STUDENT A)'s shoulder
5. A: look out the window   B: ask (STUDENT A) a question
6. A: whistle   B: leave the room
7. A: look at your watch   B: ask (STUDENT A) a question
8. A: pantomime eating (pretend to eat)   B: sit down next to (STUDENT A)
9. A: pantomime sleeping   B: take (STUDENT A)'s grammar book
10. A: pantomime drinking a glass of water   B: come in the room

☐ **EXERCISE 16:** Complete the following. Use the words in parentheses. Use the SIMPLE
PAST or the PAST PROGRESSIVE.

1. Sally (*eat*) _____ dinner last night when someone

(*knock*) _____ on the door.

2. I began to study at seven last night. Fred (*come*) _____

at seven-thirty. I (*study*) _____ when Fred (*come*)

_____ .

3. While I (*study*) _____ last night, Fred (*drop by*) _____ to visit me.

4. My roommate's parents (*call*) _____ him last night while we (*watch*) _____ TV.

5. My mother called me around five. My husband came home a little after that. When he (*come*) _____ home, I (*talk*) _____ _____ to my mother on the phone.

6. Yesterday afternoon I (*go*) _____ to visit the Parker family. When I (*get*) _____ there around two o'clock, Mrs. Parker (*be*) _____ in the yard. She (*plant*) _____ flowers in her garden. Mr. Parker (*be*) _____ in the garage. He (*work*) _____ on their car. He (*change*) _____ the oil. The children (*play*) _____ in the front yard. In other words, while Mr. Parker (*fix*) _____ the oil in the car, the children (*play*) _____ with a ball in the yard.

7. Yesterday Tom and Janice (*go*) _____ to the zoo around one o'clock. They (*see*) _____ many kinds of animals and (*have*) _____ a few adventures. While they (*walk*)

_____ by the elephant, it (*begin*) _____ to squirt water at them, so they (*run*) _____ behind a rock and (*dry*) _____ themselves. Later, while they (*pass*) _____ the giraffe area, one of the tall, purple-tongued animals (*lower*) _____ its head toward Tom and (*start*) _____ to nibble on his green hat. Janice said, "Shoo!" At that point, the giraffe (*stretch*) _____ its head toward Janice and (*try*) _____ to eat her ice cream cone. Janice (*let, not*) _____ the giraffe have the ice cream because she (*stand*) _____ right in front of a sign that said, "DO NOT FEED THE ANIMALS." She (*point*) _____ at the sign and (*say*) _____ to the giraffe, "Can't you read?"

8. A: There was a power outage in our part of town last night. (*Your lights, go out*) _____ too?

   B: Yes, they did. It (*be*) _____ terrible! I (*take*) _____ a shower when the lights went out. My wife (*find*) _____ a flashlight and rescued me from the bathroom! We couldn't cook dinner, so we (*eat*) _____ sandwiches instead. I (*try*) _____ to study by candlelight, but I couldn't see well enough, so I (*go*) _____ to bed and (*sleep*) _____. How about you?

A: I (read) _____ when the lights (go out)

_____. I (study) _____ for

a history exam. Of course, I couldn't study in the dark, so I (get up)

_____ very early this morning and finished studying

for my test.

2-8 EXPRESSING PAST TIME: USING TIME CLAUSES

(a) ⌐time clause⌐ ⌐main clause⌐ *When I went to Chicago, I visited my uncle.*	*when I went to Chicago* = a time clause* *I visited my uncle* = a main clause* (a) and (b) have the same meaning.
(b) ⌐main clause⌐ ⌐time clause⌐ *I visited my uncle when I went to Chicago.*	A time clause can: (1) come in front of a main clause, as in (a); (2) follow a main clause, as in (b).
(c) *After Mary ate dinner,* she went to the library. (d) Mary went to the library *after she ate dinner.* (e) *Before I went to bed,* I finished my homework. (f) I finished my homework *before I went to bed.* (g) *While I was watching TV,* the phone rang. (h) The phone rang *while I was watching TV.* (i) *When the phone rang,* I was watching TV. (j) I was watching TV *when the phone rang.*	**When, after, before,** and **while** introduce time clauses. *when* *after* ⎫ *before* ⎬ + subject and verb = a time clause *while* ⎭ PUNCTUATION: Put a comma at the end of a time clause when the time clause comes first in a sentence (comes in front of the main clause): **time clause + comma + main clause** **main clause + NO comma + time clause**
(k) When the phone *rang,* I *answered* it.	In a sentence with a time clause introduced by **when**, both the time clause verb and the main verb can be simple past. In this case, the action in the "**when** clause" happened first. In (i): *First: the phone rang. Then: I answered it.*

* A *clause* is a structure that has a subject and a verb.

☐ **EXERCISE 17:** Combine the two sentences into one sentence by using time clauses. Punctuate carefully.

1. *First:* I got home.
   Then: I ate dinner.

   (a) After _____*I got home, I ate dinner.*_____

   (b) _____*I ate dinner*_____ after _____*I got home.*_____

2. *First:* I washed dishes.
   Then: I watched TV.

   (a) After _____

   (b) _____ after _____

3. *First:* I unplugged the coffee pot.
   Then: I left my apartment this morning.

   (a) Before _____

   (b) _____ before _____

4. *First:* I was eating dinner.
   Then: Jim came.

   (a) While _____

   (b) _____ while _____

   (c) When _____

   (d) _____ when _____

5. *First:* It began to rain.
   Then: I stood under a tree.

   (a) When _____

   (b) _____ when _____

□ **EXERCISE 18—ORAL:** Combine the two sentences into one sentence by using a time
clause. Use the word in parentheses to introduce the time clause. Discuss
punctuation.

   1. (*before*) *First:* I did my homework.
                  Then: I went to bed.

   2. (*after*)   *First:* Bob graduated.
                  Then: He got a job.

   3. (*while*)   *First:* I was studying.
                  Then: Amanda called me on the phone.

   4. (*when*)   *First:* My alarm clock rang.
                  Then: I woke up.

   5. (*while*)   *First:* I was falling asleep last night.
                  Then: I heard a strange noise.

   6. (*when*)   *First:* I heard a strange noise.
                  Then: I turned on the light.

   7. (*when*)   *First:* I was eating lunch.
                  Then: Eric came.

   8. (*before*) *First:* I bought some flowers.
                  Then: I went to the hospital to visit my friend.

☐ **EXERCISE 19—ORAL/WRITTEN:** Pair up with a classmate.

> STUDENT A: Tell STUDENT B about your activities yesterday. Think of at least five things you did yesterday to tell STUDENT B about. Also think of two or three things you didn't do yesterday.
>
> STUDENT B: Listen carefully to STUDENT A. Make sure that STUDENT A is using past tenses correctly. Ask STUDENT A questions about his/her activities if you wish. Take notes while STUDENT A is talking.

When STUDENT A finishes talking, switch roles: STUDENT B tells STUDENT A about his/her activities yesterday.

Use the notes from the conversation to write a composition about the other student's activities yesterday. Use time clauses.

☐ **EXERCISE 20:** Complete the sentences with the correct form of the words in parentheses.

(1)   Last Friday was a holiday. It (*be*) _____ Independence

(2) Day, so I didn't have to go to classes. I (*sleep*) _____ a little

(3) later than usual. Around ten, my friend Larry (*come*) _____

(4) over to my apartment. We (*pack*) _____ a picnic basket and

(5) then (*take*) _____ the bus to Forest Park. We (*spend*)

(6) _____ most of the day there.

(7)   When we (*get*) _____ to the park, we (*find*)

(8) _____ an empty picnic table near a pond. There were some

(9) ducks on the pond, so we (*feed*) _____ them. We (*throw*)

(10) _____ small pieces of bread on the water, and the ducks

(11) (*swim*) _____ over to get them. One duck was very clever. It

(12) (*catch*) _____ the bread in midair before it (*hit*)

(13) _____ the water. Another duck was a thief. It (*steal*)

(14) _____ bread from the beaks of other ducks. While we (*feed*)

(15) _____ the ducks, Larry and I (*meet*) _____ a

(16) man who usually (*come*) _____ to the park every day to feed

(17) the ducks. We (*sit*) _____ on a park bench and (*speak*)

(18) _____ to him for fifteen or twenty minutes.

(19)   After we (*eat*) _____ our lunch, I (*take*) _____

(20) a short nap under a tree. While I

(21) (*sleep*) _____, a

(22) mosquito (*bite*) _____

(23) my arm. When I (*wake*)

(24) _____ up, my arm

(25) itched, so I scratched it. Suddenly I

(26) (*hear*) _____ a noise

(27) in the tree above me. I (*look*)

(28) _____ up and (*see*)

(29) _____ an orange and

(30) gray bird. After a few moments, it

(31) (*fly*) _____ away.

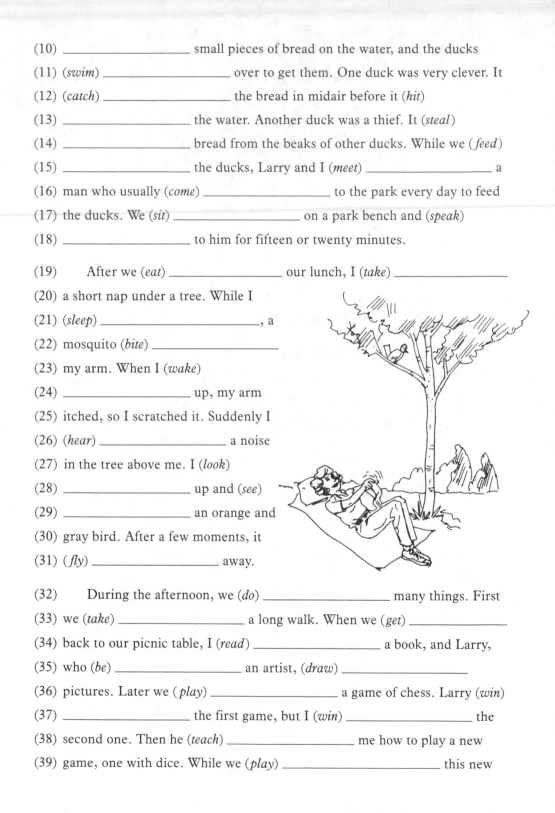

(32)   During the afternoon, we (*do*) _____ many things. First

(33) we (*take*) _____ a long walk. When we (*get*) _____

(34) back to our picnic table, I (*read*) _____ a book, and Larry,

(35) who (*be*) _____ an artist, (*draw*) _____

(36) pictures. Later we (*play*) _____ a game of chess. Larry (*win*)

(37) _____ the first game, but I (*win*) _____ the

(38) second one. Then he (*teach*) _____ me how to play a new

(39) game, one with dice. While we (*play*) _____ this new

(40) game, one of the dice (*fall*) _____ from the picnic table onto

(41) the ground. We finally (*find*) _____ it in some tall grass.

(42)   In the evening, we (*join*) _____ a huge crowd to watch

(43) the fireworks display. The fireworks (*be*) _____ beautiful.

(44) Some of the explosions (*be*) _____ very loud, however. They

(45) (*hurt*) _____ my ears. When the display (*be*)

(46) _____ over, we (*leave*) _____. All in all, it

(47) (*be*) _____ a very enjoyable day.

☐ **EXERCISE 21—WRITTEN:** Write a composition about one of the following:

    1. Write about an enjoyable day in your life. OR:
    2. Write about an important event in your life.

2-9 EXPRESSING PAST HABIT: *USED TO*

(a) I **used to live** with my parents. Now I live in my own apartment. (b) Ann **used to be** afraid of dogs, but now she likes dogs. (c) Don **used to smoke**, but he doesn't anymore.	**Used to** expresses a past situation or habit that no longer exists at present. FORM: **used to** + *the simple form of a verb*
(d) **Did** you **use to live** in Paris?	QUESTION FORM: **did** + *subject* + **use to**
(e) I **didn't use to drink** coffee at breakfast. (f) I **never used to drink** coffee at breakfast, but now I always have coffee in the morning.	NEGATIVE FORM: **didn't use to/never used to**

☐ EXERCISE 22: Make sentences with a similar meaning by using **used to**. Some of the sentences are negatives, and some of them are questions.

1. *When I was a child, I was shy. Now I'm not shy.*

   → I _____ **used to be** _____ shy, but now I'm not.

2. *Now you live in this city. Where did you live before you came here?*

   → Where _____ **did you use to live** _____ ?

3. *When I lived in my home town, I went to the beach every weekend. Now I don't go to the beach every weekend.*

   → I _____ to the beach every weekend, but now I don't.

4. *Rita worked in a law office for many years. Now she doesn't have a job.*

   → Rita _____ in a law office, but now she doesn't.

5. *Adam has a new job. He has to wear a suit every day. When he was a student, he always wore jeans.*

   → Adam _____ a suit every day, but now he does.

6. *Sara has two cats that she enjoys as pets. In the past, she hated cats. These are her first pets.*

   → Sara _____ cats. She _____ pets, but today she enjoys her two cats.

7. *Now you have a job every summer. Have you always worked during summers?*

   → What _____ in summer?

8. *When I was in high school, I wore a uniform to school.*

   → I _____ a uniform to school, but now I don't.

9. *When I was a child, I drank a lot of milk. I never drank coffee. How about you?*

   → I _____ milk with every meal. I _____

   _____ coffee, but now I have at least

   one cup every day. _____ a lot of

   milk when you were a child?

10. *When I was a child, I watched cartoons on TV. I don't watch cartoons anymore. Now I watch news programs. How about you?*

   → I _____ cartoons on TV, but I don't

   anymore. I _____ news programs,

   but now I do. What _____ on TV

   when you were a little kid?

☐ **EXERCISE 23:** Complete the sentences. Each sentence should have a form of **used to**.
Add your own words.

1. I _____ ***used to ride*** _____ my bicycle to work, but now I take the bus.

2. What time _____ ***did you use to go*** _____ to bed when you were a child?

3. I _____ ***didn't use to stay up*** _____ past midnight, but now I often go to bed
very late because I have to study.

4. I _____ wild and reckless when I was younger, but now I'm not.

5. Tom _____ tennis after work every day, but now he doesn't.

6. I _____ any physical exercise, but now
I exercise for an hour every day.

7. When you were a child, where _____ on vacation?

8. Ann _____ most of her lunches and dinners at restaurants before she got married.

9. I used to spend a lot of time with _____, but now _____.

10. When you were a little kid, what _____ after school?

11. I _____ breakfast, but now I always have something to eat in the morning because I read that students who eat breakfast do better in school.

12. I _____, but now I don't have any pets at all.

13. I _____, but now I attend _____.

14. I live in _____ now, but I _____ in _____.

15. I didn't use to _____, but _____.

16. What _____ for fun when you were _____?

17. _____ live with my parents, but now _____.

18. _____ interested in _____, but now I am.

□ EXERCISE 24—ORAL AND/OR WRITTEN: Use *used to*.

1. You are an adult now. What did you use to do when you were a child that you don't do now?

2. You are living in a foreign country. What did you use to do in your own country that you don't do now?

3. Think of a particular time in your past (e.g., when you were in elementary school, when you lived in Paris, when you worked at your uncle's store). Describe a typical day in your life at that time. What did you use to do?

2-10 PREPOSITIONS OF TIME: *IN*, *AT*, and *ON*

The prepositions *in*, *at*, and *on* are used in time expressions as follows:	
(a) Please be on time *in the future*. (b) I usually watch TV *in the evening*.	*in the past, in the present, in the future** *in the morning, in the afternoon, in the evening*
(c) We sleep *at night*. I was asleep *at midnight*. (d) I fell asleep *at 9:30 (nine-thirty)*. (e) He's busy *at present*. Please call again.	*at noon, at night, at midnight* *at + "clock time"* *at present, at the moment, at the present time*
(f) I was born *in October*. (g) I was born *in 1975*. (h) I was born *in the twentieth century*. (i) The weather is hot *in (the) summer*.**	*in + a month/a year/a century/a season*
(j) I was born *on October 31, 1975*. (k) I went to a movie *on Thursday*. (l) I have class *on Thursday morning(s)*.	*on + a date/a weekday* *on + weekday morning(s), afternoon(s), evening(s)*

* Possible in British English: *in future*. *(Please be on time in future.)*

** In expressions with the seasons, *the* is optional: *in (the) spring, in (the) summer, in (the) fall/autumn, in (the) winter*.

☐ **EXERCISE 25—PREPOSITIONS:** Complete the sentences with *in*, *at*, or *on*. All of the expressions contain time expressions.

1. History is the study of events that occurred _____ the past.

2. We don't know what will happen _____ the future.

3. Newspapers report events that happen _____ the present.

4. Last year I was a junior in high school. _____ present, I am a senior in high school.

5. I am a student _____ the present time, but I will graduate next month.

6. Ms. Walker can't come to the phone right now. She's in a meeting _____ the moment.

7. I usually take a walk _____ the morning before I go to work.

8. Frank likes to take a nap _____ the afternoon.

9. Our family enjoys spending time together _____ the evening.

10. Our children always stay home _____ night.

11. I ate lunch _____ noon.

12. I got home _____ midnight.

13. I moved to this city _____ September.

14. I moved here _____ 1990.

15. I moved here _____ September 1990.

16. I moved here _____ September 3.

17. I moved here _____ September 3, 1990.

18. I moved here _____ the fall.

19. I work _____ the morning. _____ the afternoon, I have an English class.

20. _____ Wednesday, I work all day. _____ Thursday, I have an English class.

21. _____ Thursday afternoon, I have an English class.

22. My plane was supposed to leave _____ 7:07 P.M., but it didn't take off until 8:30.

CHAPTER 3
Future Time

3-1 EXPRESSING FUTURE TIME: *BE GOING TO* AND *WILL*

FUTURE	(a) I **am going to leave** at nine tomorrow morning. (b) I **will leave** at nine tomorrow morning. (c) Marie **is going to be** at the meeting tonight. (d) Marie **will be** at the meeting tonight.	**Be going to** and **will** are used to express future time. (a) and (b) have the same meaning. (c) and (d) have the same meaning.*
(e) **I shall** leave at nine tomorrow morning. (f) **We shall** leave at nine tomorrow morning.		The use of *shall* (with *I* or *we*) to express future time is infrequent and formal.

* **Will** and **be going to** usually give the same meaning, but sometimes they express different meanings. The differences are discussed in Chart 3-4.

□ EXERCISE 1—ORAL (BOOKS CLOSED): Practice using *be going to.*

STUDENT A: Make a sentence with **be going to** about *your* future activities.
STUDENT B: Ask a question about STUDENT A's sentence.
STUDENT C: Answer the question.

Example: go/tomorrow morning
STUDENT A: I'm going to go to class tomorrow morning.
STUDENT B: What is (STUDENT A) going to do tomorrow morning?
STUDENT C: S/he's going to go to class.

1. go/tomorrow afternoon
2. write/tomorrow night
3. study/tonight
4. take/next week
5. see/later today
6. eat/in a couple of hours

7. buy/this weekend
8. go/next year
9. walk/pretty soon
10. have/after a while
11. wash/the day after tomorrow
12. travel to/sometime

☐ **EXERCISE 2—ORAL (BOOKS CLOSED):** Make sentences about *your* activities. Use present, past, or future verbs.

1. yesterday
2. tomorrow
3. right now
4. every day
5. today*
6. this morning*
7. this afternoon*
8. tonight*

9. the day before yesterday
10. the day after tomorrow
11. last week
12. this week*
13. next week
14. two days ago
15. in a few days (from now)
16. a few minutes ago

☐ **EXERCISE 3:** Complete the sentences by using *a pronoun + a form of* **be going to**.

1. I ate lunch with Alan today, and _____*I'm going to eat*_____ lunch with him tomorrow too.**

2. Jason wasn't in class today, and _____*he isn't going to be*_____ in class tomorrow either.**

3. The students took a quiz yesterday, and _____ another quiz today.

4. Margaret walked to school this morning, and _____ to school tomorrow morning too.

5. It isn't raining today, and according to the weather report, _____ _____ tomorrow either.

6. We're in class today, and _____ in class tomorrow too.

7. You didn't hitchhike to school today, and _____ to school tomorrow either.

---

* Time expressions such as *today, this morning, this afternoon, this evening, tonight, this week, this month, this year, this semester* can be used with past, present, or future verbs.
** See Chart 9-5 for more information about *too* and *either*.

8. I didn't get married last year, and _____

married this year either.

9. Peter didn't wear a clean shirt today, and _____

a clean one tomorrow either.

☐ **EXERCISE 4: ORAL:** Complete the sentences with a *pronoun + a form of **be going to***. Use a future time expression. Use ***too*** (with affirmative sentences) or ***either*** (with negative sentences).

    Example: I didn't study last night, and . . . .

    Response: I didn't study last night, and I'm not going to study tonight either.

1. I did my homework yesterday, and . . . .
2. I wasn't at home last night, and . . . .
3. We didn't have a grammar quiz today, and . . . .
4. Our teacher is in class today, and . . . .
5. It's (*cold/hot/nice*) today, and . . . .
6. I didn't go bowling today, and . . . .
7. I brought my umbrella with me today, and . . . .
8. I didn't get hit by a truck on my way to school today, and . . . .
9. The sun rose before six today, and . . . .
10. We didn't have pizza for breakfast this morning, and . . . .

3-2 FORMS WITH *WILL*

STATEMENT	{I You She He It We They} ***will come*** tomorrow.	
NEGATIVE	{I-You-She-He-It-We-They} ***will not*** (***won't***) ***come*** tomorrow.	
QUESTION	***Will*** {I-you-she-he-it-we-they} ***come*** tomorrow?	
SHORT ANSWER	Yes, {I-you-she-he-it-we-they} ***will***. No, {I-you-she-he-it-we-they} ***won't***.	
CONTRACTIONS	I'll, you'll, she'll, he'll, it'll, we'll, they'll	***Will*** is usually contracted with pronouns in both speech and informal writing.
	Bob + will = "Bob'll" the teacher will = "the teacher'll"	***Will*** is usually contracted with nouns in speech, but usually not in writing.

□ **EXERCISE 5:** Practice using contractions with *will*. Write the correct contraction for the words in parentheses. Practice pronunciation.

1. (*I will*) _____*I'll*_____ be home at eight tonight.

2. (*We will*) _____ see you tomorrow.

3. (*You will*) _____ probably get a letter today.

4. (*She will*) Karen is tired tonight. _____ probably go to bed early.

5. (*He will*) Dennis has a cold. _____ probably stay home in bed today.

6. (*It will*) _____ probably be too cold to go swimming tomorrow.

7. (*They will*) I invited some guests for dinner. _____ probably get here around seven.

□ **EXERCISE 6:** Read the following sentences aloud. Practice contracting *will* with nouns in speech.

1. Rob will probably call tonight.
2. Dinner will be at seven.
3. Mary will be here at six tomorrow.
4. The weather will probably be a little colder tomorrow.
5. The party will start at eight.
6. Sam will help us move into our new apartment.
7. My friends will be here soon.
8. The sun will rise at 6:08 tomorrow morning.

3-3 USING *PROBABLY* WITH *WILL*

(a) Ann *will **probably** go* to the park tomorrow.	People often use ***probably*** with ***will***. ***Probably*** comes between ***will*** and the main verb, as in (a). In a negative sentence, ***probably*** comes in front of
(b) Bob ***probably*** *won't go* to the park tomorrow.	
(c) FORMAL: Bob *will **probably** not go* to the park tomorrow.	***won't***, as in (b), or more formally, between ***will*** and ***not***, as in (c).*

* See Chart 7-8 for more information about placement of midsentence adverbs such as ***probably***.

☐ **EXERCISE 7:** Complete the sentences. Use a *pronoun* + *will/won't*. Use *probably*.

1. I went to the library last night, and   *I'll probably go*

   there tonight too.

2. Ann didn't come to class today, and __*she probably won't come*__

   tomorrow either.

3. I watched TV last night, and _____ TV

   tonight too.

4. I wasn't at home last night, and _____ at

   home tonight either.

5. Greg went to bed early last night, and _____

   to bed early tonight too.

6. Jack didn't hand his homework in today, and _____

   _____ it in tomorrow either.

7. It's hot today, and _____ hot tomorrow too.

8. My friends didn't come over last night, and _____

   over tonight either.

9. The students had a quiz today, and _____

   one tomorrow too.

10. Alice didn't ride her bike to school today, and _____

    _____ it to school tomorrow either.

3-4 BE GOING TO vs. WILL

(a) She *is going to succeed* because she works hard. (b) She *will succeed* because she works hard.	*Be going to* and *will* are the same when they are used to make predictions about the future. (a) and (b) have the same meaning.
(c) I bought some wood because *I am going to build* a bookcase for my apartment.	*Be going to* (but not *will*) is used to express a preconceived plan. In (c): The speaker is planning to build a bookcase.
(d) This chair is too heavy for you to carry alone. *I'll help* you.	*Will* (but not *be going to*) is used to volunteer or express willingness. In (d): The speaker is happy to help.

☐ **EXERCISE 8:** Complete the sentences with *be going to* or *will*.

1. A: Why did you buy this flour?

   B: I _____*'m going to*_____ make some bread.

2. A: Could someone get me a glass of water?

   B: Certainly. I _____*'ll*_____ get you one. Would you like some ice in it?

3. I arranged to borrow some money because I _____ buy a motorcycle tomorrow.

4. A: Could someone please open the window?

   B: I _____ do it.

5. A: Can I borrow this book?

   B: Sure. But I need it back soon.

   A: I _____ return it to you tomorrow. Okay?

6. A: I _____ wear a dark suit to the wedding reception. How about you?

   B: I'm not sure.

7. A: What are your vacation plans?

   B: I _____ spend two weeks on a Greek island.

8. A: Gee, I'd really like an ice cream cone, but I didn't bring any money with me.

   B: That's okay. I _____ get one for you.

   A: Thanks!

9. A: Hi, Josh. I hear that you _____ move into a

new apartment.

B: That's right. Sara and I found a great apartment on 45th Street.

A: I _____ help you on moving day if you like.

B: Hey, great! We'd really appreciate that.

10. A: So you _____ get married.

B: That's right. On September 22nd.

A: My congratulations.

11. A: If you can wait just a few minutes, I _____

walk to the meeting with you.

B: Okay. I _____ meet you by the elevator. Okay?

A: Okay. I _____ wait for you there.

12. A: Excuse me, but . . . .

B: I _____ be with you in a moment.

A: Thanks.

3-5 EXPRESSING FUTURE TIME IN TIME CLAUSES AND "*IF*-CLAUSES"

(a) *Before I go to class tomorrow*, I'm going to eat breakfast.	The simple present is used in a future time clause. *Be going to* and *will* are NOT used in a future time clause.
(b) I'm going to eat dinner at 6:00 tonight. *After I eat dinner*, I'm going to study in my room.	*before* *after* *when* *as soon as* } + subject and verb + a time clause*
(c) I'll give Mary your message *when I see her tomorrow*.	In (a): The speaker is talking about two events: going to class and eating breakfast. Both events are in the future. However, the speaker uses the simple present (not *be going to* or *will*) to talk about going to class because the verb occurs in a time clause: *Before I go to class tomorrow* . . . .
(d) It's raining right now. *As soon as the rain stops*, I'm going to walk downtown.	
(e) Maybe it will rain tomorrow. *If it rains tomorrow*, I'm going to stay home.	When the meaning is future, the simple present (not *be going to* or *will*) is used in an "*if*-clause." *If* + subject and verb = an "*if*-clause"*

* See Chapter 16 for other uses of "*if*-clauses."

□ **EXERCISE 9 — ORAL:** Combine the ideas of the two sentences into one sentence by using a time clause. Use the word in parentheses to introduce the time clause. Punctuate carefully.*

1. (*after*)   *First:* I'm going to finish my homework.
                 Then: I'm going to go to bed.

→   **After I finish my homework, I'm going to go to bed.** OR:

I'm going to bed after I finish my homework.

2. (*after*)   *First:* I'm going to write a letter.
                 Then: I'm going to go to bed.

3. (*when*)   *First:* I'm going to go to Chicago next week.
                 Then: I'm going to visit the art museum.

4. (*after*)   *First:* I'll go to the drug store.
                 Then: I'll go to the post office.

5. (*before*)   *First:* Ann will finish her homework.
                 Then: She will watch TV tonight.**

6. (*after*)   *First:* Jim will get home this evening.
                 Then: He's going to read the newspaper.

7. (*when*)   *First:* I'll call John tomorrow.
                 Then: I'll ask him to my party.

8. (*as soon as*) *First:* The rain will stop.
                 Then: The children are going to go outside and play.

9. (*as soon as*) *First:* The teacher will get here.
                 Then: Class will begin.

10. (*before*)   *First:* The Robertsons will get some travelers' checks.
                 Then: They will leave on vacation.

11. (*as soon as*) *First:* I will get home tonight.
                 Then: I'm going to take a hot bath.

12. (*when*)   *First:* I'm going to go shopping tomorrow.
                 Then: I'm going to buy a new pair of shoes.

---

* Notice the punctuation in the sample answer in number one. A comma is used when the time clause comes before the main clause. No comma is used when the time clause follows the main clause. See Chart 2-8 for punctuation of time clauses.

** A noun usually comes before a pronoun:
    After **Ann** *eats dinner,* **she** *is going to study.*
    Ann *is going to study after* **she** *eats dinner.*

□ **EXERCISE 10:** Complete the following sentences with your own words.

1. I'm going to eat dinner before I . . . .
2. As soon as I get home tonight, I . . . .
3. I'm going to call my friend after I . . . .
4. My life will be easy after I . . . .
5. Before I go to bed tonight, I . . . .
6. When I'm in Florida next month, I . . . .
7. I'll call you as soon as I . . . .
8. I'm going to visit my aunt and uncle when . . . .

□ **EXERCISE 11:** Combine the ideas of the two sentences into one sentence by using an "*if*-clause."

POSSIBLE CONDITION ⟶ **RESULT**

1. Maybe it will rain tomorrow. ⟶ I'm going to stay home.

→ *If it rains tomorrow, I'm going to stay home.* OR:

*I'm going to stay home if it rains tomorrow.**

2. Maybe it will be hot tomorrow. ⟶ I'm going to go swimming.

3. Maybe it will snow tomorrow. ⟶ Betsy isn't going to ride her bike to school.

4. Maybe Adam will have enough time. → He'll finish his composition tonight.

5. Maybe I won't get a letter tomorrow. → I'll call my parents.

To make sentences with "if-clauses" in the following, you need to decide which sentence is the "possible condition" and which is the "result."

6. We're going to go on a picnic. Perhaps the weather will be nice tomorrow.

7. Maybe Greg won't study for his test. He'll get a bad grade.

8. I'm probably going to go to Hawaii for my vacation. Maybe I will have enough money.

9. Maybe I won't study tonight. I probably won't pass the chemistry exam.

10. I'll probably get a good grade. Maybe I will study for the test.

---

* Notice the punctuation in the example. A comma is used when the "*if*-clause" comes before the main clause. No comma is used when the "*if*-clause" follows the main clause.

□ **EXERCISE 12—ORAL (BOOKS CLOSED):** Make sentences from the given possibilities. Use *if* and add your own ideas.

Example: Maybe you'll go downtown tomorrow.

Response: If I go downtown tomorrow, (*I'm going to buy some new clothes/I'm going to go to a department store/I can go to the post office, etc.*).

1. Maybe it'll be nice tomorrow.
2. Maybe it'll be hot/cold tomorrow.
3. Maybe it won't be nice/hot/cold tomorrow.
4. Maybe it'll rain tomorrow.
5. Maybe it won't rain tomorrow.
6. Maybe you'll be tired tonight.
7. Maybe you won't be tired tonight.
8. Maybe you'll have enough time tomorrow.

Example: Maybe you'll go downtown tomorrow.

STUDENT A: If I go downtown tomorrow, I'm going to buy some new boots.

STUDENT B: If (. . .) buys some new boots, his/her feet will be warm this winter.

9. Maybe you'll have some free time tomorrow.
10. Maybe you won't be in class tomorrow.
11. Maybe you'll be hungry after class.
12. Maybe you'll go to (*name of a local place*) tomorrow.
13. Maybe you won't have enough money to buy (*something*) when you go shopping tomorrow.
14. Maybe (. . .) will call (. . .) on the phone tonight.

□ **EXERCISE 13:** Following is a review of time clauses and "*if*-clauses." Complete the sentences by using a form of the words in parentheses. Read carefully for time expressions.

1. a. Before Tom (*go*) _____**goes**_____ to bed, he always (*brush*)

   _____**brushes**_____ his teeth.

   b. Before Tom (*go*) _____ to bed later tonight, he

   (*write*) _____ a letter to his girlfriend.

   c. Before Tom (*go*) _____ to bed last night, he

   (*take*) _____ a shower.

   d. While Tom (*take*) _____ a shower last night, the

   phone (*ring*) _____.

e. As soon as the phone (*ring*) _____ last night, Tom (*jump*) _____ out of the shower to answer it.

f. As soon as Tom (*get*) _____ up tomorrow morning, he (*brush*) _____ his teeth.

g. Tom always (*brush*) _____ his teeth as soon as he (*get*) _____ up.

2. a. After I (*get*) _____ home from school every afternoon, I usually (*drink*) _____ a cup of tea.

b. After I (*get*) _____ home from school tomorrow afternoon, I (*drink*) _____ a cup of tea.

c. After I (*get*) _____ home from school yesterday, I (*drink*) _____ a cup of tea.

d. While I (*drink*) _____ a cup of tea yesterday afternoon, my neighbor (*come*) _____ over, so I (*offer*) _____ her a cup of tea, too.

e. My neighbor (*drop*) _____ over again tomorrow. When she (*come*) _____, I (*make*) _____ a cup of tea for her.

3. Jane (*meet*) _____ me at the airport when my plane (*arrive*) _____ tomorrow.

4. If I (*see*) _____ Mike tomorrow, I (*tell*) _____ him about the party.

5. I go to New York often. When I (*be*) _____ in New York, I usually (*see*) _____ a Broadway play.

6. When I (*be*) _____ in New York next week, I (*stay*) _____ at the Park Plaza Hotel.

7. Cindy and I (*go*) _____ to the beach tomorrow if the weather (*be*) _____ warm and sunny.

8. As soon as the test (*be*) _____ over in class yesterday, the students (*leave*) _____ the room.

9. Jack (*watch*) _____ a football game on TV right now. As soon as the game (*be*) _____ over, he (*mow*) _____ the grass in the back yard.

10. As soon as I (*get*) _____ home every day, my children always (*run*) _____ to the door to meet me.

☐ **EXERCISE 14—WRITTEN:** Write two paragraphs. Show the time relationships by using words such as *before, after, when, while, as soon as, next, then, later, after that.*
　　Paragraph 1: a detailed description of your day yesterday.
　　Paragraph 2: a detailed description of your day tomorrow.

3-6 PARALLEL VERBS

V 　　**and**　　**V** (a) Jim **makes** his bed *and* **cleans** up his room every morning.	Often a subject has two verbs that are connected by **and**. We say that the two verbs are parallel: 　**V**　+ **and** +　**V** 　*makes　and　cleans* = parallel verbs
(b) Ann **is cooking** dinner *and* (*is*) **talking** on the phone at the same time. (c) I **will stay** home *and* (*will*) **study** tonight. (d) I **am going to stay** home *and* (*am going to*) **study** tonight.	It is not necessary to repeat a helping verb (an auxiliary verb) when two verbs are connected by **and**.

☐ **EXERCISE 15:** Complete the sentences with the correct forms of the words in parentheses.

1. When I (*walk*) _____ into the living room yesterday evening, Grandpa (*read*) _____ a newspaper and (*smoke*) _____ his pipe.

2. Helen will graduate next semester. She (*move*) _____ _____ to New York and (*look*) _____ for a job after she (*graduate*) _____.

3. Every day my neighbor (*call*) _____ me on the phone and (*complain*) _____ about the weather.

4. Look at Erin! She (*cry*) _____ and (*laugh*) _____ at the same time. I wonder if she is happy or sad.

5. I'm beat! I can't wait to get home. After I (*get*) _____ home, I (*take*) _____ a hot shower and (*go*) _____ to bed.

6. Yesterday my dog (*dig*) _____ a hole in the back yard and (*bury*) _____ a bone.

7. I'm tired of this cold weather. As soon as spring (*come*) _____, I (*play*) _____ tennis and (*jog*) _____ in the park as often as possible.

☐ **EXERCISE 16:** Complete the sentences by using a form of the words in parentheses.

1. It's getting late, but before I (*go*) _____ to bed, I (*finish*) _____ my homework and (*write*) _____ a couple of letters.

2. While I (*make*) _____ dinner last night, some grease (*spill*) _____ out of the frying pan and (*catch*) _____ on fire. When the smoke detector on the ceiling (*start*) _____ to buzz, my roommate (*run*) _____ into the kitchen to find out what was wrong. He (*think*) _____ that the house was on fire!

3. Mark is obsessed with video games. He (*play*) _____

   video games morning, noon, and night. Sometimes he (*cut*)

   _____ class to play the games. Right now he (*do, not*)

   _____ very well in school. If he (*study, not*)

   _____ harder and (*go*) _____ to

   class every day, he (*flunk*) _____ out of

   school.

4. Sometimes my daughter, Susie, has temper tantrums. She (*cry*)

   _____ and (*stamp*) _____ her feet when

   she (*get*) _____ angry. Yesterday when she (*get*)

   _____ angry, she (*pick*) _____ up a toy

   car and (*throw*) _____ it at her little brother. Luckily,

   the car (*hit, not*) _____ him. Susie (*feel*)

   _____ very bad. She (*apologize*) _____

   to her little brother and (*kiss*) _____ him.

5. It's October now. The weather (*begin*) _____ to get

   colder. It (*begin*) _____ to get cold every October. I (*like,*

   not) _____ winter, but I (*think*) _____

   autumn is beautiful. In a couple of weeks, my friend and I (*take*)

   _____ a weekend trip to the country if the

   weather (*be*) _____ nice. We (*drive*) _____

   _____ through the river valley and (*enjoy*) _____

   the colors of fall.

3-7 USING THE PRESENT PROGRESSIVE TO EXPRESS FUTURE TIME

(a) Don *is going to come* to the party tomorrow night. (b) Don *is coming* to the party tomorrow night. (c) We*'re going to go* to a movie tonight. (d) We*'re going* to a movie tonight. (e) I*'m going to stay* home tonight. (f) I*'m staying* home tonight. (g) Ann *is going to fly* to Chicago next week. (h) Ann *is flying* to Chicago next week. (i) Bob *is going to take* a taxi to the airport tomorrow. (j) Bob *is taking* a taxi to the airport tomorrow.	Sometimes the present progressive is used to express future time. (a) and (b) have the same meaning. The present progressive is used to express future time when the sentence concerns **a definite plan, a definite intention, a definite future activity.***
(k) A: You shouldn't buy that used car. It's in terrible condition. It costs too much. You don't have enough money. You'll have to get insurance, and you can't afford the insurance. Buying that used car is a crazy idea. B: I *am buying* that used car tomorrow morning! My mind is made up. Nobody—not you, not my mother, not my father—can stop me. I*'m buying* that car, and that's it! I don't want to talk about it anymore. A: Oh well, it's your money.	Verbs such as **come, go, stay, arrive, leave** are frequently used in the present progressive to express future time. Such verbs express definite plans. Verbs expressing planned means of transportation in the future are also frequently used in the present progressive; for example, **fly, walk, ride, drive, take** (*a bus, a taxi, etc.*). Sometimes a speaker will use the present progressive when he or she wants to make a **very strong statement** about a future activity, as in (k).

* A future meaning for the present progressive is indicated either by future time words in the sentence or by the context.

□ **EXERCISE 17:** Complete the sentences with appropriate *pronouns* + the PRESENT PROGRESSIVE.

1. I met Jane after class yesterday, and ____*I'm meeting*____ her after class again later today.

2. My friends came over last night, and _____ over this evening, too.

3. Susan didn't come to class today, and _____ to class tomorrow either.

4. We had a meeting this morning, and _____ another meeting tomorrow morning.

5. I didn't eat lunch at the cafeteria this noon, and _____

_____ lunch there tomorrow either.

6. I took a bus to work this morning, and _____

the same bus to work tomorrow morning.

7. Harry didn't go to work today, and _____ to

work tomorrow either.

8. The children went to the beach today, and _____

_____ to the beach again tomorrow.

☐ **EXERCISE 18:** Practice using the PRESENT PROGRESSIVE to express future time by completing the dialogues. Use the words in the list or your own words. Are there any sentences in this exercise in which the present progressive expresses present, not future, time?

| call | drive | go | meet |
| come | fly | make | stay |

1. A: What are you doing tomorrow afternoon?

B: I ____*am going*____ downtown. I ____*am going*____

_____ shopping. How about you? What ____*are*____

you ____*doing*____ tomorrow afternoon?

A: I _____ to a movie with Tom. After the movie,

we _____ out to dinner. Would you like to come

with us?

B: No, thanks. I can't. I _____ Heidi at 6:30 at the

new seafood restaurant on Fifth Street.

2. A: What courses _____ you _____ this year?

B: I _____ English, biology, math, and

psychology.

A: What courses _____ you _____ next year?

B: I _____ English literature, chemistry, calculus,

and history.

A: That should keep you busy!

3. A: I _____ on vacation tomorrow.

   B: Where _____ you _____?

   A: To San Francisco.

   B: How are you getting there? _____ you

   _____ or _____ your car?

   A: I _____. I have to be at the airport by seven

   tomorrow morning.

   B: Do you need a ride to the airport?

   A: No, thanks. I _____ a taxi. Are you planning to

   go somewhere over vacation?

   B: No. I _____ here.

4. A: My sister and her husband _____ over to my

   house for dinner tomorrow night. It's my sister's birthday, so I

   _____ a special birthday dinner for her. I

   _____ her favorite food: roast beef and mashed

   potatoes.

   B: _____ anyone else _____ over for the

   birthday dinner?

   A: Yes. Rick and Olga Walker.

5. A: I'm going to call the doctor. You have a fever, chills, and a stomach

   ache.

   B: No, don't call a doctor. I'll be okay.

   A: I'm worried. I _____ the doctor! And that's it!

3-8 USING THE SIMPLE PRESENT TO EXPRESS FUTURE TIME

(a) My plane **arrives** at 7:35 *tomorrow evening*. (b) Tom's new job **starts** *next week*. (c) The semester **ends** *in two more weeks*. (d) There **is** a meeting at ten *tomorrow morning*.	The simple present can express future time when events are on a definite schedule or timetable. Only a few verbs are used in the simple present to express future time. The most common are **arrive**, **leave**, **start**, **begin**, **end**, **finish**, **open**, **close**, **be**.

Use the SIMPLE PRESENT of the verb in parentheses *if possible*. Otherwise, use *be going to*/the PRESENT PROGRESSIVE.

1. (*start*)   The game _____**starts**_____ *(also possible: is starting/is going to start)* at one tomorrow afternoon.

2. (*have*)   We ___**are having/are going to have**___ chicken and pasta for dinner tonight.

3. (*walk*)   I _____ to school tomorrow morning. I need the exercise.

4. (*leave*)   The bus _____ at 8:15 tomorrow morning.

5. (*begin,*   The exam _____ at 9:00 tomorrow morning

    end)   and _____ at 11:00.

6. (*open,*   Tomorrow the museum _____ at 10:00 and

    close)   _____ at 5:00. Let's go around 2:30, okay?

7. (*get*)   Have you heard the news? Laura and Jason _____ married in August.

8. (*watch*)   I _____ the championship game on TV at Jim's house tomorrow.

9. (*arrive,*   Alex's plane _____ at 10:14 tomorrow

    take)   morning. I can't pick him up, so he _____ the airport bus into the city center.

10. (*be*)   There _____ a flight to Dallas at 7:02 tomorrow morning.

3-9 PRESENT PLANS FOR FUTURE ACTIVITIES: USING *INTEND, PLAN, HOPE*

(a) I'm *intending*/I *intend* **to go** to Paris. (b) I'm *planning*/I *plan* **to take** a trip next month. (c) I'm *hoping*/I *hope* **to fly** to Paris next month.	*Intend*, *plan*, and *hope* are used in present tenses to express present ideas about future activities. INCORRECT: *I intend to go to Paris next month.*
TO + THE SIMPLE FORM OF A VERB (d) I intend **to** + **go** I plan **to** + **take**	*Intend*, *plan*, and *hope* are followed by an infinitive (**to** + the simple form of a verb).*

* See Chapter 10 for more information about infinitives.

☐ **EXERCISE 20—ORAL:** Make sentences that communicate the same or a similar meaning. Use the verbs in parentheses.

1. I think that I will graduate next June. (*hope*)
   → *I am hoping/hope to graduate next June.*
2. I think that I will be at the meeting on time tomorrow. (*intend*)
3. Tom thinks that he will buy a new red bicycle tomorrow. (*plan*)
4. Jane thinks that she is going to get a good job after she graduates. (*hope*)
5. I think I will stay in London for two weeks after I leave Paris. (*plan*)
6. I think I will finish my education, get a good job, start a family, and live happily ever after. (*intend*)

3-10 IMMEDIATE FUTURE: USING *BE ABOUT TO*

(a) Ann's bags are packed, and she is wearing her coat. She *is about to leave* for the airport.	The idiom *be about to do something* expresses an activity that will happen in the **immediate future**, usually within five minutes. In (a): Ann is going to leave sometime in the next few minutes.
(b) Shhh. The movie *is about to begin.*	

☐ **EXERCISE 21—ORAL:** What are the following people probably about to do?

1. Jack is holding his camera to his eye. He has his finger on the button.
   → *He's about to take a picture.*
2. Sally has her hand on the door knob.
3. Ben is putting on his coat and heading for the door.
4. Nancy has dirty hands from working in the garden. She is holding a bar of soap. She is standing at the bathroom sink.
5. Eric is on the last question of the examination.
6. Rita is holding a fly swatter and staring at a fly on the kitchen table.

☐ **EXERCISE 22—WRITTEN:** Write a short paragraph on each of the following topics.

    1. Write about an interesting experience you had when you were a child (six to twelve years old).

    2. Write about your plans for the future.

☐ **EXERCISE 23—PREPOSITIONS:** Complete the sentences with prepositions. (See Appendix 1 for a list of preposition combinations.)

    1. I borrowed this dictionary _____ Pedro.

    2. Could you please help me _____ these heavy suitcases?

    3. Sue, I'd like to introduce you _____ Ed Jones.

    4. You shouldn't stare _____ other people. It's not polite.

    5. Marco Polo traveled _____ China in the thirteenth century.

    6. Do you believe _____ ghosts?

    7. Are you laughing _____ my mistake?

    8. I admire my father _____ his honesty and intelligence.

    9. I argued _____ Jack _____ politics.

   10. I discussed my educational plans _____ my parents.

   11. I applied _____ the University of Massachusetts. I applied _____ admission to the University of Massachusetts.

   12. Joanna applied _____ a job at the automobile factory.

CHAPTER 4
Nouns and Pronouns

□ **EXERCISE 1—PRETEST:** Identify each italicized word in the sentences as a:
- NOUN
- ADJECTIVE
- PREPOSITION or
- PRONOUN.

1. Eric is wearing a new *shirt* today. shirt _____ **noun** _____

2. Algeria is *in* North Africa. in _____ **preposition** _____

3. Steve is in Asia. *He* is traveling. he _____ **pronoun** _____

4. I'm *thirsty*. thirsty _____ **adjective** _____

5. We have class in this *room* every day. room _____

6. I know my *way* to Joanna's house. way _____

7. The *happy* children squealed with joy. happy _____

8. I walked to class *with* Maria. with _____

9. Hawaii has eight principal *islands*. islands _____

10. The *hungry* man stuffed his mouth with rice. hungry _____

11. Tokyo is the capital of *Japan*. Japan _____

12. Athens is a *beautiful* city. beautiful _____

13. My history book is *under* my desk. under _____

14. Do you like classical *music*? music _____

15. I don't eat sour oranges. I don't like *them*. them _____

Number a piece of paper from 1 to 22. This is a spelling test. Write the plural forms of the given nouns.

Example: one chair, two...
Written: **chairs**

1. glass	12. roof
2. problem	13. hero
3. match	14. radio
4. bush	15. zero
5. animal	16. foot
6. sex	17. mouse
7. library	18. sheep
8. monkey	19. woman
9. family	20. child
10. wife	21. phenomenon
11. shelf	22. offspring

4-1 PLURAL FORMS OF NOUNS

SINGULAR	PLURAL	
(a) one bird one street one rose	two **birds** two **streets** two **roses**	To make most nouns plural, add **-s**.
(b) one dish one match one class one box	two **dishes** two **matches** two **classes** two **boxes**	Add **-es** to nouns ending in **-sh**, **-ch**, **-ss**, and **-x**.
(c) one baby one city	two **babies** two **cities**	If a noun ends in a consonant + **-y**, change the "**i**" to "**i**" and add **-es**. (NOTE: If **-y** is preceded by a vowel, add only **-s**: *boys, days, keys*.)
(d) one knife one shelf	two **knives** two **shelves**	If a noun ends in **-fe** or **-f**, change the ending to **-ves**. (Exceptions: *beliefs, chiefs, roofs, cuffs*.)

(e) one tomato
one zoo
one zero
	two **tomatoes**
	two **zoos**
	two **zeroes**/**zeros**
		The plural form of nouns that end in **-o** is sometimes **-oes** and sometimes **-os**.
		    -oes: *tomatoes, potatoes, heroes, echoes, mosquitoes*
		    -os: *zoos, radios, studios, pianos, solos, sopranos, photos, autos*
		    -oes or **-os**: *zeroes/zeros, volcanoes/volcanos, tornadoes/tornados*

(f) one child	two *children*	Some nouns have irregular plural forms.
one foot	two *feet*	(NOTE: The singular form of *people* can be *person*,
one goose	two *goose*	*woman*, *man*, *child*. For example, one man and one
one man	two *men*	child = two people.)
one mouse	two *mice*	
one tooth	two *teeth*	
one woman	two *women*	
—	two *people*	
(g) one deer	two *deer*	The plural form of some nouns is the same as the
one fish	two *fish*	singular form.
one sheep	two *sheep*	
one offspring	two *offspring*	
one species	two *species*	
(h) one bacterium	two *bacteria*	Some nouns that English has borrowed from other
one cactus	two *cacti*	languages have foreign plurals.
one crisis	two *crises*	
one phenomenon	two *phenomena*	

☐ **EXERCISE 3:** Write the plural forms of the nouns.

1. one potato, two _____ *potatoes* _____

2. a dormitory, many _____

3. one child, two _____

4. a leaf, a lot of _____

5. a wish, many _____

6. one fish, two _____

7. an opinion, many _____

8. a mouse, several _____

9. a sandwich, some _____

10. a man, many _____

11. one woman, two _____

12. a flash, three _____

13. one tomato, a few _____

14. one tooth, two _____

15. one half, two _____

16. a tax, a lot of _____

17. a possibility, several _____

18. a thief, many _____

19. a volcano, many _____

20. a goose, a lot of _____

21. an attorney, a few _____

22. a butterfly, several _____

23. one category, two _____

24. a mosquito, a lot of _____

25. one sheep, two _____

26. a wolf, some _____

27. one stitch, two _____

28. one foot, three _____

29. one piano, two _____

30. a belief, many _____

4-2 SUBJECTS, VERBS, AND OBJECTS

(a) The **sun shines**.
     (noun) (verb)
 	
(b) **Plants grow**.
    (noun) (verb)
	An English sentence has a SUBJECT (**S**) and a VERB (**V**).
	
	The SUBJECT is a **noun**. In (a): *sun* is a noun; it is the subject of the verb *shines*.

(c) **Plants need water**.
   (noun) (verb) (noun)
 	
(d) **Bob is reading** a **book**.
  (noun) (verb)   (noun)
	Sometimes a VERB is followed by an OBJECT (**O**).
	
	The OBJECT of a verb is a **noun**. In (c): *water* is the object of the verb *need*.

☐ **EXERCISE 4:** Find the SUBJECT (S) and VERB (V) of each sentence. Also find the OBJECT (O) of the verb if the sentence has an object.

                  S   V   O

1. The <u>carpenter</u> <u>built</u> a <u>table</u>.

           S   V

2. <u>Birds</u> <u>fly</u>.

3. Cows eat grass.

4. My dog barked.

5. The dog chased the cat.

6. Accidents happen.

7. My roommate opened the window.

8. Most birds build nests.

9. Our guests arrived.

10. Teachers assign homework.

11. Steam rises.

12. Jack raised his hand.

13. Irene is watching her sister's children.

4-3 OBJECTS OF PREPOSITIONS

S V O PREP O of PREP (a) Ann put her books **on** the **desk**. (noun) **S V PREP O of PREP** (b) A leaf fell **to** the **ground**. (noun)	Many English sentences have prepositional phrases. In (a): "on the desk" is a prepositional phrase. A prepositional phrase consists of a PREPOSITION (**PREP**) and an OBJECT OF A PREPOSITION (**O of PREP**). The object of a preposition is a *noun*.

REFERENCE LIST OF PREPOSITIONS

about	*before*	*despite*	*of*	*to*
above	*behind*	*down*	*off*	*toward(s)*
across	*below*	*during*	*on*	*under*
after	*beneath*	*for*	*out*	*until*
against	*beside*	*from*	*over*	*up*
along	*besides*	*in*	*since*	*upon*
among	*between*	*into*	*through*	*with*
around	*beyond*	*like*	*throughout*	*within*
at	*by*	*near*	*till*	*without*

□ **EXERCISE 5:** Find the SUBJECTS, VERBS, and OBJECTS in the following. Identify the PREPOSITION (PREP) and the noun that is used as the OBJECT OF THE PREPOSITION (O of PREP).

S   V   O   PREP   O of PREP
1. Sara saw some pictures on   the wall.

2. Sara looked at the pictures.

3. Emily waited for her friend at a restaurant.

4. The sun rises in the east.

5. Sue lost her ring in the sand at the beach.

6. The moon usually disappears from view during the day.

7. Eric talked to his friend on the phone for thirty minutes.

8. Children throughout the world play with dolls.

9. Astronauts walked on the moon in 1969.★

10. A woman in a blue suit sat beside me until the end of the meeting.

★ Note: In a typical English sentence, "**place**" (e.g., *on the moon*) is mentioned before "**time**" (e.g., *in 1969*). INCORRECT: *Astronauts walked in 1969 on the moon.*

□ **EXERCISE 6—ORAL:** Review prepositions of place by using the following phrases in sentences. Demonstrate the meaning of the preposition by some action.

Example: above my head
Oral response: I'm holding my hand above my head. (*The student demonstrates this action.*)

1. across the room
2. against the wall
3. among my books and papers
4. between two pages of my book
5. around my wrist
6. at my desk
7. on my desk
8. in the room
9. into the room
10. behind me
11. below the window
12. beside my book
13. near the door
14. far from the door
15. off my desk
16. out the window
17. under my desk
18. through the door
19. throughout the room
20. toward(s) the door

4-4 USING ADJECTIVES TO DESCRIBE NOUNS

(a) Bob is reading a **good** book. (adjective + noun)	Words that describe nouns are called *adjectives*. In (a): *good* is an adjective; it describes the book.
(b) The **tall** *woman* wore a **new** *dress*. (c) The **short** *woman* wore an **old** *dress*. (d) The **young** *woman* wore a **short** *dress*.	We say that adjectives "modify" nouns. "Modify" means "change a little." An adjective changes the meaning of a noun by giving more information about it.
(e) Roses are **beautiful** *flowers*. INCORRECT: Roses are beautifuls flowers.	Adjectives are neither singular nor plural. They do NOT have a plural form.
(f) He wore a **white** *shirt*. INCORRECT: He wore a shirt white. (g) Roses *are* **beautiful**. (h) His shirt *was* **white**.	Adjectives can come immediately before nouns, as in (f). Adjectives can also follow main verb *be*, as in (g) and (h).

□ **EXERCISE 7:** Find the ADJECTIVES (ADJ) in the sentences. Also discuss subjects, verbs, and objects.

Adj.

1. The students wrote <u>long</u> compositions.

2. Deserts are dry.

3. The audience laughed at the funny joke.

4. Sensible people wear comfortable shoes.

5. Knives are sharp.

6. Crocodiles have big teeth.

7. Dark places frighten small children.

8. Steve cleaned the shelves of the refrigerator with soapy water.

9. The local police searched the stolen car for illegal drugs.

10. Before the development of agriculture, primitive people gathered wild plants for food.

4-5 USING NOUNS AS ADJECTIVES

(a) I have a *flower* garden. (b) The *shoe* store also sells socks. (c) INCORRECT: a flowers garden INCORRECT: the shoes store	Sometimes words that are usually used as nouns are used as adjectives. For example, *flower* is usually a noun, but in (a) it is used as an adjective to modify *garden*. When a noun is used as an adjective, it is singular in form, NOT plural.

☐ **EXERCISE 8:** Identify the nouns. Use a noun in the first sentence as an adjective in the second sentence.

         NOUN   **NOUN**   **NOUN**   **NOUN**

1. My garden has vegetables. It is a _____*vegetable*_____ garden.*

2. The program is on television. It's a _____ program.

3. He climbs mountains. He is a _____ climber.

---

* When one noun modifies another noun, the spoken stress is usually on the first noun: a **vegetable** garden.

4. The lesson concerned history. It was a _____ lesson.

5. Tom works for the government. He is a _____ worker.

6. The soup has beans. It is _____ soup.

7. The factory makes automobiles. It's an _____ factory.

8. Janet forecasts the weather. She's a _____ forecaster.

9. This book is about grammar. It's a _____book.

10. An album that contains photographs is called a_____ album.

□ **EXERCISE 9:** The following sentences have many mistakes in the use of nouns.
- Find each noun.
- Decide if the noun should be plural.
- Write the correct plural form as necessary.

Do not change any of the words in the sentences.

1. The mountain in Chile are beautiful.

   → ***The mountains in Chile are beautiful.***

2. Cat hunt mouse.

3. Mosquito are small insect.

4. Everyone has eyelash.

5. Goose are larger than duck.

DUCK

GOOSE

6. What are your favorite radio program?

7. Forest sometimes have fire. Forest fire endanger wild animal.

8. Sharp kitchen knife can be dangerous weapon.

9. There are many different kind of people in the world.

10. I applied to several foreign university because I want to study abroad next year.

11. Ted lives with three other university student.

12. The offspring of animal like horse, zebra, and deer can run soon after they are born.

13. I like to read book and magazine article about true personal experience.

14. Many modern device require battery to work. Flashlight, pocket calculator, portable radio, tape recorder, and many kind of toy often need battery.

☐ **EXERCISE 10:** Find the nouns. Make them plural if necessary.

Whales

(1)   Whale look like fish, but they aren't. They are mammal. Mouse, tiger,

(2) and human being are other examples of mammal. Whale are intelligent

(3) animal like dog and chimpanzee. Even though they live in sea, ocean, and

(4) river, whale are not fish. Fish lay egg and do not feed their offspring.

(5) Mammal give birth to live offspring and feed them.

(6)   There are many kind of whale. Most whale are huge creature. The

(7) largest whale are called blue whale. They can grow to 100 foot (30 meter) in

(8) length and can weigh 150 ton (135,000 kilogram). Blue whale are much

(9) larger than elephant and larger than any of the now extinct dinosaur. The

RELATIVE SIZES OF A BLUE WHALE AND AN AFRICAN ELEPHANT

(10) heart of an adult blue whale is about the size of a compact car. Its main

(11) blood vessel, the aorta, is large enough for a person to crawl through.

(12)   Human being have hunted and killed whale since ancient times. Aside

(13) from people, whale have no natural enemy. Today many people are trying to

(14) stop the hunting of whale.

4-6 PERSONAL PRONOUNS: SUBJECTS AND OBJECTS

PERSONAL PRONOUNS					
SUBJECT PRONOUNS:	**I**	**we**	**you**	**she, he, it**	**they**
OBJECT PRONOUNS:	**me**	**us**	**you**	**her, him, it**	**them**

S (a) **_Kate_** is married. **_She_** has two children. O (b) **_Kate_** is my friend. I know **_her_** well.	A pronoun refers to a noun. It is used in place of a noun. In (a): "she" is a pronoun. It refers to "Kate." It is used in place of the noun "Kate." In (b): "her" is a pronoun. It refers to "Kate." **_She_** is a subject pronoun; **_her_** is an object pronoun. A pronoun is used in the same ways as a noun: as a subject or as an object of a verb or preposition.
(c) Mike has **_a new blue bicycle_**. He bought **_it_** yesterday.	A pronoun can refer to a single noun, as in (a) and (b). A pronoun can also refer to a noun phrase. In (c): "it" refers to the whole noun phrase "a new blue bicycle."
S (d) _[Eric and I]_ are good friends. O (e) Ann met _[Eric and me]_ at the museum. O of **PREP** (f) Ann walked between _[Eric and me]_.	Sometimes nouns and pronouns are connected by **_and_**. The choice of a pronoun after **_and_** can be troublesome.* If the pronoun is used as part of the subject, use a subject pronoun (e.g., _I_), as in (d). If it is part of the object, use an object pronoun, (e.g., _me_) as in (e) and (f).

SINGULAR PRONOUNS:	**I**	**me**	**you**	**she, he, it**	**her, him**
PLURAL PRONOUNS:	**we**	**us**	**you**	**they**	**them**

(g) **_Mike_** is in class. **_He_** is taking a test. (h) The **_students_** are in class. **_They_** are taking a test. (i) **_Kate and Tom_** are married. **_They_** have two children.	_Singular_ = one. _Plural_ = more than one. Singular pronouns refer to singular nouns, plural pronouns to plural nouns. In (g): "Mike" is singular (one person), so a singular pronoun (_he_) is used. In (h): "students" is plural, so a plural pronoun (_they_) is used.

*Pronoun usage after **_and_** can be troublesome for native speakers, too!

□ **EXERCISE 11:** Choose the correct words in italics.

1. Ms. Lee wrote a note on my test paper. (_She,_) _Her_ wanted to talk to _I,_ (_me_) after class.

2. Nick ate dinner with _I, me_.

3. Nick ate dinner with Betsy and _I, me_.

4. _I, me_ had dinner with Nick last night.

5. Betsy and _I, me_ had dinner with Nick last night.

6. Nick ate dinner with _we, us_.

7. Nick ate dinner with the Robertsons and *we, us*.

8. My brother drove Emily and *I, me* to the store. He didn't come in. He waited for *we, us* in the car. *We, Us* hurried.

9. A: I want to get tickets for the soccer game.

   B: You'd better get *it, them* right way. *It, They* *is, are* selling fast.

10. Alex bought a ticket to the soccer game. He put *it, them* in his pocket and forgot about *it, them*. The next day, he put his shirt in the wash. The ticket came out of the washing machine and dryer crumpled and nearly illegible. But when Alex took *it, them* to the game, the ticket taker accepted *it, them* and let Alex in.

11. Please take these food scraps and give *it, them* to the dog.

12. I talked to Jennifer and Mike. I told *they, them* about the surprise birthday party for Lizzy. *They, them* won't tell *she, her* about *it, them*. *She, Her* is really going to be surprised!

13. Ted invited *I, me* to go to the game with *he, him*.

14. Ted invited Adam and *I, me* to go to the game with Tina and *he, him*.

15. Between you and *I, me,* I think Brian made a bad decision when he quit his job. Brian and *I, me* see things differently.

4-7 POSSESSIVE NOUNS

SINGULAR: (a) I know the ***student's*** name. PLURAL: (b) I know the ***students'*** names. PLURAL: (c) I know the ***children's*** names.	An apostrophe (') and an *-s* are used with nouns to show possession. Notice the patterns:
SINGULAR the student ⟶ the ***student's*** name my baby ⟶ my ***baby's*** name a man ⟶ a ***man's*** name	SINGULAR POSSESSIVE NOUN: noun + apostrophe (') + *-s*

PLURAL
the students ⟶ the ***students'*** names
my babies ⟶ my ***babies'*** names
men ⟶ ***men's*** names
the children ⟶ the ***children's*** names
	PLURAL POSSESSIVE NOUN:
	    noun + *-s* + apostrophe (')
	IRREGULAR PLURAL* POSSESSIVE NOUN:
	    noun + apostrophe (') + *-s*

*An irregular plural noun is a plural noun that does not end in *-s*: *children, men, people, women*. See Chart 4-1.

☐ **EXERCISE 12:** Use the correct possessive form of the noun in italics to complete the sentence.

1. *student*   One student asked several questions. I answered the
    ___**student's**___ questions.

2. *students*   Many students had questions after the lecture. I answered the
    ___**students'**___ questions.

3. *daughter*   We have one child, a girl. Our _____

    bedroom is right next to ours.

4. *daughters*   We have two children, both girls. They share a bedroom. Our

    _____ bedroom is next to ours.

5. *man*   Keith is a _____ name.

6. *woman*   Heidi is a _____ name.

7. *men*   Keith and Jeremy are _____ names.

8. *women*   Emily and Colette are _____ names.

9. *people*   It's important to be sensitive to other _____

    feelings.

10. *person*   I always look straight into a _____ eyes

    during a conversation.

11. *earth*   The _____ surface is about seventy per cent water.

12. *elephant*   An _____ skin is gray and wrinkled.

13. *teachers*   We have class in this building, but all of the _____

    offices are in another building.

14. *teacher*   My grammar _____ husband is an

    engineer.

15. *enemy*   Two soldiers, each faceless and nameless to the other, fought

    to the death on the muddy river bank. At the end, the winner

    could not help but admire his _____

    courage and wonder why he'd had to die.

16. *enemies*   Through the years in public office, he made many political

    enemies. He made a list of his _____

    names so that he could get revenge when he achieved

    political power.

4-8 POSSESSIVE PRONOUNS AND ADJECTIVES

This pen belongs to me. (a) It's **mine**. (b) It is **my** pen.	(a) and (b) have the same meaning; they both show possession. "Mine" is a possessive pronoun; "my" is a possessive adjective.

POSSESSIVE PRONOUNS	POSSESSIVE ADJECTIVES	
(c) I have **mine**.	I have **my** pen.	A **possessive pronoun** is used alone, without a noun following it. A **possessive adjective** is used only with a noun following it. In (j): the possessive **its** is used only with a noun following it. Note that possessive **its** has no apostrophe.*
(d) You have **yours**.	You have **your** pen.	
(e) She has **hers**.	She has **her** pen.	
(f) He has **his**.	He has **his** pen.	
(g) We have **ours**.	We have **our** pens.	
(h) You have **yours**.	You have **your** pens.	
(i) They have **theirs**.	They have **their** pens.	
(j) _____	I have a book. **Its** cover is black.	

***its** = possessive adjective

it's = *it is* (or *it has* when used in the present perfect)

☐ **EXERCISE 13:** Choose the correct words in italics.

1. Children should obey   *his, their*   parents.

2. A: Excuse me. Is this   *my, mine*   dictionary or *your, yours*?

   B: This one is   *my, mine.   Your, Yours*   is on   *your, yours*   desk.

3. The bird cleaned   *its, it's*   feathers with   *its, it's*   beak.

4. A: What kind of bird is that?

   B: *Its, It's*   a crow.

5. Paula had to drive my car to work.   *Hers, Her*   had a flat tire.

6. Julie fell off her bicycle and broke   *hers, her*   arm.

7. Fruit should be a part of   *your, yours*   daily diet.   *It, They*   *is, are* good for   *you, them*.

8. a. Adam and Amanda are married.   *They, Them*   live in an apartment building.

   b. *Their, There, They're★*   apartment is on the fifth floor.

   c. We live in the same building.   *Our, Ours*   apartment has one bedroom, but   *their, theirs*   has two.

   d. *Their, There, They're*   sitting in the kitchen of   *their, there, they're*   apartment right now.

   e. *Their, There, They're*   sitting   *their, there, they're*   now because *their, there, they're*   waiting for a phone call from   *their, there, they're*   son.

4-9   *A FRIEND OF* + POSSESSIVE

(a) Do you know Greg Smith? He is ***a friend of mine***.★ (b) We ate dinner with ***a friend of Bill's***. INCORRECT: *a friend of **Bill***	***A friend of*** + *a possessive noun/pronoun* is a special or idomatic expression. It is used to identify another person as one friend among many friends. In (a): *a friend of mine* = one of my friends, but not my only friend. In (b): *a friend of Bill's* = one of Bill's friends; Bill has other friends. In (d): The expression can also be used in the plural.
(c) The Smiths are ***friends*** *of mine*.	

★*He is my friend* may give the idea that the speaker has only one friend. A speaker would normally say *He is one of my friends* or *He is a friend of mine*.

★***Their, there,*** and ***they're*** have the same pronunciation (but not meaning).

   Their = possessive adjective. ***There*** = expression of place. ***They're*** = *They are*.

☐ **EXERCISE 14—ORAL (BOOKS CLOSED):** Make sentences with *a friend of/friends of.*

> *Example:* You have a friend (in Chicago). You wrote a letter to this person.
> *Response:* I wrote a letter to a friend of mine in Chicago.
>
> *Example:* (. . .) has a friend (in Miami). He wrote a letter to this person.
> *Response:* Pedro wrote a letter to a friend of his in Miami.

1. (. . .) has a friend in (*a city*). He/She wrote a letter to this person.
2. You have a good friend in (*a city*). You wrote a letter to this person.
3. (. . .) and (. . .) have friends in (*a city*). They visited them.
4. You have a good friend. You want to introduce me to this person.
5. You and I have a mutual friend. We ran into this person at (*name of a place*).
6. (. . .) has a good friend. You met this person.
7. You have a friend. You invited this person to spend the weekend with your family.
8. (. . .) and (. . .) have some friends. They usually have dinner with these people.

4-10 REFLEXIVE PRONOUNS

myself	(a) *I saw* **myself** *in the mirror.*	Reflexive pronouns end in **-self/-selves**. They are used when the subject (e.g., *I*) and the object (e.g., *myself*) are the same person. The action of the verb is pointed back to the subject of the sentence. INCORRECT: *I saw me in the mirror.*
yourself	(b) *You* (one person) *saw* **yourself**.	
herself	(c) *She saw* **herself**.	
himself	(d) *He saw* **himself**.	
itself	(e) *It* (e.g, the kitten) *saw* **itself**.	
ourselves	(f) *We saw* **ourselves**.	
yourselves	(g) *You* (plural) *saw* **yourselves**.	
themselves	(h) *They saw* **themselves**.	
(i) Greg lives **by himself**. (j) I sat **by myself** on the park bench.		**By** + *a reflexive pronoun* = alone. In (i): Greg lives alone, without family or roommates.
(k) I **enjoyed myself** at the fair.		*Enjoy* and a few other verbs are commonly followed by a reflexive pronoun. See the list below.

VERBS AND PHRASES COMMONLY FOLLOWED BY A REFLEXIVE PRONOUN

believe in yourself	*hurt yourself*	*take care of yourself*
blame yourself	*give yourself (something)*	*talk to yourself*
cut yourself	*introduce yourself*	*teach yourself*
enjoy yourself	*kill yourself*	*tell yourself*
feel sorry for yourself	*pinch yourself*	*work for yourself*
help yourself	*be proud of yourself*	*wish yourself (luck)*

☐ **EXERCISE 15—ORAL (BOOKS CLOSED):** Using a mirror in the classroom, describe who is looking at whom.

> *Example:* (*Spyros*) holds the mirror and looks into it.
> TEACHER: What is (Spyros) doing?
> STUDENT A: He is looking at himself in the mirror.
> TEACHER: What are you doing, Spyros?
> SPYROS: I am looking at myself in the mirror.
> TEACHER: Tell Spyros what he is doing.
> STUDENT B: Spyros, you are looking at yourself in the mirror.

> *Example:* (. . .) and (. . .) hold the mirror and look into it.
> TEACHER: What are (Min Sok) and (Ivonne) doing?
> Etc.

☐ **EXERCISE 16:** Complete the sentences with reflexive pronouns.

1. Are you okay, Heidi? Did you hurt _____*yourself*_____?

2. David was really embarrassed when he had to go to the job interview with a bandage on his face. He had cut _____ while he was shaving.

3. Do you ever talk to _____? Most people talk to _____ sometimes.

4. It is important for all of us to have confidence in our own abilities. We need to believe in _____.

5. Sara is self-employed. She doesn't have a boss. She works for

_____.

6. Steve, who is on the wrestling team, wishes _____ good luck before each match.

7. There's plenty of food on the table. Would all of you please simply help _____ to the food?

8. Brian, don't blame _____ for the accident. It wasn't your fault. You did everything you could to avoid it.

9. I couldn't believe my good luck! I had to pinch _____ to make sure I wasn't dreaming.

10. A newborn puppy can't take care of _____.

11. I know Nicole and Paul have had some bad luck, but it's time for them to stop feeling sorry for _____ and get on with their lives.

12. Jane and I ran into someone she knew. I'd never met this person before. I waited for Jane to introduce me, but she forgot her manners. I finally introduced _____ to Jane's friend.

☐ **EXERCISE 17—ORAL/WRITTEN:** Make up sentences with reflexive pronouns. Use imaginary situations.

Example: pinch herself
Response: When Graciela won the lottery, she pinched herself to make sure she wasn't dreaming.

Example: wish myself
Response: Last week I took my first lesson in skydiving. Before I jumped out of the airplane, I wished myself good luck.

1. talk to himself
2. hurt myself
3. enjoy themselves
4. take care of herself
5. cut himself
6. wish yourself

7. be proud of yourselves
8. blame ourselves
9. feel sorry for myself
10. introduce herself
11. believe in myself
12. pinch yourself

4-11   SINGULAR FORMS OF *OTHER; ANOTHER* vs. *THE OTHER*

ANOTHER

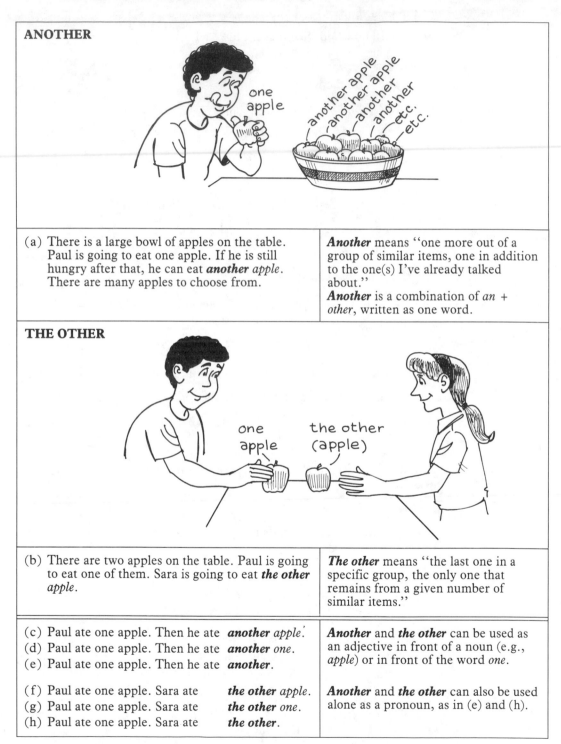

(a) There is a large bowl of apples on the table. Paul is going to eat one apple. If he is still hungry after that, he can eat **another** *apple*. There are many apples to choose from.	**Another** means "one more out of a group of similar items, one in addition to the one(s) I've already talked about." **Another** is a combination of *an* + *other*, written as one word.

THE OTHER

(b) There are two apples on the table. Paul is going to eat one of them. Sara is going to eat **the other** *apple*.	**The other** means "the last one in a specific group, the only one that remains from a given number of similar items."
(c) Paul ate one apple. Then he ate **another** *apple*. (d) Paul ate one apple. Then he ate **another** *one*. (e) Paul ate one apple. Then he ate **another**.	**Another** and **the other** can be used as an adjective in front of a noun (e.g., *apple*) or in front of the word *one*.
(f) Paul ate one apple. Sara ate **the other** *apple*. (g) Paul ate one apple. Sara ate **the other** *one*. (h) Paul ate one apple. Sara ate **the other**.	**Another** and **the other** can also be used alone as a pronoun, as in (e) and (h).

□ **EXERCISE 18:** Complete the sentences with *another* or *the other*.

1. There are many kinds of animals in the world. The elephant is one kind. The tiger is _____*another*_____.

2. There are two colors on this page. One is white. _____*The other*_____ is black.

3. Alex's bicycle was run over by a truck and destroyed. He needs to get _____ one.

4. The Smiths have two bicycles. One belongs to Mr. Smith. _____ bike belongs to Mrs. Smith.

5. There are three books on my desk. Two of them are dictionaries. _____ one is a telephone directory.

6. The puppy chewed up my telephone directory, so I went to the telephone company to get _____ phone book.

7. Vietnam is a country in Southeast Asia. Thailand is _____.

8. It rained yesterday, and from the looks of those dark clouds, we're going to have _____ rainstorm today.

9. Nicole and Michelle are identical twins. The only way you can tell them apart is by looking at their ears. One of them has pierced ears and _____ doesn't.

10. Of the fifty states in the United States, forty-nine are located on the North American continent. Where is _____ located?

11. I have two brothers. One is named Nick. _____ is named Matt.

12. There are five names in this list. One is Adam. _____ is Greg. _____ is Nick. _____ one of the names is Eric. _____ name on the list (the last of the five) is Jessica.

People I need to call

✓ Adam
Greg
Eric
Nick
Jessica

4-12 PLURAL FORMS OF *OTHER: OTHER(S)* vs. *THE OTHER(S)*

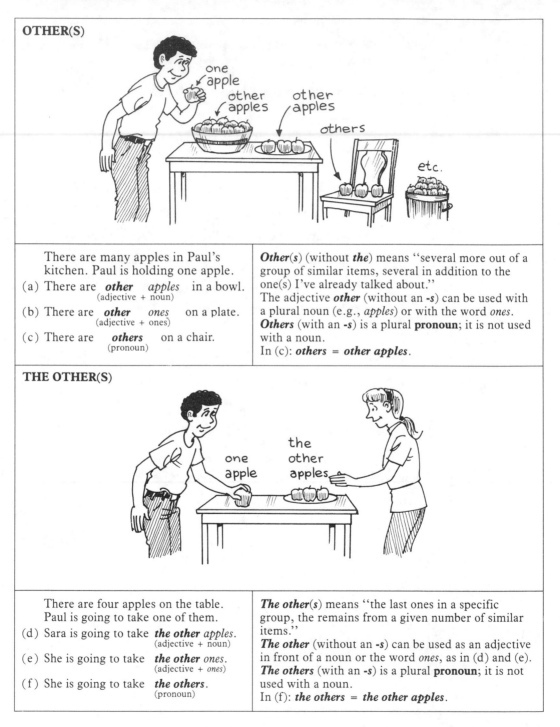

OTHER(S)

one apple
other apples
other apples
others
etc.

There are many apples in Paul's kitchen. Paul is holding one apple.

(a) There are **other** *apples* in a bowl.
    (adjective + noun)

(b) There are **other** *ones* on a plate.
    (adjective + ones)

(c) There are **others** on a chair.
    (pronoun)

Other(*s*) (without *the*) means "several more out of a group of similar items, several in addition to the one(s) I've already talked about."
The adjective *other* (without an *-s*) can be used with a plural noun (e.g., *apples*) or with the word *ones*.
Others (with an *-s*) is a plural **pronoun**; it is not used with a noun.
In (c): *others* = *other apples*.

THE OTHER(S)

one apple
the other apples

There are four apples on the table. Paul is going to take one of them.

(d) Sara is going to take **the other** *apples*.
    (adjective + noun)

(e) She is going to take **the other** *ones*.
    (adjective + ones)

(f) She is going to take **the others**.
    (pronoun)

The other(*s*) means "the last ones in a specific group, the remains from a given number of similar items."
The other (without an *-s*) can be used as an adjective in front of a noun or the word *ones*, as in (d) and (e).
The others (with an *-s*) is a plural **pronoun**; it is not used with a noun.
In (f): *the others* = *the other apples*.

□ **EXERCISE 19:** Complete the sentences with *other(s)* or *the other(s)*.

1. There are many kinds of animals in the world. The elephant is one kind.

   Some _____*others*_____ are tigers, horses, and whales.

2. There are many kinds of animals in the world. The elephant is one kind.

   Some _____*other*_____ kinds are tigers, horses, and whales.

3. There are three colors in the U.S. flag. One of the colors is red.

   _____*The others*_____ are white and blue.

4. There are three colors in the U.S. flag. One of the colors is red.

   _____*The other*_____ colors are white and blue.

5. There are four seasons. Spring and summer are two.

   _____ are fall and winter.

6. Spring and summer are two of the four seasons. _____

   seasons are fall and winter.

7. There are many kinds of geometric figures. Some are circles.

   _____ figures are squares. Still _____

   are rectangular.

8. There are four geometric figures in the above drawing. One is a square.

   _____ figures are a rectangle, a circle, and a triangle.

9. Of the four geometric figures in the drawing, only the circle has curved

   lines. _____ have straight lines.

10. Some ships are fueled by petroleum. _____ are

    propelled by atomic power.

11. Some boats are used for pleasure. _____ boats are used for commercial fishing.

12. Many people like to get up very early in the morning. _____ like to sleep until noon.

13. Out of the twenty students in the class, eighteen passed the exam. _____ failed.

14. Out of the twenty students in the class, only two failed the exam. _____ students passed.

4-13 SUMMARY OF FORMS OF *OTHER*

	ADJECTIVE	PRONOUN	
SINGULAR	another apple	another	Notice that the word ***others*** (*other* + final -*s*) is used only as a plural pronoun.
PLURAL	other apples	others	
SINGULAR	the other apple	the other	
PLURAL	the other apples	the others	

☐ **EXERCISE 20:** Complete the sentences with correct forms of *other: **another, other, others, the other, the others***.

1. Jake has only two suits, a blue one and a gray one. His wife wants him to buy _____*another*_____ one.

2. Jake has two suits. One is blue, and _____ is gray.

3. Some suits are blue. _____ are gray.

4. Some suits have two buttons. _____ suits have three buttons.

5. Our physical education class was divided into two groups. Half of the students stayed inside and played basketball. _____ students went outside and played soccer.

6. If you really hate your job, why don't you look for _____ one? You don't have to be a dishwasher all your life. There are lots of _____ jobs in the world.

7. An automobile consists of many parts. The motor is one, and the steering wheel is _____. _____ parts are the brakes, the trunk, and the fuel tank.

8. Some people keep dogs as pets. _____ have cats. Still _____ people have fish or birds as pets. Can you name _____ kinds of animals that people keep for pets?

9. When I was a kid, I had two pets. One was a black dog. _____ was an orange cat.

10. When I walked into the classroom on the first day, the room was empty. I sat down at a desk and wondered if I was in the right room. Soon _____ student came and took a seat. Then a few _____ followed, and the room slowly began to fill.

11. The students in our class had two choices: basketball or soccer. Half of the students played basketball. _____ played soccer.

12. Here, children. I have two coins. One is for you, Tommy. _____ is for you, Jimmy.

13. My boyfriend gave me a ring. I tried to put it on my ring finger, but it didn't fit. So I had to put it on _____ finger.

14. People have two thumbs. One is on the right hand. _____ is on the left hand.

15. The telephone and the automobile are twentieth-century inventions. _____ are the computer, television, and the airplane. Can you name _____ twentieth-century inventions?

☐ **EXERCISE 21—ORAL (BOOKS CLOSED):** Complete the sentences or answer the questions using a form of ***other***.

          Example: Please give me your pen.

To STUDENT A: Would you please give me your pen? Thank you.

To STUDENT B: I now have two pens, (STUDENT A's) pen and my pen. I'm holding a total of two pens. Mine is one. Is (STUDENT A's) pen another or the other?

       Response: The other.

To STUDENT C: Please give me your pen. Now I'm holding three pens. Mine is one. Is (STUDENT A's) the other or another?

       Response: Another.

To STUDENT C: And your pen? Another or the other?

       Response: The other.

1. To STUDENTS A and B: Please write your names on the board.
   To STUDENT C: There are two names on the board. (. . .) is one of the names. (. . .) is . . . .
   To STUDENT D: Please write your name on the board.
   To STUDENT E: There are three names on the board. (. . .) is one of the names. (. . .) is . . . . (. . .) [the last of the three names] is . . . .
   [Students should continue to write their names on the board and discuss them in terms of *another, other, the others,* etc.]

2. What is one name in this class? And another? And others? And still another? And still others?

3. You have two hands. One is your right hand. Is your left hand another or the other?

4. Look at your right hand. You have five fingers. Your thumb is one finger. Your index finger is . . . . Your middle finger is . . . . Your ring finger is . . . . And your little finger, the last of the five, is . . . .

5. To STUDENTS A and B: Would you please come and stand in front of the class?
   To STUDENT C: There are only two people standing in front of the class. One of them is (. . .). How would you describe (. . .), using a form of *other*?
   [Continue by having more students join the group in front of the class and discuss who is *another, others, the other, the others,* etc.]

4-14 CAPITALIZATION

CAPITALIZE: 1. The first word of a sentence	(a) **W**e saw a movie last night. **I**t was very good.	*Capitalize* = use a big letter, not a small letter.
2. The names of people	(b) I met **G**eorge **A**dams yesterday.	
3. Titles used with the names of people	(c) I saw **D**octor (**D**r.) Smith. Do you know **P**rofessor (**P**rof.) Alston?	COMPARE: I saw a **d**octor. I saw **D**octor Wilson.
4. Months, days, holidays	(d) I was born in **A**pril. Bob arrived last **M**onday. It snowed on **T**hanksgiving **D**ay.	NOTE: Seasons are not capitalized: *spring, summer, fall/autumn, winter*
5. The names of places: city state/province country continent	(e) He lives in **C**hicago. She was born in **C**alifornia. They are from **M**exico. Tibet is in **A**sia.	COMPARE: She lives in a **c**ity. She lives in New York **C**ity.
ocean lake river desert mountain	They crossed the **A**tlantic **O**cean. Chicago is on **L**ake **M**ichigan. The **N**ile **R**iver flows north. The **S**ahara **D**esert is in Africa. We visited the **R**ocky **M**ountains.	COMPARE: They crossed a **r**iver. They crossed the Yellow **R**iver.
school business	I go to the **U**niversity of **F**lorida. I work for the **G**eneral **E**lectric **C**ompany.	COMPARE: I go to a **u**niversity. I go to the **U**niversity of Texas.
street, etc. building park, zoo	He lives on **G**rand **A**venue. We have class in **R**itter **H**all. I went jogging in **F**orest **P**ark.	COMPARE: We went to a **p**ark. We went to Central **P**ark.
6. The names of courses	(f) I'm taking **C**hemistry 101 this term.	COMPARE: I'm reading a book about **p**sychology. I'm taking **P**sychology 101 this term.
7. The names of languages and nationalities	(g) She speaks **S**panish. We discussed **J**apanese customs.	Words that refer to the names of nations, nationalities and languages are always capitalized.
8. The names of religions	(h) **B**uddism, **C**hristianity, **H**induism, **I**slam, and **J**udaism are major religions in the world. Talal is a **M**oslem.	Words that refer to the names of religions are always capitalized.
9. The pronoun "I."	(i) Yesterday **I** fell off my bicycle.	The pronoun "I" is always capitalized.

Add capital letters where necessary.

$$W \qquad\qquad T$$

1. we're going to have a test next tuesday.

2. do you know richard smith? he is a professor at this university.

3. i know that professor smith teaches at the university of arizona.

4. the nile river flows into the mediterranean sea.

5. john is a catholic. ali is a moslem.

6. anna speaks french. she studied in france for two years.

7. i'm taking a history course this semester.

8. i'm taking modern european history 101 this semester.

9. we went to vancouver, british columbia, for our vacation last summer.

10. venezuela is a spanish-speaking country.

11. canada is in north america.*

12. canada is north of the united states.

13. the sun rises in the east.

14. the mississippi river flows south.

□ EXERCISE 23: Add capital letters where necessary.

1. We don't have class on saturday.

2. I'm taking biology 101 this semester.

3. I'm taking history, biology, english, and calculus this semester.

4. We went to a zoo. We went to brookfield zoo in chicago.

5. I live on a busy street. I live at 2358 olive street.

6. We went to canada last summer. We went to montreal in july.

7. I like vietnamese food.

8. The religion of saudi arabia is islam.

9. She works for the xerox corporation. It is a very large corporation.

10. Pedro is from latin america.

---

*When **north, south, east,** and **west** refer to the direction on a compass, they are not capitalized: *Japan is **east** of China.*

When they are part of a geographical name, they are capitalized: *Japan is in the Far **East.***

11. My uncle lives in st. louis. I'm going to visit uncle bill next spring.

12. On valentine's day (february 14), sweethearts give each other presents.

13. We went to a park. We went to woodland park.

14. Are you going to go to the university of oregon or oregon state university?

15. Alice goes to a university in oregon.

□ **EXERCISE 24—PREPOSITIONS:** Complete the sentences with prepositions. (See Appendix 1 for a list of preposition combinations.)

1. Tom paid _____*for*_____ his airplane ticket in cash.

2. Joan graduated _____ high school two years ago.

3. I waited _____ the bus.

4. Jim is a waiter. He waits _____ customers at a restaurant.

5. I have a different opinion. I don't agree _____ you.

6. I arrived _____ this city last month.

7. I arrived _____ the airport around eight.

8. I listened _____ the news on TV last night.

9. This exercise consists _____ verbs that are followed by certain prepositions.

10. Jack invited me _____ his party.

11. I complained _____ the landlord _____ the leaky faucet in the kitchen.

12. Did you talk _____ Professor Adams _____ your grades?

CHAPTER **5**
Modal Auxiliaries

5-1 THE FORM OF MODAL AUXILIARIES

The verbs in the list below are called *modal auxiliaries*. They are helping verbs that express a wide range of meanings (ability, permission, possibility, necessity, etc.). Most of the modals have more than one meaning.

AUXILIARY + THE SIMPLE FORM OF A VERB		*Can*, *could*, *may*, *might*, *should*, *had better*, *must*, *will*, and *would* are followed by the simple form of a verb.
can	(a) I *can speak* English.	They are not followed by *to*:
could	(b) He *couldn't come* to class.	CORRECT: *I can speak English.*
may	(c) It *may rain* tomorrow.	INCORRECT: *I can to speak English.*
might	(d) It *might rain* tomorrow.	
should	(e) Mary *should study* harder.	The main verb never has a final *-s*.
had better	(f) I *had better study* tonight.	CORRECT: *Olga can speak English.*
must	(g) Joe *must see* a doctor today.	INCORRECT: *Olga can speaks English.*
will	(h) I *will be* in class tomorrow.	
would	(i) *Would* you please *close* the door?	
AUXILIARY + *TO* + THE SIMPLE FORM OF A VERB		
have to	(j) I *have to study* tonight.	*Have*, *have got*, and *ought* are followed by an infinitive (*to* + *the simple form of a verb*).
have got to	(k) I *have got to study* tonight.	
ought to	(l) Kate *ought to study* harder.	

☐ **EXERCISE 1:** Add *to* where necessary. If no *to* is necessary, write Ø in the blank.

1. I have ____**to**____ go downtown tomorrow.

2. Tom can ____**Ø**____ play soccer.

3. Could you please _____ open the window?

4. The students must _____ learn all of the irregular verbs.

5. Sally has _____ do her history report tonight.

6. I think you should _____ take better care of yourself.

7. I ought _____ go to the post office this afternoon.

8. Would you _____ speak more slowly, please?

9. We may _____ go to Argentina for our vacation.

10. Will you please _____ mail this letter for me?

11. Tom and I might _____ play tennis after work tomorrow.

12. You had better _____ see a doctor.

13. We can _____ go shopping tomorrow.

14. The students have _____ take a test next Friday.

15. I have got _____ go to the post office this afternoon.

16. Shouldn't you _____ save a little money for a rainy day?

17. Poor Edward. He has _____ go to the hospital for an operation.

18. Alex! Stop! You must not _____ run into the street when there's traffic!

19. May I please _____ have the salt and pepper? Thanks.

20. You'd better not _____ come to the meeting late. The boss will _____ be angry if you're late.

21. I've had a lot of trouble sleeping the last few nights. I've got _____ get a good night's sleep! I can barely _____ stay awake in class.

5-2 EXPRESSING ABILITY: *CAN* AND *COULD*

(a) Bob *can play* the piano.* (b) You *can buy* a screwdriver at a hardware store.	*Can* expresses *ability* in the present or future.
(c) I $\left\{ \begin{array}{l} can't \\ cannot \\ can not \end{array} \right\}$ understand that sentence.	The negative form of *can* may be written: *can't*, *cannot*, or *can not*.
(d) Our son *could talk* when he was two years old.	The past form of *can* is *could*.
(e) They $\left\{ \begin{array}{l} couldn't \\ could not \end{array} \right\}$ come to class yesterday.	The negative of *could*: *couldn't* or *could not*.

*Notice: CORRECT: *Bob can play the piano.*
INCORRECT: *Bob can to play the piano.*
INCORRECT: *Bob can plays the piano.*

□ **EXERCISE 2:** Complete the sentences with *can* and *can't*.

1. A cat _____**can**_____ climb trees, but it _____**can't**_____ fly.

2. A fish _____ walk, but it _____ swim.

3. A dog _____ bark, but it _____ sing.

4. You _____ buy stamps at the post office, but you _____ buy shoes there.

5. A tiny baby _____ cry, but it _____ talk.

6. I _____ write with a pen, but I _____ write with a paper clip.

7. I _____ read a book by moonlight, but I _____ read in sunlight.

8. Trees _____ produce oxygen, but rocks _____.

9. Fish _____ live in air, but they _____ live in water.

10. You _____ store water in a glass jar, but you _____ store it in a paper bag.

11. You _____ drive from the Philippines to Australia, but you _____ drive from Italy to Austria.

12. You _____ ride on the back of a cat, but you _____ ride on the back of a horse.

13. Jack's friends are going to the park to play soccer. Jack wants to play too, but he has a broken toe, so he's on crutches. Jack _____ go to the park and watch the game, but he _____ play in the game.

14. Laurie has to go to the airport. The airport is 25 miles (40 kilometers) from her house. She _____ walk to the airport. It's too far. She _____ take a bus, however.

□ **EXERCISE 3—ORAL (BOOKS CLOSED):** Use *can*.

1. What abilities and talents do you have? Tell the class about some of the things you can do. Can you swim? Whistle? Play the piano? Cook?

2. Tell the class about some abilities or talents that you don't have—things that you can't do.

3. Ask a classmate if he or she has a certain ability or talent.

   Example: STUDENT A: (...), can you play pool?
   STUDENT B: Yes, I can. OR: No, I can't.

4. (...) wants to go to the zoo. Tell him/her what he/she can see at the zoo. *and so om (기타 등등)*

5. (...) wants to buy a hammer. Tell him/her where he/she can get a hammer. A wristwatch? Some bananas? Tennis balls? A haircut? *at the hardware store 철물점*

6. (...) has to go to the airport tomorrow. How can he/she get there? *she can get there by taxi*

7. (...) is bored on weekends. Tell him/her some things he/she can do on weekends in (*this city*). *she can she can*

8. (...) wants to go out to eat tonight. Where can he/she get a good meal? *she can go to eat T.G.I*

9. (...) is interested in science. What are some of the courses he/she can take at a university? *he can take biology, physics, earth science,*

10. What are some things you can find in (a library, a computer room, a language lab, etc.)? *I can find lots of books, people, desks and chairs computer, marine biology*

11. (...) has four days to take a trip somewhere. She/He is going to drive her/his friend's car. Where can she/he go? Where can't she/he go? *environment science* *a circulation desk 대출 and on*

12. The temperature is around ten degrees today. It's a (cold, hot, nice, etc.) day. (...) and (...) don't have class later today. They don't want to go home. Where can/can't they go?

13. (...) is going to a dinner party at a fancy restaurant tonight. He/She doesn't know what to wear. Suggest to him/her things that he/she can and can't wear.

14. You are going to a department store this afternoon. You have (a certain amount of money). You intend to spend all of it. What can and can't you buy?

☐ **EXERCISE 4—ORAL (BOOKS CLOSED):** Use *could*.

1. What could you do when you were a child that you can't do now?
2. What could you do when you were living in your own country or hometown that you can't do now?
3. What did you want to do yesterday or last week but couldn't do? Why couldn't you do it?
4. Who has missed class recently? When? Why?
5. Who has had a cold or the flu recently? What couldn't you do when you were sick?

5-3 EXPRESSING POSSIBILITY: *MAY* AND *MIGHT*
EXPRESSING PERMISSION: *MAY* AND *CAN*

(a) It *may rain* tomorrow. (b) It *might rain* tomorrow. (c) A: Why isn't John in class? B: I don't know. He $\left\{\begin{array}{l}\textit{may}\\\textit{might}\end{array}\right\}$ be sick today.	*May* and *might* express *possibility* in the present or future. They have the same meaning. There is no difference in meaning between (a) and (b).
(d) It *may not rain* tomorrow. (e) It *might not rain* tomorrow.	Negative: *may not* and *might not*. (Do not contract *may* and *might* with *not*.)
(f) *Maybe* it will rain tomorrow. (g) *Maybe* John is sick. (h) John *may be* sick.	*Maybe* (spelled as one word) is an adverb meaning "perhaps." Notice (f) and (g). *May be* (spelled as two words) is a verb form, as in (h): the auxiliary *may* + the main verb *be*.
(i) Yes, children, you *may have* a cookie after dinner. (j) Okay, kids, you *can have* a cookie after dinner.	*May* is also used to give *permission*. Often *can* is used to give *permission*, too. (i) and (j) have the same meaning, but *may* is more formal than *can*.
(k) You *may not* have a cookie. You *can't have* a cookie.	*May not* and *cannot* (*can't*) are used to deny permission (i.e., to say "no").

☐ **EXERCISE 5—ORAL (BOOKS CLOSED):** Answer the questions. Include at least three possibilities in the answer to a question, using *may, might,* and *maybe* as in the example.

    Example: What are you going to do tomorrow?

    Response: I don't know. I *may* go downtown. Or I *might* go to the laundromat. *Maybe* I'll study all day. Who knows?
              세탁소

1. What are you going to do tomorrow night?
2. What's the weather going to be like tomorrow? Maybe It will be sunny.
3. What is (. . .) going to do tonight? He may go home tonight.
4. I'm taking something out of my briefcase/purse/pocket/wallet. It's small and I'm holding it in my fist. What is it? It maybe a key
5. What does (. . .) have in her purse?
6. What does (. . .) have in his pants pockets? 작은지갑
7. (. . .) isn't in class today. Where is he/she?

8. You have another class after this one. What are you going to do in that class?

9. We have a vacation (*during a certain time*). What are you going to do during vacation?

10. What are you going to do this weekend?

11. What is (. . .) going to do after class today?

12. What are you going to do after you graduate?

☐ **EXERCISE 6—ORAL:** Make sentences with *may, might,* and *maybe* based on given situations. Notice: Some of the situations are future, and some of them are present.

1. You don't have any special plans for this coming weekend.
   (*I may . . . . Or I might . . . . Maybe I'll . . . .*)

2. It's midnight. Your roommate/spouse isn't home. Where is he/she?

3. (. . .) wants to buy a sandwich. The sandwich costs (*a certain amount of money*). (. . .) has only (*a lesser amount of money*) in her/his pocket. What is she/he going to do?

4. Your friends are coming to your home for dinner. What are you going to make (i.e., cook) for them?

5. You want to go on a picnic tomorrow, but the weather forecaster predicts rain for tomorrow. What are you going to do if you can't go on a picnic?

6. It is late at night. You hear a strange noise. What is it?

7. What is your (younger sister/younger brother/daughter/son/niece/ nephew) going to be when she or he grows up?

8. Look at the picture. What is the man's occupation? What is the woman's occupation?

5-4 USING *COULD* TO EXPRESS POSSIBILITY

(a) A: Why isn't Greg in class? B: I don't know. He ***could be*** sick.	***Could*** can mean *past ability* (see Chart 5-2). But that is not its only meaning. Another meaning of ***could*** is *possibility*. In (a): "He ***could*** be sick" has the same meaning as "He ***may/might*** be sick," i.e., "It is possible that he is sick."
(b) Look at those dark clouds. It ***could start*** raining any minute.	In (a), ***could*** expresses a **present** possibility. In (b), ***could*** expresses a **future** possibility.

□ EXERCISE 7—ORAL (BOOKS CLOSED): Listen to the clues; then make guesses. Use *could, may,* and *might*.

> *Example:* made of metal and you keep it in a pocket
> TEACHER: I'm thinking of something made of metal that you can find in my pocket. What could it be?
> STUDENTS: It could be a pen. It could be some keys. It might be a paper clip. It may be a small pocket knife. It could be a coin.
> TEACHER: (. . .) was right! I was thinking of the keys in my pocket.

1. has wheels and a motor
2. is made of plastic and can be found in my purse/pocket
3. is brown, is made of leather, and is in this room
4. is flat and rectangular
5. is white, hard, and in this room
6. is played with a ball on a large field
7. has (*three*) stories/storeys and is made of (*brick*)
8. has four legs and is found on a farm
9. is green and we can see it out that window
10. is sweet and you can eat it

5-5 ASKING FOR PERMISSION: *MAY I, COULD I, CAN I*

POLITE QUESTION	POSSIBLE ANSWERS	People use ***may I, could I,*** * and ***can I***
(a) ***May I*** please borrow your pen? (b) ***Could I*** please borrow your pen? (c) ***Can I*** please borrow your pen?	Yes. Yes. Of course. Yes. Certainly. Of course. Certainly.	to ask polite questions. The questions ask for someone's permission. (a), (b), and (c) have basically the same meaning. Note: ***can I*** is less formal than ***may I*** and ***could I***.
	Sure. (*informal*) Okay. (*informal*)	***Please*** can come at the end of the question: *May I borrow your pen, please?*
	Uh-huh. (*meaning* "yes")	***Please*** can be omitted from the question: *May I borrow your pen?*

*In a polite question, ***could*** is NOT the past form of ***can***.

□ **EXERCISE 8:** Following are some phone conversations. Complete the dialogues. Use *may I, could I,* or *can I* + a verb from the list. Note: The caller is SPEAKER B.

> *help   leave   speak/talk   take*

1. A: Hello?
   B: Hello. Is Dick there?
   A: Yes, he is.
   B: _____May I speak_____ to him?
   A: Just a minute. I'll get him.

2. A: Hello. Dean Black's office.
   B: _____May I speak_____ to Dean Black?
   A: May I ask who is calling?
   B: Susan Abbott.
   A: Just a moment, Ms. Abbott. I'll connect you.

3. A: Hello?
   B: Hi. This is Bob. _____Can I speak_____ to Steve?
   A: Sure. Hang on.
      점깐만요 ~

4. A: Good afternoon. Dr. Anderson's office. _____may I ~~speak~~ help_____ you?
   B: Yes. I'd like to make an appointment with Dr. Anderson.
   A: Fine. Is Friday morning at ten all right?
   B: Yes. Thank you.
   A: Your name?

5. A: Hello?
   B: Hello. _____may I speak_____ to Emily?
   A: She's not at home right now. _____take ✗_____ a message?
   B: No thanks. I'll call later.

6. A: Hello?
   B: Hello. _____may I talk_____ to Mary?
   A: She's not here right now.
   B: Oh. _____may I leave_____ a message?
   A: Certainly. Just a minute. I have to get a pen.

7. A: Hello?
   B: Hello. _____may I speak_____ to Jack?
   A: Who?
   B: Jack. Jack Butler.
   A: There's no one here by that name. I'm afraid you have the wrong
      number.   You've got the wrong number.
   B: Is this 221–3892?
   A: No, it's not.
   B: Oh. I'm sorry.
   A: That's okay.

I promise not to tell a lie.

I would like to make an appointment.
나는 약속을 잡는다.
I have an appointment.
나 약속 있어.

Ask a classmate a polite question. Use *may I, could I,* or *can I.*

Handwritten left margin:
May I ~?
Yes. You may.
Certainly.
Sure.
Here it is.
of course.
Go ahead.
거절 → I'm afraid, I can't
I'm sorry, I can't
< 정중하게 ·····! >

Example: (...) has a book. You want to see it for a minute.
STUDENT A: May/Could/Can I (please) see your book for a minute?
STUDENT B: Of course./Sure./etc.
STUDENT A: Thank you./Thanks.

1. (...) has a dictionary. You want to see it for a minute.
2. (...) has a pen. You want to use it for a minute.
3. (...) has a calculator. You want to borrow it.
4. (...) has a camera. You want to see it for a minute.
5. You want to see something that a classmate has.
6. You want to use something that a classmate has.
7. You want to borrow something that a classmate has.
8. You are at a restaurant. (...) is your waiter/waitress. You have finished your meal. You want the check.
9. You are at (...)'s house. You want to use the phone.
10. (...) is carrying some heavy packages. What are you going to say to him/her?
11. You are speaking to one of your teachers. You want to leave class early today.
12. You're in a store. Your bill is (*a certain amount of money*). You have only (*a lesser amount of money*). What are you going to say to your friend?
13. You have a job at (*name of a local store*). A customer walks to your counter. What are you going to say to the customer?

Handwritten: shopping talk → I'm just looking 2분 봐기 위한 건거예요.

5-6 ASKING FOR ASSISTANCE: WOULD YOU, COULD YOU, WILL YOU, CAN YOU

Handwritten: when you need me, please let me know.

POLITE QUESTION	POSSIBLE ANSWERS *	
(a) **Would you** please open the door? (b) **Could you** please open the door? (c) **Will you** please open the door? (d) **Can you** please open the door?	Yes. Yes. Of course. Yes. Certainly. Of course. Certainly. I'd be happy to. I'd be glad to. Of course. I'd be happy/glad to. Certainly. I'd be happy/glad to. Sure. (*informal*) Okay. (*informal*) My pleasure. (*informal*) Uh-huh. (*meaning "yes"*)	People use **would you, could you, will you,** and **can you** to ask polite questions. The questions ask for someone's help or cooperation. (a), (b), (c), and (d) have basically the same meaning. The use of **can,** as in (d), is less formal than the others.
		NOTE: **May** is NOT used when **you** is the subject of a polite question. INCORRECT: *May you please open the door?*

*Answers to polite questions are usually affirmative. Examples of possible polite negative responses follow:
I'm sorry, but (I can't, I don't have enough time, my arms are full, etc.).
I'd like to, but (I can't, I don't have enough time, my arms are full, etc.).

☐ **EXERCISE 10:** Complete the dialogues. Use a polite question with *would you/could you/will you/can you* in each. Use the expressions in the list or your own words.

> answer the phone for me   say that again
> get the door for me   turn it down 피나 훈익다
> open the window   turn the volume up
> pick some up

1. TEACHER: It's getting hot in here. ___**Would/Could/Will/Can you**___

   ___**please open the window?**___

   STUDENT: ___**Of course, I'd be happy to./Sure./etc.**___

   TEACHER: ___**Thank you./Thanks.**___

   STUDENT: You're welcome.

2. FRIEND A: The phone is ringing, but my hands are full. _____
   Would you please answer the phone for me?

   FRIEND B: of course, ~~I'd be happy to~~

   FRIEND A: Thanks.

   FRIEND B: No problem.

3. ROOMMATE A: I'm trying to study, but the radio is too loud. would
   you please turn ~~the volume up~~ ?   it down

   ROOMMATE B: Sure.

   ROOMMATE A: thank you, very much.

   ROOMMATE B: That's okay. No problem.

4. SISTER: I'm trying to listen to the news on television, but I can't
   hear it. Could you please turn the volume up?

   BROTHER: Sure.

   SISTER: thanks

   BROTHER: Don't mention it.   ~가 다떨어지다

5. HUSBAND: Honey, I'm out of razor blades. When you go to the
   store, Can you please pick some up?

   WIFE: of course, I'd happy to.

   HUSBAND: thank you. Honey ~

   WIFE: Anything else?

6. STRANGER A: Excuse me. _Would you please get the door for me?_
   STRANGER B: _Sure_
   STRANGER A: _Thank you._
   STRANGER B: You're welcome.

7. PERSON A: Hi.

   PERSON B: Hi. Walabaxitinpundoozit?

   PERSON A: Excuse me? _Could you please say that again?_

   PERSON B: Walabaxitinpundoozit.

   PERSON A: I'm sorry, but I don't understand.

□ **EXERCISE 11—ORAL (BOOKS CLOSED):** Ask a classmate a polite question.

> *Example:* You want someone to open the door.
> STUDENT A: (*...*) would/could/will/can you please open the door?
> STUDENT B: Certainly./Sure./I'd be happy to./etc.
> STUDENT A: Thank you./Thanks.

You want someone to . . .

1. close the door.
2. lend you his/her eraser.
3. tell you the time.
4. hand you (*something*).
5. shut the window.
6. lend you a quarter.
7. help you.
8. spell (*a particular word*) for you.
9. hold your books for a minute.
10. give (*something*) to (. . .).
11. (*...*) is at your apartment. The phone is ringing, but your hands are full. You want him/her to answer it for you.
12. You and (*...*) are on vacation together. You'd like to have a picture of the two of you together. You see a stranger who looks friendly. You want her to take a picture of you.

13. You wrote a letter to a university. You want your teacher to read it and correct the mistakes.

14. (/...) is going to the library. You want him/her to return a book for you.

15. (...) and you are at (*name of a nearby restaurant*). You want (...) to lend you (*a certain amount of money*).

사람이름들어갈 뿐

borrow   lend
빌려오다   빌려주다

5-7 EXPRESSING ADVICE:
SHOULD, OUGHT TO, HAD BETTER

(a) My clothes are dirty. I	*should* *ought to* *had better*	*wash* them.	*Should*, *ought to*, and *had better* have basically the same meaning. They mean: "*This is a good idea. This is good advice.*"
(b) You need your sleep. You *shouldn't* stay up late.			Negative: *should* + *not* = *shouldn't*.*
(c) *I'd* better *You'd* better *He'd* better *She'd* better *We'd* better *They'd* better	study tonight.		Contraction of *had* = 'd. NOTE: Usually *had* is the past form of *have*. However, in the expression *had better*, *had* is used as part of an idiom and the meaning is not past. The meaning is present or future.

Ought to is usually not used in the negative.
The negative of *had better* is *had better not*, and it often carries a warning of bad consequences.
You had better not be late! If you are late, you will get into a lot of trouble.

☐ EXERCISE 12: Complete the sentences. Use *shouldn't* + the expressions in the list or your own words.

be cruel to animals 동물한테 동물을 하다 ✗ give too much homework 숙제가 많다
∧에 늦다 ← be late for an appointment   miss any classes 수업 빼먹다
drive a long distance 장거리 운전
exceed the speed limit 과속   smoke
    throw trash out of your car window 쓰레기를 함부로 버리다

1. If you are tired, you ____**shouldn't drive a long distance.**____

2. Cigarette smoking is dangerous to your health. You _____

3. A good driver _____

4. A teacher _____

5. A student _____

6. Animals have feelings, too. You _____

7. It is important to be punctual. You _____

8. Littering is against the law. You _____

☐ **EXERCISE 13:** Complete the dialogues. Use *should, ought to,* or *had better.* Choose from the expressions in the list or use your own words.

borrow some money	*marry somebody who is rich* 부자와 결혼
call the landlord and complain	*put cotton in your ears*
call the police	*see a dentist*
drink a glass of water	*send her a dozen roses*
find a new apartment	*soak it in cold water* 찬물에물건담기
find a new girlfriend	*speak English outside of class every day*
get a job	*take it back to the store* 환불
go back to the restaurant and ask if	*use a dictionary when he writes*
someone found them 레스토랑에 잃어버린 물건 찾기	*watch TV a lot*
hold your breath 숨을 참다	

1. A: I have a toothache. This tooth hurts. What should I do?★

   B: ___***You should/ought to/had better see a dentist.***___

2. A: I have the hiccups. What should I do?
   딸꾹질

   B: _____

3. A: Ali wants to improve his English. What should he do?

   B: _____

4. A: I don't have any money. I'm broke. I can't pay my rent. I don't have enough money to pay my bills. What should I do?

   B: _____

★*Should,* not *ought to* or *had better,* is usually used in a question. The answer, however, can contain *should, ought to,* or *had better,* as in the example answer in number one.

5. A: Someone stole my bicycle. What should I do?

   B: _____

6. A: I cut my finger. I got blood on my sweater. My finger is okay, but I'm worried about my sweater. What should I do?

   B: _____

7. A: Tom's spelling isn't very good. He makes a lot of mistakes when he writes compositions. What should he do?

   B: _____

8. A: Ann bought a new tape recorder. After two days, it stopped working. What should she do?

   B: _____

9. A: The refrigerator in my apartment doesn't work. The stove doesn't work. The air conditioner doesn't work. And there are cockroaches in the kitchen. What should I do?

   B: _____

10. A: I asked Mary to marry me. She said no. What should I do?

    B: _____

11. A: I left my sunglasses at a restaurant yesterday. What should I do?

    B: _____

12. A: My husband/wife snores. I can't get to sleep at night. What should I do?

    B: _____

☐ **EXERCISE 14—ORAL:** Discuss problems and give advice.

STUDENT A: Think of a problem. It can be your problem or a friend's problem. Tell your classmates about the problem and then ask them for advice.

OTHER STUDENTS: Give STUDENT A some advice. Use ***should/ought to/had better***.

Example: A: I can't study at night because the dorm is too noisy. What should I do?

B: You ought to study at the library.

C: You shouldn't stay in your dorm room in the evening.

D: You'd better get some ear plugs.

E: (Etc.)

5-8 EXPRESSING NECESSITY:
HAVE TO, HAVE GOT TO, MUST

(a) I have a very important test tomorrow. I $\begin{cases} \textit{have to} \\ \textit{have got to} \\ \textit{must} \end{cases}$ *study* tonight.	*Have to*, *have got to*, and *must* have basically the same meaning. They express the idea that something is *necessary*.
	Have to is used much more frequently than *must* in everyday speech and writing.* *Have got to* is generally used only in informal speech and writing.
(b) I *have to* ("hafta") *go* downtown today. (c) Rita *has to* ("hasta") *go* to the bank. (d) I've *got to* ("gotta") *study* tonight.	Usual pronunciation: *have to* = "hafta" *has to* = "hasta" (*have*) *got to* = "gotta"
(e) I *had to study* last night.	The past form of *have to*, *have got to*, and *must* (meaning necessity) is *had to*.

*__Must__ means that something is **very** necessary; there is no other choice. __Must__ is used much less frequently than __have to__ in everyday speech and writing. __Must__ is a "strong" word.

☐ **EXERCISE 15:** Complete the sentences. Use *have to*, *has to*, or *had to* in each.

1. I went downtown yesterday because _____ *I had to go to City Hall.*

2. I can't go to the movie tonight because _____

3. I couldn't go to Pete's party last Saturday because _____

4. Josh can't go downtown with us this afternoon because _____

5. When I was in high school, _____

6. If you want to travel abroad, _____

7. I'm sorry I was absent from class yesterday, but _____

8. Erica can't come to class tomorrow because _____

9. I need a car because _____

10. When I worked in my uncle's restaurant, _____

11. If you want to enter the university, _____

12. We wanted to go on a picnic yesterday, but we couldn't because _____

_____

13. I wanted to _____ yesterday, but _____

_____ instead.

□ **EXERCISE 16—ORAL (BOOKS CLOSED):** Practice using *have to, have got to, must,* and *should*.

> *Example:* Tell me something you have to do this evening.
> STUDENT A: I have to go to a meeting.
> TEACHER: What does (STUDENT A) have to do this evening?
> STUDENT B: He/She has to go to a meeting.
> TEACHER: How about you, (. . .)? Tell me something you have to do this evening.

1. Use *have to*:
   a. Tell me something you have to do today or tomorrow.
   b. Tell me something you have to do every day.
   c. Tell me something you had to do yesterday or last week.
2. Use *have got to*:
   d. Tell me something you have got to do today or tomorrow.
   e. Tell me something you've got to do tonight.
   f. Tell me something you've got to do after class today.
3. Use *must* or *should*:
   g. Tell me something very important that you must do today or tomorrow.
   h. Tell me something that you should do today or tomorrow (but which you may or may not do).
   i. Tell me something a driver must do, according to the law.
   j. Tell me something a good driver should always do.
   k. Tell me something a person should do in order to stay healthy.
   l. Tell me something a person must do to stay alive. (If a person doesn't do this, he or she will die.)
   m. I don't have a driver's license for this state/province, but I want to get one. Tell me something I must do to get a driver's license.

5-9   EXPRESSING LACK OF NECESSITY: *DO NOT HAVE TO* EXPRESSING PROHIBITION: *MUST NOT*

(a) I finished all of my homework this afternoon. I *don't have to study* tonight. (b) Tomorrow is a holiday. Mary *doesn't have to go* to class.	*Don't/doesn't have to* expresses the idea that something is *not necessary*.
(c) Children, you *must not play* with matches! (d) We *must not use* that door. The sign says: PRIVATE: DO NOT ENTER.	*Must not* expresses *prohibition*. (DO NOT DO THIS!)
(e) You *mustn't play* with matches.	*Must + not = mustn't.* (Note: The first "t" is not pronounced.)

not have to ～する X .

□ **EXERCISE 17:** Complete the sentences with *don't/doesn't have to* or *must not*.

1. The soup is too hot. You _____**must not**_____ eat it yet. Wait for it to cool.

2. You _____**don't have to**_____ have soup for lunch. You can have a sandwich if you like.

3. Liz finally got a car, so now she usually drives to work. She _____*doesn't*_____ _____*have to*_____ take the bus.

4. Tommy, you _____*musn't*_____ say that word. That's not a nice word.

5. Mr. Moneybags is very rich. He _____*doesn't have to*_____ work for a living.

6. If you are in a canoe, you _____*musn't*_____ stand up and walk around. If you do, the canoe will probably tip over.

7. According to the rules of the game, one player _____*musn't*_____ hit or (trip) another player.
   방해하다

8. The review class before the final exam is optional. We _____*don't have to*_____ go unless we want to.

9. Most vegetables can be eaten raw. You _____*don't have to*_____ cook them.
   날것으로

10. You _____ **must not** _____ use a pencil to write a check because someone could change the amount you have written on it.

11. When the phone rings, you _____ **don't have to** _____ answer it. It's up to you.

12. When you have a new job, you _____ **must not** _____ be late the first day. In fact, it is a good idea to be a few minutes early.

13. A: You _____ **must not** _____ tell Jim about the surprise birthday party. Do you promise?

    B: I promise.

14. A: Did Professor Adams make an assignment?

    B: Yes, she assigned Chapters 4 and 6, but we _____ **don't have to** _____ read Chapter 5.

15. A: I _____ **must not** _____ forget to set my alarm for 5:30.

    B: Why do you have to get up at 5:30?   *Set my alarm for* (00:00)

    A: I'm going to meet Ron at 6:00. We're going fishing.

16. A: Listen to me carefully, Annie. If a stranger offers you a ride, you
    _____ **must not** _____ get in the car. Never get in a car with a
    ~에게 차를 태워줄 것을 제안하다
    I offered my friend a ride.
    친구에게 차태워줄것을 제안하다
    stranger. Do you understand?

    B: Yes, Mom.

17. A: Do you have a stamp?

    B: Uh-huh. Here.

    A: Thanks. Now I _____ **don't have to** _____ go to the post office to buy stamps.

18. A: Children, your mother and I are going to go out this evening. I want you to be good and follow these rules: You must do everything the baby-sitter tells you to do. You _____ **must not** _____ go outside after dark. It's Saturday night, so you _____ **don't have to** _____ go to bed at eight. You can stay up until eight-thirty. And remember: you _____ **must not** _____ pull the cat's
    꼬리를 잡아 당기다
    tail. Okay?

    B: Okay, Dad.

5-10 MAKING LOGICAL CONCLUSIONS: *MUST*

(a) A: Nancy is yawning. B: She ***must be*** sleepy.	In (a): SPEAKER B is making a logical guess. He bases his guess on the information that Nancy is yawning. His logical conclusion, his "best guess," is that Nancy is sleepy. He uses ***must*** to express his logical conclusion.
(b) LOGICAL CONCLUSION: Amy plays tennis every day. She ***must like*** to play tennis. (c) NECESSITY: If you want to get into the movie theater, you ***must buy*** a ticket.	COMPARE: ***Must*** can express: • a logical conclusion, as in (b). • necessity, as in (c).
(d) NEGATIVE LOGICAL CONCLUSION: Eric ate everything on his plate except the pickle. He ***must not like*** pickles. (e) PROHIBITION: There are sharks in the ocean near our hotel. We ***must not go*** swimming there.	COMPARE: ***Must not*** can express: • a negative logical conclusion, as in (d). • prohibition, as in (e).

□ **EXERCISE 18:** Make logical conclusions. Use ***must*** or ***must not***.

1. Tim has been working in the hot sun for the last hour. He just drank one glass of water. Right now he is refilling his glass. (*thirsty?*)
   → Tim _____ **must be thirsty.**

2. I am at Eric's apartment door. I've knocked on the door and have rung the doorbell several times. Nobody has answered the door. (*at home?*)
   → Eric _____ **must not be at home.**

3. Brian has a red nose and has been coughing and sneezing. 개네기 (*have a cold?*)
   → Brian _____ must (have a cold

4. Sally looks tired. She's been coughing and sneezing. (*feel well?*)
   → Sally _____ must not feel well

5. Adam has already eaten one sandwich. Now he's making another sandwich. (*hungry?*)
   → Adam _____ must be hungry

6. When Joe takes a problem to his grandmother, she always knows how to help him solve it. (*very wise?*) 자식을 잘 해야하봐
   → Joe's grandmother _____ must ∧ very wise
                                              be

7. Kate has a full <u>academic schedule</u>, plays on the volleyball team, has the lead in the school play, is a cheerleader, takes piano lessons, and has a part-time job at the ice cream store. (*have a lot of spare time? busy all the time?*)
   → Kate _____ must not spare time. 여유
                She must be busy.

떡떡하게 ←
깐샵
스케쥴w

8. David goes to the video store and rents three movies every night. (*like movies a lot? spend much time with his friends and family in the evenings?*)

→ David _must like movies a lot. He must not his friends and family in the evenings._

9. Jennifer reads all the time. She sits in a corner and reads even when people come to visit her. (*love books? like books better than people?*)

→ Jennifer _must love books. She must not like books better than people._

10. Jake called Betsy and asked her to go to a movie. Betsy told him that she had to study. She has just hung up, and now she's going to get ready for bed and go to sleep. (*want to go to a movie? be tired? want to hurt Jake's feelings?*)

→ Betsy _must not want to go to a movie. she must not hurt be tired? Jacke's feeling. hurt James feeling_

11. The teacher just asked Jason a question. Jason is looking down at the floor and not answering. His ears are getting red. (*know the answer? be embarrassed?*)

→ Jason _must not know the answer. He must be embarrassed._

12. Debbie just got home from school. She slammed the front door, threw her books on the floor, and ran to her room. Now her parents can hear music through Debbie's closed door. (*be upset? want to be alone? want to talk to her parents right now? like loud music?*)

→ Debbie _must be upset. He must be alone. He must not want to parents right now. He must like music._

13. A crow is a large black bird. It is a scavenger. That means that it eats dead and rotting animal remains. A crow that lives near a beach looks for shellfish left behind when the tide goes out. It first tries to open a shellfish with its beak, but if it can't, it picks the shellfish up and flies over a hard surface such as a paved road or sidewalk. From this height, it drops the shellfish so that the shell will crack open. After that, it flies down to claim its dinner. (*smart birds?*)

→ Crows _must be smart birds._

5-11 GIVING INSTRUCTIONS: IMPERATIVE SENTENCES

<table>
<tr>
<td>
COMMAND
  (a) <i>General:</i> Open the door!
     Soldier: Yes, sir!
REQUEST
  (b) <i>Teacher:</i> Open the door, please.
     Student: Okay, I'd be happy to.
DIRECTIONS
  (c) <i>Barbara:</i> Could you tell me how to get to the post office?
     Stranger: Certainly. Walk two blocks down this street. Turn left and walk three more blocks. It's on the right hand side of the street.
</td>
<td>
Imperative sentences are used to give commands, make polite requests, and give directions.
The difference between a command and a request lies in the speaker's tone of voice and the use of please.
Please can come at the beginning or end of a request:
   Open the door, please.
   Please open the door.
</td>
</tr>
<tr>
<td>
  (d) Close the window.
  (e) Please sit down.
  (f) Be quiet!
  (g) Don't walk on the grass.
  (h) Please don't wait for me.
  (i) Don't be late.
</td>
<td>
The simple form of a verb is used in imperative sentences. The understood subject of the sentence is <i>you</i> (meaning the person the speaker is talking to): (<i>You</i>) <i>close the window.</i>
Negative form:
   Don't + the simple form of a verb.
</td>
</tr>
</table>

☐ **EXERCISE 19:** Complete the dialogues with imperative sentences. Try to figure out something the first speaker might say in the given situation.

1. THE TEACHER: *__Read this sentence, please./Look at page 33./etc.__*
  THE STUDENT: Okay.

2. THE DOCTOR: _____
  THE PATIENT: All right.

3. THE MOTHER: _____
  THE SON: I will. Don't worry.

4. MRS. JONES: _____
  THE CHILDREN: Yes, ma'am.

5. THE GENERAL: _____
  THE SOLDIER: Yes, sir! Right away, sir!

6. THE FATHER: _____
  THE DAUGHTER: Okay, Dad.

7. A FRIEND: _____
  A FRIEND: Why not?

8. THE WIFE: _____
  THE HUSBAND: Okay.

9.   THE HUSBAND: _____
      THE WIFE: Why?

10.   THE BOSS: _____
      THE EMPLOYEE: I'll do it immediately.

11.   THE FATHER: _____
      THE SON: Okay. I won't.

□ EXERCISE 20—ORAL: Use imperative sentences.

1. Using an imperative sentence, tell another classmate to perform some
    action in the classroom.
    (STUDENT A to B: *Write your name on the board.* [STUDENT B writes on the
                       board.]
    STUDENT B to C: *Change desks.* [STUDENT C changes desks.]
    STUDENT C to D: *etc.*)

2. Using an imperative sentence, tell a classmate either what to do or what
    NOT to do in classroom.
    (STUDENT A to B: *Don't interrupt while another student is speaking.*
    STUDENT B to C: *Raise your hand if you want to speak.*
    STUDENT C to D: *etc.*)

3. Tell your listeners what to do in their daily lives to help preserve the
    earth's environment and natural resources. (*Recycle aluminum cans. Walk
    instead of driving your car. . . .etc.*)

4. Direct a classmate whose eyes are closed (or who is blindfolded) from
    one spot in the room to another. Make sure your classmate doesn't
    bump into any tables or chairs or other people! (*Take two steps straight
    ahead. Now turn to your left and take one step . . . .etc.*)

5. Give a classmate explicit directions on how to get to a place that is near
    the classroom building. Don't name the place. Let your classmate figure
    out which place you are thinking about from listening to your directions.
    (*Go out the main door. Turn left and . . . etc.*)

□ EXERCISE 21—WRITTEN: Write about one of the following.

1. Give general advice to people who want to (*choose one*):

    a. improve their health.   e. find a job.
    b. get good grades.   f. live life fully every day.
    c. improve their English.   g. get married.
    d. make a good first impression.

    Tell your readers: Do this. Don't do that. You should do this. You
    shouldn't do that. You ought to do this. You have to do this. You don't have
    to do that. You must do this. You must not do that. You can do this. You had
    better do that, etc.

2. One of your friends wants to come to this city. He/She wants to go to school here or get a job here. Write your friend a letter. Give your friend advice about coming to this city to study or work.

3. Explain how to get a date for Saturday night.

5-12 MAKING SUGGESTIONS: *LET'S* AND *WHY DON'T*

(a) A: It's hot today. **Let's go** to the beach. B: Okay. Good idea. (b) A: It's hot today. **Why don't we go** to the beach? B: Okay. Good idea.	**Let's** (*do something*) and **why don't we** (*do something*) have the same meaning. They are used to make suggestions about activities for you and me. **Let's** = *let us*.
(c) A: I'm tired. B: **Why don't you take** a nap? A: That's a good idea. I think I will.	People use **why don't you** (*do something*) to make a friendly suggestion, to give friendly advice.

☐ **EXERCISE 22:** Complete the dialogues. Use *let's* or *why don't we*.

1. A: The weather's beautiful today. _____

   B: Good idea.

2. A: I'm bored.

   B: Me too. _____

   A: Great idea!

3. A: Are you hungry?

   B: Yes. Are you?

   A: Yes. _____

   B: Okay.

4. A: What are you going to do over spring break?

   B: I don't know. What are you going to do?

   A: I haven't made any plans.

   B: _____

   A: That sounds like a terrific idea, but I can't afford it.

   B: Actually, I can't either.

5. A: I need to go shopping.

   B: So do I.

   A: _____

   B: I can't go then. _____

   A: Okay. That's fine with me.

6. A: Do you have any plans for this weekend?

   B: Not really.

   A: I don't either. _____

   B: Okay. Good idea.

7. A: What time should we leave for the airport?

   B: _____

   A: Okay.

8. A: What should we do tonight?

   B: _____

   A: Sounds okay to me.

9. A: _____

   B: Let's not. _____ instead.

   A: Okay.

□ **EXERCISE 23—ORAL:** Give suggestions. Use *"Why don't you...?"*

1. I'm thirsty.
2. I'm sleepy.
3. I have a headache.
4. I have a toothache.
5. It's too hot in this room.
6. Brrr. I'm cold.
7. I'm broke.
8. I'm hungry.
9. I have to take a science course next semester. What should I take?
10. Tomorrow is my sister's birthday. What should I give her?
11. I'd like to go to (...)'s party tonight, but I should probably stay home and study. What do you think I should do?
12. I'm going to take a vacation this summer. Where should I go?

☐ **EXERCISE 24:** Make sentences by combining one of the ideas in Column A with one of the ideas in Column B. Use *if* with the ideas in Column A.*

> *Example:* *If you need some help when you move into your new apartment, please call me.*

COLUMN A (*conditions*)

✔1. You may need some help when you move into your new apartment.

2. The weather may be nice tomorrow.

3. You may have a problem with your visa.

4. I may not be at the airport when your plane gets in.

5. Matt may want to lose some weight.

6. You may be tired.

7. Sara may not get better soon.

8. You may not know the answer to a question on the test.

9. Alice may call while I'm out.

10. You may be hungry.

COLUMN B (*suggestions*)

1. Guess.

2. You should see the International Student Advisor.

3. Why don't you take a nap?

4. Wait for me by the United Airlines counter.

5. Please take a message.

6. I could make a sandwich for you.

7. He should stop eating candy.

✔8. Please call me.

9. She should see a doctor.

10. Let's go sailing.

_____

*Use the simple present in the "**if**-clause." (See Chart 3-2.) Do not use **may** in the "**if**-clause."

5-13 STATING PREFERENCES: *PREFER, LIKE...BETTER, WOULD RATHER*

(a) I **prefer** apples **to** oranges.	*prefer* + NOUN + *to* + NOUN
(b) I **prefer** *watching* TV **to** *studying*.	*prefer* + -ING VERB + *to* + -ING VERB
(c) I **like** apples **better than** oranges.	*like* + NOUN + *better than* + NOUN
(d) I **like** *watching* TV **better than** *studying*.	*like* + -ING VERB + *better than* + -ING VERB
(e) Ann **would rather have** an apple **than** (*have*) an orange. (f) **I'd rather visit** a big city **than live** there.	In (e) and (f): **would rather** and **than** are followed immediately by the simple form of a verb (e.g., *have, visit, live*).*
(g) **I'd/You'd/She'd/He'd/We'd/They'd** rather have an apple.	Contraction of **would** = **'d**.
(h) **Would you rather** have an apple **or** an orange?	In (h): In a polite question, **would rather** can be followed by **or** to offer someone a choice.

*INCORRECT: *Ann would rather has an apple.*
INCORRECT: *I'd rather visit a big city than to live there.*
INCORRECT: *I'd rather visit a big city than living there.*

□ **EXERCISE 25:** Complete the sentences with *than* or *to*.

1. When I'm hot and thirsty, I **prefer** cold drinks ___**to**___ hot drinks.

2. When I'm hot and thirsty, I **like** cold drinks **better** ___**than**___ hot drinks.

3. When I'm hot and thirsty, I **'d rather have** a cold drink ___**than**___ a hot drink.

4. I **prefer** chicken ___to___ beef.

5. I **like** chicken **better** ___than___ beef.

6. I **'d rather** eat chicken ___than___ beef.

7. When I choose a book, I **prefer** nonfiction ___to___ fiction.

8. I **like** rock 'n roll **better** ___than___ classical music.

9. Tina **would rather lie** on the beach ___than___ **go** swimming.

10. Tina **likes lying** on the beach **better** _____ **going** swimming.

11. Tina **prefers lying** on the beach _____ **going** swimming.

Modal Auxiliaries □ **119**

12. My parents **would rather work** _____than_____ **retire.** They enjoy their jobs.

13. Do you **like** fresh vegetables **better** _____than_____ frozen or canned vegetables?

14. I **would rather take** a picture of a wild animal _____than_____ **kill** it with a gun.

15. Mr. Kim **prefers** tea _____to_____ coffee with his evening meal.

16. I **prefer visiting** my friends in the evening _____to_____ **watching** TV by myself.

17. My brother **would rather read** a book in the evening _____ **visit** with friends.

18. My sister **likes** her math class **better** _____than_____ her biology class.

□ **EXERCISE 26—ORAL (BOOK CLOSED):** Answer the questions **in complete sentences.**

Example: Which do you prefer, apples or oranges?
Response: I prefer (oranges) to (apples).

Example: Which do you like better, bananas or strawberries?
Response: I like (bananas) better than (strawberries).

Example: Which would you rather have right now, an apple or a banana?
Response: I'd rather have (a banana).

1. Which do you like better, rice or potatoes?
2. Which do you prefer, rice or potatoes?
3. Which would you rather have for dinner tonight, rice or potatoes?
4. Which do you prefer, fish or beef?
5. Which do you like better, fish or beef?
6. Which would you rather have for dinner tonight, fish or beef?
7. Which do you like better, Chinese food or Mexican food?
8. Which do you prefer, tea or coffee?
9. Would you rather have a cup of tea after class or a cup of coffee?
10. Which do you like better, hot weather or cold weather?
11. Which do you prefer, rock music or classical music?
12. What kind of music would you rather listen to, rock or classical?

13. Name two vegetables. Which do you prefer?

14. Name two kinds of fruit. Which do you like better?

15. Name two sports. Which do you like better?

16. Name two sports that you play. Which sport would you rather play this afternoon?

17. Name two TV programs. Which do you like better?

18. Name two movies. Which one would you rather see?

☐ **EXERCISE 27—ORAL (BOOKS CLOSED):** Answer the questions in complete sentences. Use **would rather . . . than . . . .**

Would you rather. . .

1. have a cup of coffee or (have) a cup of tea right now?

2. be a doctor or (be) a dentist?

3. be married or (be) single?

4. live in an apartment or (live) in a house?*

5. go to Moscow or (go) to London for your vacation?

6. visit Niagara Falls or (visit) the Grand Canyon?

7. take a nap or go downtown this afternoon?

8. watch TV or read a good book?

9. study chemistry or (study) accounting?

10. be a plumber or (be) a carpenter?

11. go to a football game or (go) to a soccer game?

12. take a long walk this afternoon or go swimming?

13. after dinner, wash the dishes or dry the dishes?

14. go to (*name of a place in this city*) or go to (*name of a place in this city*)?

15. have straight hair or (have) curly hair?

16. be a student or (be) a teacher?

17. have six children or (have) two children?

18. take your vacation in Greece or (take your vacation) in Brazil?

19. have a car or (have) an airplane?

20. be a bird or (be) a fish?

---

*It is possible but not necessary to repeat a preposition after **than**.
    CORRECT: I'd rather live in an apartment *than in a house.*
    CORRECT: I'd rather live in an apartment *than a house.*

    1. A: Do you feel like going to a show tonight?

        B: Not really. I'd rather _____

    2. A: Which do you like better, _____ or _____

        B: I like _____ better _____

    3. A: What are you going to do this weekend?

        B: I may _____, but I'd rather _____

    4. A: What kind of music do you like?

        B: All kinds. But I prefer _____ to _____

    5. A: What are you going to do tonight?

        B: I should _____, but I'd rather _____

    6. A: Let's go on a picnic next Saturday.

        B: That sounds good, but I'd rather _____

    7. A: I like _____ better _____

        B: Oh? Why?

        A: _____

    8. A: Are you going to _____ tonight?

        B: I'd like to, but I can't. I have to _____,

        but I'd much rather _____

□ **EXERCISE 29—PREPOSITIONS:** Complete the sentences with prepositions. This exercise contains prepositions that follow adjectives. (See Appendix 1 for a list of preposition combinations.)

be clear to

    1. Alex is afraid ___*of*___ snakes.

    2. I don't understand that sentence. It isn't clear __to__ me.

    3. Mark Twain is famous __for__ his novels about life on the

    Mississippi in the nineteenth century.

    4. I'm hungry __for__ some chocolate ice cream.

    5. Our daughter graduated from the university. We're very proud

    __of__ her.

6. A lot of sugar isn't good _____for_____ you. Sugar is especially bad

   _____for_____ your teeth.

7. Who was responsible _____for_____ the accident?

8. My coat is similar _____to_____ yours, but different _____from_____ Ben's. 근본상 차이가

9. Some people aren't friendly _____to_____ strangers.

10. My daughter is crazy _____about_____ horses. She is very interested

    _____in_____ horses.

11. Sara knows what she's talking about. She's sure _____of_____ her facts.

12. Are you aware _____of_____ the number of children who die each day

    throughout the world? According to one report, 40,000 children die

    each day throughout the world, mostly due to malnutrition and lack of

    minimal medical care.

    due to ~때문에

CHAPTER 6
Asking Questions

6-1 YES/NO QUESTIONS AND SHORT ANSWERS

YES/NO QUESTIONS	SHORT ANSWER (+ LONG ANSWER)	A *yes/no question* is a question that can be answered by "yes" or "no" (or their equivalents, such as "yeah" or "nah," and "uh huh" or "huh uh").
(a) ***Do you know*** Jim Smith?	***Yes, I do.*** (I know Jim Smith.) ***No, I don't.*** (I don't know Jim Smith.)	
(b) ***Did it rain*** last night?	***Yes, it did.*** (It rained last night.) ***No, it didn't.*** (It didn't rain last night.)	
(c) ***Are you studying*** English?	***Yes, I am.*** * (I'm studying English.) ***No, I'm not.*** (I'm not studying English.)	
(d) ***Was Ann*** in class?	***Yes, she was.*** (Ann was in class.) ***No, she wasn't.*** (Ann wasn't in class.)	
(e) ***Will Rob be*** here soon?	***Yes, he will.*** * (Rob will be here soon.) ***No, he won't.*** (Rob won't be here soon.)	
(f) ***Can you swim?***	***Yes, I can.*** (I can swim.) ***No, I can't.*** (I can't swim.)	

*NOTE: In an affirmative answer (*yes*), a helping verb is not contracted with the subject.
    In (c): CORRECT: *Yes, I am.* (The spoken emphasis is on ***am***.)
             INCORRECT: *Yes, I'm.*
    In (e): CORRECT: *Yes, he will.* (The spoken emphasis is on ***will***.)
             INCORRECT: *Yes, he'll.*

☐ **EXERCISE 1:** In the following dialogues, the long answer is given in parentheses. Look at the long answer, and then make the appropriate YES/NO QUESTION and SHORT ANSWER to complete each dialogue. Do not use a negative verb in the question.

1. A: _____*Do you know my brother?*_____

   B: No, ____*I don't.*____ (I don't know your brother.)

2. A: _____

   B: Yes, _____ (Jane eats lunch at the cafeteria every day.)

3. A: *Does this pen belong to you?*

   B: No, _____ (That pen doesn't belong to me.)

4. A: *Do the students*

   B: Yes, *they do* (The students in this class speak English well.)

5. A: *Did you sleep well last night?*

   B: Yes, _____ (I slept well last night.)

6. A: _____

   B: No, *they didn't* (Ann and Jim didn't come to class yesterday.)

7. A: _____

   B: Yes, *I am* (I'm studying my grammar book.)

8. A: _____

   B: No, _____ (The children aren't watching TV.)

9. A: _____

   B: Yes, _____ (Tim Wilson is in my astronomy class.)

10. A: *Was it foggy yesterday?*

    B: No, _____ (It wasn't foggy yesterday.)

11. A: *Will you be at home tonight?*

    B: No, _____ (I won't be at home tonight.)

12. A: *Is Jason going to be*

    B: No, _____ (Jason isn't going to be at work tomorrow.)

13. A: ___Will_____

    B: Yes, _she will_. (Karen will finish her work before she
       goes to bed.)

14. A: _____

    B: No, _____ (I can't play the piano.)

15. A: _____

    B: Yes, _____ (Some birds can swim under water.)

16. A: _____

    B: Yes, _____ (You should make an appointment to see
       the doctor.)

17. A: ___Do I_____

    B: Yes, _you do_. (You need to make an appointment to see
       the doctor.)

18. A: _____

    B: Yes, _I do_. (I have a bicycle.)*

19. A: _____

    B: No, _____ (Greg doesn't have a roommate.)

20. A: _Do you have to study tonight?_

    B: Yes, _____ (I have to study tonight.)

☐ **EXERCISE 2—ORAL (BOOKS CLOSED):** Answer the questions. Use short answers.

Example: Do you know how to swim?
Response: Yes, I do. OR: No, I don't.

Example: Is (. . .) wearing blue jeans today?
Response: Yes, s/he is. OR: No, s/he isn't.

1. Is (. . .) in class today?
2. Does (. . .) have a mustache?
3. Is (. . .) wearing a sweater today?
4. Was (. . .) in class yesterday?
5. Did (. . .) come to class yesterday?

6. Is (. . .) from (*name of a country*)?
7. Does (. . .) speak (*name of a language*)?
8. Are you going downtown tomorrow?
9. Will you be in class tomorrow?
10. Can you play the piano?

---

*In American English, a form of **do** is usually used when **have** is the main verb:
   Do you have a car?

In British English, a form of **do** with main verb **have** is not necessary:
   Have you a car?

11. Do you know how to play the violin?
12. Are we going to have a test tomorrow?
13. Can turtles swim?
14. Should people smoke cigarettes?
15. Did you watch TV last night?
16. Do you have a bicycle?
17. Will class begin at (*time*) tomorrow?

18. Does class begin at (*time*) every day?
19. Do giraffes eat meat?
20. Were all of the students in class yesterday?
21. Should I speak more slowly?
22. Is English grammar easy?
23. Was this exercise difficult?

☐ **EXERCISE 3—ORAL (BOOKS CLOSED):** Make questions and give short answers.

> *Example:* (. . .) is wearing jeans today.
> STUDENT A: Is (. . .) wearing jeans today?
> STUDENT B: Yes, s/he is.

> *Example:* (. . .) isn't wearing jeans today.
> STUDENT A: Is (. . .) wearing jeans today?
> STUDENT B: No, s/he isn't.

1. (. . .) has curly hair.
2. (. . .) doesn't have a mustache.
3. (. . .) is going to be in class tomorrow.
4. (. . .) won't be in class tomorrow.
5. (. . .) studied at the library last night.
6. (. . .) can't play the piano.
7. (. . .) has to study tonight.
8. (. . .) went to a party last night.
9. (. . .) is wearing earrings.
10. (. . .) has dark eyes.
11. (. . .)'s grammar book isn't open.

12. (. . .) should close his/her grammar book.
13. That book belongs to (. . .).
14. (. . .) and (. . .) came to class yesterday.
15. (. . .) wasn't in class yesterday.
16. This book has an index.
17. Most books have indexes.
18. This exercise is easy.
19. (. . .) will be at home tonight.
20. An ostrich can't fly.

6-2 YES/NO QUESTIONS AND INFORMATION QUESTIONS

A yes/no question = a question that may be answered by "yes" or "no."
    A: *Does Ann live in Montreal?*
    B: *Yes, she does.* OR: *No, she doesn't.*
An information question = a question that asks for information by using a question word: *where, when, why, who, whom, what, which, whose, how.*
    A: *Where does Ann live?*
    B: *In Montreal.*

(QUESTION WORD)	HELPING VERB	SUBJECT	MAIN VERB	(REST OF SENTENCE)	
(a)	**Does**	*Ann*	**live**	in Montreal?	The same subject-verb word order is used in both yes/no and information questions:
(b) Where	**does**	*Ann*	**live**?		
(c)	**Is**	*Sara*	**studying**	at the library?	HELPING VERB + SUBJECT + MAIN VERB
(d) Where	**is**	*Sara*	**studying**?		
(e)	**Will**	*you*	**graduate**	next year?	
(f) When	**will**	*you*	**graduate**?		
(g)	**Did**	*they*	**see**	Jack?	In (i) and (j): Main verb **be** in simple present and simple past (**am, is, are, was, were**) precedes the subject. It has the same position as a helping verb.
(h) Who(m)*	**did**	*they*	**see**?		
(i)	**Is**	*Heidi*		at home?	
(j) Where	**is**	*Heidi*?			
(k)		*Who*	**came**	to dinner?	When the question word (e.g., **who** or **what**) is the subject of the question, the usual question word order is not used. No form of **do** is used. Notice (k) and (l).
(l)		*What*	**happened**	yesterday?	

*See Chart 6-3 for a discussion of **who(m)**.

□ **EXERCISE 4—ORAL:** Make questions from the following sentences. Make (a) a YES/NO QUESTION and (b) an INFORMATION QUESTION with *where.*

Example: I live there.
Response: (a) Do you live there?
            (b) Where do you live?

1. She lives there.
2. The students live there.
3. Bob lived there.
4. I'm living there.
5. Mary is living there.
6. I was living there.

7. He was living there.
8. They are going to live there.
9. John will live there.

10. The students can live there.
11. Alice should live there.
12. Tom has to live there.*

☐ **EXERCISE 5:** Make information questions. Use *where, why, when,* or *what time.*

1. A: ___*When/What time*** *did you get up this morning?*___
   B: At 7:30. (I got up at 7:30 this morning.)

2. A: _____
   B: At the cafeteria. (I ate lunch at the cafeteria today.)

3. A: _____
   B: At 12:15. (I ate lunch at 12:15.)

4. A: _____
   B: Because the food is good. (I eat lunch at the cafeteria because the food is good.)

5. A: _____
   B: In Chicago. (My aunt and uncle live in Chicago.)

6. A: _____
   B: Next week. (I'm going to visit my aunt and uncle next week.)

7. A: _____
   B: Around six. (I'll get home around six tonight.)

8. A: _____
   B: At the library. (George is going to study at the library tonight.)

9. A: _____
   B: Because it's quiet. (George studies at the library because it's quiet.)

10. A: _____
    B: At that corner. (You can catch a bus at that corner.)

11. A: _____
    B: Ten o'clock. (I have to leave at ten o'clock.)

12. A: _____
    B: In Japan. (I was living in Japan in 1988.)

_____

*In a question, a form of *do* is used with *have to.*
　　Do you have to go there? Where do you have to go?
　　Does she have to go there? Where does she have to go?
**A question with *what time* usually asks about time on a clock. The answer can be *7:30, a quarter past ten, around five o'clock,* etc.
　A question with *when* can be answered by any time expression: *7:30, around five o'clock, last night, next week, in a few days, yesterday,* etc.

13. A: _____
    B: Because they're working on an exercise. (The students are writing in their books because they're working on an exercise.)

14. A: _____
    B: Around seven. (You should call me around seven.)

15. A: _____
    B: Because she's flying her kite in the park. (Yoko is absent because she's flying her kite in the park.)

□ **EXERCISE 6:** Make information questions. Use *where, why, when, what time,* or *what.*

1. A: _____
   B: Tomorrow. (I'm going to go downtown tomorrow.)

2. A: _____
   B: Because I didn't feel good. (I stayed home yesterday because I didn't feel good.)

3. A: _____
   B: To a movie. (I went to a movie last night.)

4. A: _____
   B: At a hardware store. (You can buy a hammer at a hardware store.)

5. A: _____
   B: At 1:10. (Class begins at 1:10.)

6. A: _____
   B: Because I need to buy some stamps. (I have to go to the post office because I need to buy some stamps.)

7. A: _____
   B: Next June. (My daughter will graduate from college next June.)

8. A: _____
   B: At Lincoln Elementary School. (My children go to school at Lincoln Elementary School.)

9. A: _____
   B: Four years ago. (I met the Smiths four years ago.)

10. A: _____
    B: "Try." ("Attempt" means "try.")

11. A: _____
    B: An amphibian. (A frog is an amphibian.)

12. A: _____
    B: An animal that can live on land or in water. (An amphibian is an animal that can live on land or in water.)

13. A: _____
    B: Mostly insects. (Frogs eat mostly insects.)

14. A: _____
    B: "Job or profession." ("Occupation" means "job or profession.")

15. A: _____
    B: Because I need to know it in order to study in the United States.
    (I'm studying English because I need to know it in order to study in
    the United States.)

☐ **EXERCISE 7—ORAL:** Pair up with a classmate. Practice asking questions with **why**.

STUDENT A's book is open. STUDENT B's book is closed.
STUDENT A: Say the sentence in the book. (Then listen carefully to B's
question with **why** and make sure it is correct.)
STUDENT B: Ask a question using **why**.*
STUDENT A: Make up an answer to the question.

Example: A: I'm tired today.
          B: Why are you tired today?
          A: Because I stayed up late last night.

1. A: I was absent from class yesterday.
2. A: I'm going to the bank after class.
3. A: I went downtown yesterday.
4. A: I took a taxi to school today.
5. A: I need to go to the drugstore.
6. A: I'm going to buy a new dictionary.

---

*In normal daily conversation, the second speaker (STUDENT B) would usually ask only
"Why?" or "Why not?" However, to practice question word order, STUDENT B should
ask the full question in this exercise.

Example: A: I didn't study last night.

B: Why didn't you study last night?

(*Notice: Use a negative verb in the question with* **why**.)

A: Because I was tired.

7. A: I didn't do my homework last night.

8. A: I'm not coming to class tomorrow.

9. A: I can't come to your party this weekend.

10. A: I didn't eat breakfast this morning.

11. A: I won't be in class tomorrow.

12. A: I don't like the weather in this city.

6-3 USING *WHO, WHO(M),* AND *WHAT*

QUESTION	ANSWER	
(a) **Who** came? *(S)*	**Someone** came. *(S)*	In (a): **Who** is used as the subject (**S**) of a question. In (b): **Who(m)** is used as the object (**O**) in a question. **Whom** is used in formal English. In everyday spoken English, **who** is usually used instead of **whom**: FORMAL: *Whom did you see?* INFORMAL: *Who did you see?*
(b) **Who(m)** did you see? *(O S)*	I saw **someone**. *(S O)*	
(c) **What** happened? *(S)*	**Something** happened. *(S)*	**What** can be used as either the subject or the object in a question. Notice in (a) and (c): When **who** or **what** is used as the subject of a question, usual question word order is not used; no form of **do** is used. CORRECT: *Who came?* INCORRECT: *Who did come?*
(d) **What** did you see? *(O S)*	I saw **something**. *(S O)*	

☐ **EXERCISE 8:** Make questions. Use *what, who,* or *who(m)*.

1. A: _____*What did you see*?_____

B: An accident. (I saw an accident.)

2. A: _____

B: An accident. (Mary saw an accident.)

WHO   WHAT

3. A: _____
   B: Mary. (Mary saw an accident.)

4. A: _____
   B: John. (Mary saw John.)

WHO   WHO(M)

5. A: _____
   B: Mary. (Mary saw John.)

6. A: _____
   B: An accident. (An accident happened.)

7. A: _____
   B: A new coat. (Alice bought a new coat.)

8. A: _____
   B: Alice. (Alice bought a new coat.)

9. A: _____
   B: A map of the world. (I'm looking at a map of the world.)*

10. A: _____
    B: Jane. (I'm looking at Jane.)

11. A: _____
    B: The secretary. (I talked to the secretary.)

12. A: _____
    B: His problems. (Tom talked about his problems.)

13. A: _____
    B: The board. (The teacher looked at the board.)

14. A: _____
    B: The teacher. (The teacher looked at the board.)

15. A: _____
    B: The students. (The teacher looked at the students.)

---

*A preposition may come at the beginning of a question in very formal English:
    At what *are you looking?*
    At whom (NOT ***who***) *are you looking?*
In everyday English, a preposition usually does not come at the beginning of a question.

1. Where is my book?★
2. What is in that drawer?★
3. Why is Mary absent?
4. Who is that man?★
5. Who are those men?
6. Where are you going?
7. What are you doing?
8. Where did Bob go last night?
9. What did you say?
10. Why did you say that?
11. Who did you see at the party?
12. Where will you be?
13. When will you arrive?
14. Who will meet you at the airport?

□ EXERCISE 10: Make any appropriate question for the given answer.

1. A: _____
   B: Yesterday.

2. A: _____
   B: A new pair of shoes.

3. A: _____
   B: Mary.

4. A: _____
   B: Six-thirty.

5. A: _____
   B: To the zoo.

6. A: _____
   B: Because I was tired.

7. A: _____
   B: A sandwich.

8. A: _____
   B: I don't know.

9. A: _____
   B: Tomorrow.

10. A: _____
    B: My brother.

★Often *is* is contracted with *where, what,* and *who* in informal writing as well as in spoken English.
Where's my pen?
What's that?
Who's he?

6-4 USING *WHAT* + A FORM OF *DO*

What + *a form of do* is used to ask questions about activities.
(Examples of forms of *do:* am doing, will do, are going to do, did, etc.)

QUESTION	ANSWER
(a) *What* **does** Bob **do** every morning? ⟶	He *goes to class.*
(b) *What* **did** you **do** yesterday? ⟶	I *went downtown.*
(c) *What* **is** your roommate **doing**? ⟶	She's *studying.*
(d) *What* **are** you **going to do** tomorrow? ⟶	I'm *going to go to the beach.*
(e) *What* **do** you **want to do** tonight? ⟶	I *want to go to a movie.*
(f) *What* **would** you **like to do** tomorrow? ⟶	I *would like to visit Jim.*
(g) *What* **will** you **do** tomorrow? ⟶	I'll *go downtown.*
(h) *What* **should** I **do** about my headache? ⟶	You *should take an aspirin.*

☐ **EXERCISE 11:** Make questions. Use *what* + a form of *do.*

1. A: ___**What are you doing?**_____ right now?
   B: I'm studying.

2. A: _____ last night?
   B: I studied.

3. A: _____ tomorrow?
   B: I'm going to visit my relatives.

4. A: _____ tomorrow?
   B: I want to go to the beach.

5. A: _____ tomorrow?
   B: I need to go to the library.

6. A: _____ tomorrow?
   B: I would like to go to a movie.

7. A: _____ tomorrow?
   B: I'm planning to stay home and relax most of the day.

8. A: _____ in class every day?
   B: I study English.

9. A: _____ (for a living)?*
   B: I'm a teacher. (I teach.)

---

*What do you do? has a special meaning. It means *What is your occupation, your job?* Another
way of asking the same question: *What do you do for a living?*

10. A: _____ if it snows tomorrow
    and you can't get to the airport?
    B: I'll cancel my reservation and book a flight for the next day.

11. A: _____ to improve my English?
    B: You should speak English as much as possible.

12. A: _____ after class yesterday?
    B: He (Steve) went to the post office.

13. A: _____ after class yesterday?
    B: She (Jane) went swimming.

14. A: _____ when he stopped you
    for speeding?
    B: He (the police officer) gave me a ticket.

15. A: _____ ?
    B: She (Yoko) is writing in her book.

16. A: _____ in the winter?
    B: It (a bear) hibernates.

17. A: I have the hiccups. _____ ?
    B: You should drink a glass of water.

18. A: Mike is in trouble with the law. _____?
    B: He should see a lawyer.

19. A: _____?
    B: He (my husband) is a businessman. He works for General Electric.

20. A: _____?
    B: She (my wife) is a computer programmer. She works for the
    telephone company.

□ **EXERCISE 12—ORAL (BOOKS CLOSED):** Ask a classmate a question. Use **what + do**.

Example: tomorrow
STUDENT A: What are you going to do tomorrow?/What do you want to do
tomorrow?/What would you like to do tomorrow?/etc.
STUDENT B: *(Answer the question.)*

1. last night
2. right now
3. next Saturday
4. this afternoon
5. tonight
6. yesterday
7. every day
8. yesterday afternoon

9. this morning
10. last weekend
11. on weekends
12. tomorrow afternoon
13. after class yesterday
14. after class today
15. every morning
16. the day after tomorrow

6-5 USING *WHAT KIND OF*

QUESTION	ANSWER	

(a) **What kind of** *shoes* did you buy? ⟶	Boots.
	Sandals.
	Tennis shoes.
	Loafers.
	Running shoes.
	High heels.
	(etc.)
		What kind of asks for information about a specific type (a specific kind) in a general category.
		
		In (a):
		general category = shoes
		specific kinds = boots
		       sandals,
		       tennis shoes,
		       etc.

(b) **What kind of** *fruit* do you like best? ⟶	Apples. Bananas. Oranges. Grapefruit. Grapes. Strawberries. (etc.)	

Complete each question. Give other possible answers to the question.

1. A: What kind of _____shoes_____ are you wearing?

   B: Boots. (*Other possible answers:* ____loafers /running shoes /etc.____)

2. A: What kind of _____meat_____ do you eat most often?

   B: Beef. (*Other possible answers:* ____chicken /lamb /pork /etc.____)

3. A: What kind of _____ do you like best?

   B: Rock 'n roll. (*Other possible answers:*_____)

4. A: What kind of _____ would you like to have?

   B: A Mercedes-Benz. (*Other possible answers:* _____)

5. A: What kind of _____ do you like to read?

   B: Science fiction. (*Other possible answers:*_____)

6. A: What kind of _____ do you like best?

   B: Chocolates. (*Other possible answers:*_____)

7. A: What kind of _____ do you prefer to use?

   B: A Macintosh.* (*Other possible answers:*_____)

8. A: What kind of _____ do you have?

   B: _____. (*Other possible answers:*_____)

□ EXERCISE 14—ORAL (BOOKS CLOSED): Answer the questions.

1. What kind of music do you like best?
2. What kind of shoes are you wearing?
3. What kind of food do you like best?
4. What kind of books do you like to read?
5. Who has a car? What kind of car do you have?**
6. I'm going to buy a car. What kind of car should I buy?
7. Who is wearing a watch? What kind of watch do you have?
8. Who has a camera? What kind of camera do you have?
9. Who had a sandwich yesterday/for lunch today? What kind of sandwich did you have?

---

*"Macintosh" is a brand name of a type of computer.

**When a question with *what kind of* involves manufactured products, the answer may either name a particular brand or describe the product's particular attributes (qualities).

    A: *What kind of car do you have?*   A: *What kind of car do you have?*

    B: *A Ford.*   B: *A four-door station wagon.*

10. Who had soup yesterday/for lunch today? What kind of soup did you have?

11. Who has a TV? A VCR? What kind?

12. What kind of government does your country have?

13. What kind of job would you like to have?

14. What kind of person would you like to marry?

15. What kind of products can we recycle?

6-6 USING *WHICH*

<table>
<tr>
<td>
(a) <i>Tom:</i> May I borrow a pen from you?
    Ann: Sure. I have two pens. This pen has black ink. That pen has red ink. Which (pen/one) do you want?
    Tom: That one. Thanks.
(b) Which pen do you want?
(c) Which one do you want?
(d) Which   do you want?
</td>
<td>
In (a): Ann uses <i>which</i> (not <i>what</i>) because she wants Tom to choose.
Which is used when the speaker wants someone to make a choice, when the speaker is offering alternatives: this one or that one; these or those.
(b), (c), and (d) have the same meaning.
</td>
</tr>
<tr>
<td>
(e) <i>Sue:</i> I like these earrings, and I like those earrings.
    Bob: Which (earrings/ones) are you going to buy?
    Sue: I think I'll get these.
(f) Which earrings are you going to buy?
(g) Which ones   are you going to buy?
(h) Which   are you going to buy?
</td>
<td>
Which can be used with either singular or plural nouns.
(f), (g), and (h) have the same meaning.
</td>
</tr>
</table>

□ **EXERCISE 15:** Make questions. Use *which* or *what*.

1. A: I have two books. _**Which book/ Which one/ Which do you want?**_

   B: That one. (I want that book.)

2. A: _____**What did you buy when you went shopping?**_____

   B: A book. (I bought a book when I went shopping.)

3. A: Could I borrow your pen for a minute?

   B: Sure. I have two. _____

   A: That one. (I would like that one.)

4. A: _____

   B: A pen. (Chris borrowed a pen from me.)

5. A: Do you like this tie?

   B: Yes.

   A: Do you like that tie?

   B: It's okay.

   A: _Which are you going to buy?_

   B: This one. (I'm going to buy this one.)

6. A: _What did Tony get when he went shopping?_

   B: A tie. (Tony got a tie when he went shopping.)

7. A: These shoes are comfortable, and so are those shoes. _Which should I buy_ I can't decide.

   B: These. (You should buy these shoes.)

8. A: There are flights to Atlanta at 7:30 A.M. and 8:40 A.M. _Which are you going to take_

   B: The 7:30 flight. (I'm going to take the 7:30 flight.)

9. A: _What does huge means?_

   B: "Very big." ("Huge" means "very big.")

10. A: _What is meaning of rapid?_

    B: "Fast." (The meaning of "rapid" is "fast.")

11. A: Would you please hand me a sharp knife?

    B: I'd be happy to. _Which would you like?_

    A: That one. (I'd like that one.)

12. A: Are you a student in the English program?

    B: Yes, I am.

    A: _Which are you in?_ = which class are you in?

    B: The beginning class. (I'm in the beginning class.)*

13. A: Did you enjoy your trip to Europe?

    B: Yes, I did. Very much. (_What did you visit?_

    A: _What country did you visit?_

    B: I visited Poland, Germany, Czechoslovakia, and Italy.

    A: _____

    B: Poland. (I enjoyed visiting Poland the most.)

---

*The differences between *what class* and *which class* and between *what country* and *which country* are often very small.

6-7 USING WHOSE

QUESTION	ANSWER	
(a) **Whose** (**book**) is this?	It's John's (book).	**Whose** asks about possession. Notice in (a): the speaker of the question may omit the noun (*book*) if the meaning is clear to the listener.
(b) **Whose** (**books**) are those?	They're mine (OR: my books).	
(c) **Whose car** did you borrow?	I borrowed Karen's (car).	
COMPARE:		**Who's** and **whose** have the same pronunciation.
(d) **Who's** that?	Mary Smith.	**Who's** = a contraction of **who is**.
(e) **Whose** is that?	Mary's.	**Whose** = asks about possession.*

*See Charts 4-7 and 4-8 for ways of expressing possession.

☐ **EXERCISE 16:** Make questions with **whose** or **who**. The things near Susan belong to her. The things near Eric belong to him.

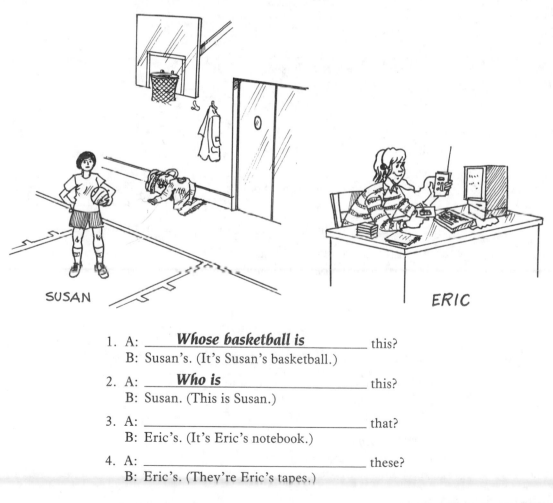

SUSAN   ERIC

1. A: _____**Whose basketball is**_____ this?
   B: Susan's. (It's Susan's basketball.)

2. A: _____**Who is**_____ this?
   B: Susan. (This is Susan.)

3. A: _____ that?
   B: Eric's. (It's Eric's notebook.)

4. A: _____ these?
   B: Eric's. (They're Eric's tapes.)

5. A: _____ that?
   B: Eric. (That is Eric.) ~~Who's~~

6. A: ~~Which they are~~ clothes ~~are~~ those?
   B: Susan's. (They're Susan's clothes.)

7. A: ___whose_____ that?
   B: Susan's. (It's Susan's coat.)

8. A: ___who is___~~that~~_____ in a gym?
   B: Susan. (Susan is in a gym.)

9. A: ___who is_____ sitting down?
   B: Eric. (Eric is sitting down.)

10. A: ___who's___~~hair~~_____ hair is longer?
    B: Eric's. (Eric's hair is longer than Susan's.)

11. A: ~~who~~_____
    B: Pedro's. (I borrowed Pedro's umbrella.)

12. A: _____
    B: Linda's. (I used Linda's book.)

13. A: ___whose book_____
    B: Nick's. (Nick's book is on the table.)

14. A: ___whose___~~on the phone~~? ___
    B: Nick. (Nick is on the phone.)

15. A: _____
    B: Pat's. (That's Pat's house.)

16. A: _____
    B: Pat. (Pat is living in that house.)

17. A: ___whose student in your class who is that?___
    B: Sue Smith. (That's Sue Smith.) She's a student in my class.

18. A: ___who's one is that?_____
    B: Sue's. (That's Sue's.) This one is mine.

☐ **EXERCISE 17—ORAL:** Ask questions with *whose.*

STUDENT A: Pick up, touch, or point to an object in the classroom. Ask a question with *whose.*

STUDENT B: Answer the question.

Example: (*Student A picks up a book.*)

STUDENT A: Whose (book) is this?

STUDENT B: It's Maria's (book).

Example: (*Student A points to some books.*)
STUDENT A: Whose (books) are those?
STUDENT B: They're Kim's (books).

□ **EXERCISE 18—ORAL:** Ask and answer questions about possession. Follow the pattern in the examples. Talk about things in the classroom.

Example: pen
STUDENT A: Is this your pen?/Is this (pen) yours?
STUDENT B: No, it isn't.
STUDENT A: Whose is it?
STUDENT B: It's Ali's.

Example: pens
STUDENT A: Are these Yoko's (pens)?/Are these (pens) Yoko's?
STUDENT B: No, they aren't.
STUDENT A: Whose are they?
STUDENT B: They're mine.

1. dictionary	5. bookbag	9. purse
2. books	6. briefcase	10. calculator
3. notebook	7. glasses	11. things
4. papers	8. backpack	12. stuff*

□ **EXERCISE 19—WRITTEN:** Make questions for the given answers. Use any appropriate question word. Write **both** the question (A:) and the answer (B:). Use your own paper.

Example: A: ...? B: I'm reading.
Written dialogue: **A: What are you doing?**
B: I'm reading.

1. A: ...? B: They're mine.
2. A: ...? B: I'm going to study.
3. A: ...? B: A Toyota.
4. A: ...? B: Mr. Miller.
5. A: ...? B: It's Bob's.
6. A: ...? B: It means "small."
7. A: ...? B: Jazz.
8. A: ...? B: Because I didn't feel good.
9. A: ...? B: This one, not that one.
10. A: ...? B: You should buy that shirt.
11. A: ...? B: A couple of days ago.
12. A: ...? B: I would like to go to India.

*Stuff is used in informal spoken English to mean miscellaneous things. For example, when a speaker says, "This is my stuff," the speaker may be referring to pens, pencils, books, papers, notebooks, clothes, etc. (Note: **stuff** is a noncount noun; it never has a final **-s**.)

6-8 USING *HOW*

QUESTION	ANSWER	
(a) *How* did you get here? ⟶	⎰ I drove./By car. ⎱ I took a taxi./By taxi. I took a bus./By bus. I flew./By plane. I took a train./By train. I walked./On foot.	*How* has many uses. One use of *how* is to ask about means (ways) of transportation.
(b) *How old* are you? ⟶ (c) *How tall* is he? ⟶ (d) *How big* is your apartment? ⟶ (e) *How sleepy* are you? ⟶ (f) *How hungry* are you? ⟶ (g) *How soon* will you be ready? ⟶ (h) *How well* does he speak English? ➤ (i) *How quickly* can you get here? ⟶	Twenty-one. About six feet. It has three rooms. Very sleepy. I'm starving. In five minutes. Very well. I can get there in 30 minutes.	*How* is often used with adjectives (e.g., *old, big*) and adverbs (e.g., *well, quickly*).

(handwritten notes near (a): "do 하지 않", "are하지", "ㅁㅁ하")

☐ **EXERCISE 20:** Make questions with *how*.

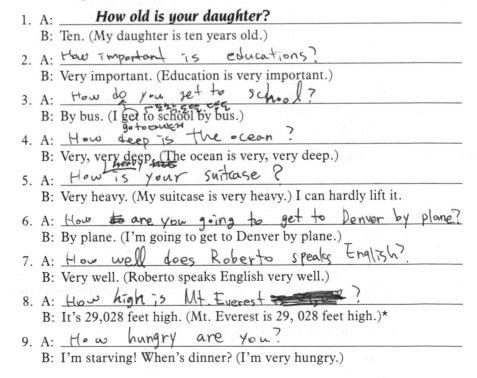

1. A: _____**How old is your daughter?**_____
   B: Ten. (My daughter is ten years old.)

2. A: How important is educations?
   B: Very important. (Education is very important.)

3. A: How do you get to school?
   B: By bus. (I get to school by bus.)

4. A: How deep is the ocean?
   B: Very, very deep. (The ocean is very, very deep.)

5. A: How heavy is your suitcase?
   B: Very heavy. (My suitcase is very heavy.) I can hardly lift it.

6. A: How are you going to get to Denver by plane?
   B: By plane. (I'm going to get to Denver by plane.)

7. A: How well does Roberto speaks English?
   B: Very well. (Roberto speaks English very well.)

8. A: How high is Mt. Everest?
   B: It's 29,028 feet high. (Mt. Everest is 29, 028 feet high.)*

9. A: How hungry are you?
   B: I'm starving! When's dinner? (I'm very hungry.)

---

*29,028 feet = 8,848 meters.

10. A: How did you get to school today?
    B: I walked. (I walked to school today.)
11. A: How should I send that letter?
    B: By express mail. (You should send that letter by express mail.)
12. A: How safe is that neighborhood at night?
    B: It's not very safe at all. (That neighborhood isn't very safe at night.)
13. A: How difficult was the test?
    B: Not very. (The test wasn't very difficult.)
14. A: How tall is Mary?
    B: About 5½ feet. (Mary is about 5½ feet tall.)*
15. A: How fast do you drive? 165cm
    B: Not very fast. Usually about 55 miles per hour. (I don't drive very fast.)**

6-9 USING *HOW OFTEN*

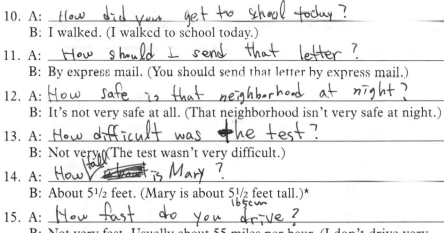

QUESTION	ANSWER	*How often* asks about frequency.
(a) **How often** do you go shopping?	Every day. Once a week. About twice a week. Every other day or so.* Three times a month.	
(b) **How many times a day** do you eat? **How many times a week** do you go shopping? **How many times a month** do you go to the bank? **How many times a year** do you take a vacation?	Three or four. Two. Once. Once or twice.	Other ways of asking **how often**: **how many times** { a day a week a month a year

Every other day means Monday yes, Tuesday no, Wednesday yes, Thursday no, etc. *Or so* means *approximately*.

☐ **EXERCISE 21—ORAL:** Ask and answer questions about frequency.

STUDENT A: Ask a question with **how often** or **how many times a day/week/month/year.**

STUDENT B: Answer the question. (Possible answers are suggested in the list of frequency expressions.)

---

*5 ½ feet = 165 cm.
**55 mph = 88 kilometers per hour.

FREQUENCY EXPRESSIONS

a lot	*every* 매일
*occasionally** 때때로	*every other* 매 일
once in a while 가끔	*once a* 한번 } day/week/month/year
not very often 자주 아니	*twice a* 두번 } 매일 매주 매달 매견
hardly ever 거의 X	*three times a* 세번
almost never	*ten times a* 열번
never 절대 X	

Example: eat lunch at the cafeteria

STUDENT A: How often do you eat lunch at the cafeteria?
STUDENT B: About twice a week.

1. go to a movie
2. watch TV
3. go out to eat
4. cook your own dinner
5. play cards
6. read a newspaper
7. get your hair cut
8. write a letter to your parents

9. see a dentist
10. buy a toothbrush
11. wake up during the night
12. go to a laundromat
13. go swimming
14. be late for class
15. attend a wedding
16. see a falling star

6-10 USING *HOW FAR*

(a) *It is* 289 miles *from* St. Louis *to* Chicago.** (b) *It is* 289 miles { *from* St. Louis *to* Chicago. *from* Chicago *to* St. Louis. *to* Chicago *from* St. Louis. *to* St. Louis *from* Chicago.	The most common way of expressing distance: *It is* + *distance* + *from/to* + *to/from.* In (b): All four expressions with *from* and *to* have the same meaning.

(c) A: *How far is it* from St. Louis to Chicago?
    B: 289 miles.
 (d) A: *How far do you live* from school?
    B: Four blocks.
	How far is used to ask questions about distance.

(e) *How many miles* is it from St. Louis to Chicago?
 (f) *How many kilometers* is it to Montreal from here?
 (g) *How many blocks* is it to the post office?
	Other ways to ask *how far:*
	    how many miles
	    how many kilometers
	    how many blocks

**1 mile = 1.609 kilometers.
  1 kilometer = 0.614 mile.

———————

*Notice: *Occasionally* is spelled with *two "c's"* but only *one "s."*

☐ **EXERCISE 22:** Make questions.

1. A: _____
   B: 237 miles. (It's 237 miles from New York City to Washington, D.C.)

2. A: _____
   B: 257 kilometers. (It's 257 kilometers from Montreal to Quebec.)

3. A: _____
   B: 919 miles. (It's 919 miles to Chicago from New Orleans).

4. A: *How many blocks is it to the post office?*
   B: Six blocks. (It's six blocks to the post office.)

5. A: *How many ~~far~~ blocks is it to the book store?*
   B: Two and a half blocks. (It's two and a half blocks to the bookstore from here.)

6. A: *How far do you live from school?*
   B: About three miles. (I live about three miles from school.)

7. A: Karen is really into physical fitness. She jogs every day. *be into something 에 빠지다*
   B: Oh? *How many miles ~~does karen jog?~~ ~~every day~~?*
   A: Five miles. (She jogs five miles every day.)
   B: That's great. I usually don't even walk five miles a day.

8. A: I had a terrible day yesterday.
   B: What happened?
   A: I ran out of gas while I was driving to work.
   B: *How far did you get* _____ before you ran out of gas?
   A: To the junction of I-90 and 480. (I got to the junction of I-90 and 480.) Luckily, there was a gas station about half a mile down the road.

☐ **EXERCISE 23—ORAL:** In small groups, look at a map of your area and ask each other questions with *how far*.

6-11 EXPRESSING LENGTH OF TIME: *IT + TAKE*

How long

IT + TAKE + (SOMEONE) + TIME EXPRESSION + INFINITIVE*				
(a) **It** takes	*us*	six hours *we 걸리다*	**to drive**	to Chicago from here.
(b) **It** took	Janet	a long time	**to finish**	her composition.

*An infinitive = **to** + *the simple form of a verb*. See Chart 10-1.

□ **EXERCISE 24:** Make sentences using *it* + *take* to express length of time.

1. I drove to Los Angeles. (*Length of time: three days*)
   It took me three days to drive to Los Angeles.

2. I walk to class. (*Length of time: twenty minutes*)
   It takes me ∧ to walk to class
   twenty minutes

3. George finished the test. (*Length of time: an hour and a half*)

4. We will drive to the airport. (*Length of time: forty-five minutes*)
   It take will orty-five minutes to the airport.
   이것 will   drive

5. Ann made a dress. (*Length of time: six hours*)

6. Alan hitchhiked to Alaska. (*Length of time: two weeks*)

7. Jennifer puts on her makeup. (*Length of time: five minutes*)
   It takes Jennifer five minutes (to) put on her make up.

8. I wash my clothes at the laundromat. (*Length of time: two hours*)
   It

6-12 USING *HOW LONG*

QUESTION	ANSWER	
(a) **How long** *does it take* to drive to Chicago from here?	Two days.	**How long** asks for information about length of time.
(b) **How long** did you study last night?	Four hours.	
(c) **How long** will you be in Florida?	Ten days.	
(d) **How many days** will you be in Florida?	Ten.	Other ways of asking **how long**: **how many** + { minutes, hours, days, weeks, months, years

□ EXERCISE 25: Make questions using *how long*.

1. A: ___*How long did it take you to drive to New York?*___
   B: Five days. (It took me five days to drive to New York.)

2. A: _____
   B: Twenty minutes. (It takes me twenty minutes to walk to class.)

3. A: _____
   B: Two hours. (It took Mike two hours to finish his composition.)

4. A: _____
   B: Thirty minutes. (It will take us thirty minutes to drive to the
   stadium.)

5. A: _____
   B: For a week. (Mr. McNally is going to be in the hospital for a week.)

6. A: _____
   B: Four years. (I'll be at the University of Maryland for four years.)

7. A: _____
   B: About an hour. (It takes about an hour to bake a cake.)
   A: How about cookies? _____
   B: Oh, it depends. Maybe thirty minutes. (It takes maybe thirty
   minutes to bake cookies.)

8. A: _____
   B: Five days. (I was out of town for five days.)
   A: How about Amy? _____
   B: A week. (She was out of town for a week.)

9. A: _____
   B: About fifteen minutes. (It takes me about fifteen minutes to change a
   flat tire.)
   A: How about the oil? _____
   B: Not long. Maybe twenty minutes. (It takes me maybe twenty
   minutes to change the oil.)

10. A: _____
    B: A long time. (It takes a long time to learn a second language.)
    A: How about a computer language? _____
    B: That takes a long time, too. (It takes a long time to learn a computer
    language.)

☐ **EXERCISE 26:** Make questions. Use any appropriate question words.

1. A: _____**What are you going to do this weekend?**_____

   B: I'm going to go to a baseball game. (I'm going to go to a baseball game this weekend.)

2. A: There are two games this weekend, one on Saturday and one on Sunday. _____

   B: The one on Sunday. (I'm going to go to the one on Sunday.)

3. A: _____

   B: No, I didn't. (I didn't go to the game yesterday.)

4. A: _____

   B: Sara and Jim. (Sara and Jim went to the game yesterday.)

5. A: _____

   B: About once a month. (I go to a baseball game about once a month.)

6. A: _____

   B: Bob. (I'm going to go to the game with Bob on Sunday.)

7. A: _____

   B: At the corner of Fifth and Grand. (The stadium is at the corner of Fifth and Grand.)

8. A: _____

   B: Six miles. (It's six miles to the stadium from here.)

9. A: _____

   B: Twenty minutes. (It takes twenty minutes to get there.)

10. A: _____

    B: One o'clock. (The game starts at one o'clock.)

11. A: _____

    B: Because I have fun. (I like to go to baseball games because I have fun.)

12. A: _____

    B: I yell, enjoy the sunshine, eat peanuts, and drink beer. (I yell, enjoy the sunshine, eat peanuts, and drink beer when I go to a baseball game.)

☐ **EXERCISE 27—ORAL (BOOKS CLOSED):** Make questions. Use question words.

Example: I'm studying English grammar.
Response: What are you doing? OR: What are you studying?

1. I studied last night.
2. I studied at the library.
3. I studied for two hours at the library last night.
4. I'm going to study tonight.
5. I'm going to study at home.
6. I'm going to study with (. . .).
7. We're going to study together because we have a test tomorrow.
8. I saw (. . .) yesterday.
9. (. . .) called me last night.
10. I talked to (. . .) last night.
11. I go to the library twice a week.
12. The library is two blocks from here.
13. I live in (*name of this city*).
14. I was born in (*name of town*).
15. I grew up in (*name of town*).
16. I stayed home yesterday because I didn't feel good.
17. I'm looking at the board.
18. I'm looking at (. . .).
19. That is (. . .)'s pen.
20. I want this pen, not that one.
21. (. . .) is wearing (*kind of shoes*).
22. I'm going to wear jeans tomorrow.
23. I'm going to write a letter to (. . .).
24. (. . .) wrote me a letter.
25. It's (*distance*) to (*name of city*) from here.
26. I have a (*kind of car*).
27. It takes (*length of time*) to drive to (*name of city*) from here.
28. I drive to (*name of city*) once or twice a year.
29. "Glad" means "happy."
30. The first oil well in history was drilled near Titusville, Pennsylvania, in the year 1859.

6-13 MORE QUESTIONS WITH *HOW*

QUESTION	ANSWER	
(a) *How do you spell* "coming"? (b) *How do you say* "yes" in Japanese? (c) *How do you say/pronounce* this word?	C-O-M-I-N-G. *Hai.* _____	To answer (a): Spell the word. To answer (b): Say the word. To answer (c): Pronounce the word.
(d) *How are you getting along?* (e) *How are you doing?* (f) *How's it going?*	Great. Fine. Okay. So-so.	In (d), (e), and (f): How is your life? Is your life okay? Do you have any problems? NOTE: (f) is often used in greetings: *Hi, Bob. How's it going?*

(g) *How do you feel?*
   How are you feeling?
	Terrific!
	Wonderful!
	Great!
	Fine.
	Okay.
	So-so.
	A bit under the
	   weather.
	Not so good.
	Terrible!
	Lousy.
	Awful!
		The questions in (g) ask about health or about general emotional state.

(h) *How do you do?*	How do you do?	*How do you do?* is used by both speakers when they are introduced to each other in a somewhat formal situation.*

*A: *Dr. Erickson, I'd like to introduce you to a friend of mine, Dick Brown. Dick, this is my biology professor, Dr. Erickson.*
B: *How do you do*, *Mr. Brown?*
C: *How do you do*, *Dr. Erickson? I'm pleased to meet you.*

□ **EXERCISE 28—ORAL (BOOKS CLOSED):** Ask another student how to spell the given word.

    Example: country
STUDENT A: How do you spell "country"?
STUDENT B: C-O-N-T-R-Y
STUDENT A: Yes, that's right. OR: No, that isn't right. The correct spelling is C-O-U-N-T-R-Y.

1. together	4. planned	7. different
2. purple	5. rained	8. foreign
3. daughter	6. neighbor	9. studying

10. bought	13. beginning	16. occasionally
11. people	14. intelligent	17. family
12. beautiful	15. writing	18. Mississippi

☐ **EXERCISE 29—ORAL:** Ask your classmates how to say these words in their native languages:

> *Example:* yes
> STUDENT A: How do you say "yes" in Japanese?
> STUDENT B: *Hai.*

1. Yes.   3. Thank you.
2. No.   4. I love you.

☐ **EXERCISE 30—ORAL:** Ask your classmates how to pronounce these words.

> *Example:*
> STUDENT A: How do you pronounce number 9?
> STUDENT B: (STUDENT B *pronounces the word.*)
> STUDENT A: Good. OR: No, I don't think that's right.

GROUP A:	(1)	(2)	(3)	(4)	(5)	(6)	(7)	(8)	(9)	(10)
	beat	bit	bet	bite	bait	bat	but	boot	boat	bought

GROUP B:	(1)	(2)	(3)	(4)	(5)	(6)	(7)	(8)	(9)	(10)
	zoos	Sue's	shoes	chews	choose	chose	those	toes	doze	dose

☐ **EXERCISE 31—WRITTEN:** Make questions for the given answers. Write **both** the question (A:) and the answer (B:). Use your own paper.

> *Example:* A: ...? B: I'm reading.
> *Written dialogue:* **A: What are you doing?**
> **B: I'm reading.**

1. A: ...?	B:	It means "big."		10. A: ...?	B:	Because I....
2. A: ...?	B:	Three days ago.		11. A: ...?	B:	This one, not that one.
3. A: ...?	B:	Once a week.		12. A: ...?	B:	100 (miles/kilometers).
4. A: ...?	B:	Fine.		13. A: ...?	B:	I'm going to study.
5. A: ...?	B:	By bus.		14. A: ...?	B:	A bit under the weather.
6. A: ...?	B:	Mine.		15. A: ...?	B:	How do you do?
7. A: ...?	B:	Nonfiction.		16. A: ...?	B:	Two hours.
8. A: ...?	B:	B-E-A-U-T-I-F-U-L.		17. A: ...?	B:	Six o'clock.
9. A: ...?	B:	The park.		18. A: ...?	B:	Mary.

6-14 USING *HOW ABOUT* AND *WHAT ABOUT*

(a) A: We need one more player. B: ***How about (what about)* Jack?** Let's ask him if he wants to play. (b) A: What time should we meet? B: ***How about (what about)* three o'clock?**	***How about*** and ***what about*** have the same meaning and usage. They are used to make suggestions or offers. ***How about*** and ***what about*** are followed by a noun (or pronoun) or the *-ing* form of a verb.
(c) A: What should we do this afternoon? B: ***How about* going** to the zoo? (d) A: ***What about* asking** Sally over for dinner next Sunday? B: Okay. Good idea.	Note: ***How about*** and ***what about*** are used in informal spoken English frequently, but are usually not used in writing.
(e) A: I'm tired. ***How about you?*** B: Yes, I'm tired too. (f) A: Are you hungry? B: No. ***What about you?*** A: I'm a little hungry.	***How about you?*** and ***What about you?*** are used to ask a question that refers to the information or question that immediately preceded. In (e): *How about you? = Are you tired?* In (f): *What about you? = Are you hungry?*

☐ **EXERCISE 32—ORAL (BOOKS CLOSED):** Respond by using *how about* or *what about*.

> *Example:* I'm looking for a good book to read. Do you have any suggestions?
>
> *Response:* How about (What about) *Tom Sawyer* by Mark Twain? It's a good book.

1. You and I are having dinner together this evening, (. . .). What time should we get together?
2. I can't figure out what to give my sister for her birthday.
3. I'm hungry, but I'm not sure what I want to eat.
4. We have a whole week of vacation. Where should we go?
5. What time should I call you?
6. Where should we go for dinner tonight?
7. I've already asked (. . .) and (. . .) to my party. Who else should I ask?
8. Some friends are coming to visit me this weekend. They said they wanted to see some of the interesting places in the city. I'm wondering where I should take them.

☐ **EXERCISE 33:** Complete the dialogues by using ***how about you*** or ***what about you*** and an appropriate response.

> *Example:* A: What are you going to do over vacation?
>
> B: I'm staying here. _____ ***What about (How about) you?***_____
>
> A: _____ ***I'm going to Texas to visit my sister.***_____

1. A: Did you like the movie?

   B: It was okay, I guess. _____

   A: _____

2. A: Are you going to summer school?

   B: I haven't decided yet. _____

   A: _____

3. A: Do you like living in the dorm?

   B: Sort of. _____

   A: _____

4. A: What are you going to have?

   B: Well, I'm not really hungry. I think I might have just a salad.

   _____

   A: _____

5. A: Where are you planning to go to school next year?

   B: I've been accepted by the state university. _____

   A: _____

6. A: Are you married?

   B: _____

   A: _____

☐ **EXERCISE 34—ORAL:** Pair up with another member of the class. One of you will be
STUDENT A and the other will be STUDENT B. During your conversation, find
out as much information about each other on the given topics as you can.

STUDENT A: The following questions are conversation openers. Glance at a
question quickly, then look up—directly into the eyes of
STUDENT B—and initiate the conversation. After the two of you
have explored the topic, go on to the next question (or make
up one of your own).

STUDENT B: Do not look at your text. Answer STUDENT A's questions. Then
ask *How about you?* or *What about you?* to continue the
conversation.

1. How long have you been living in (this city or country)?
2. How do you like living here?
3. Where are you staying?
4. What are you going to do after class today?

5. What are your plans for this evening?

6. What are you going to do this weekend?

7. What are you planning to do at the end of this term/semester?

8. Do you come from a large family?

9. What kind of sports do you enjoy?

10. Do you speak a lot of English outside of class?

6-15 TAG QUESTIONS

AFFIRMATIVE	NEGATIVE	
(a) *You **know** Bob Wilson,*	***don't** you?*	A tag question is a question that is added onto the end of a sentence. An auxiliary verb is used in a tag question.
(b) *Mary **is** from Chicago,*	***isn't** she?*	
(c) *Jerry **can play** the piano,*	***can't** he?*	In (a), (b), and (c): When the main verb is affirmative, the tag question is negative.
NEGATIVE	**AFFIRMATIVE**	In (c), (d), and (e): When the main verb is negative, the tag question is affirmative.
(d) *You **don't know** Jack Smith,*	***do** you?*	
(e) *Mary **isn't** from New York,*	***is** she?*	
(f) *Jerry **can't speak** Arabic,*	***can** he?*	

Notice in the following: I (the speaker) use a tag question because I expect you (the listener) to agree with me. I give my idea while asking a question at the same time.*

THE SPEAKER'S IDEA	THE SPEAKER'S QUESTION	EXPECTED ANSWER
(g) I think that you know Bob Wilson.	You **know** Bob Wilson, **don't** you?	**Yes,** I **do.**
(h) I think that you don't know Jack Smith.	You **don't know** Jack Smith, **do** you?	**No,** I **don't.**
(i) I think that Mary is from Chicago.	Mary **is** from Chicago, **isn't** she?	**Yes,** she **is.**
(j) I think that Mary isn't from New York.	Mary **isn't** from New York, **is** she?	**No,** she **isn't.**
(k) I think that Jerry can play the piano.	Jerry **can play** the piano, **can't** he?	**Yes,** he **can.**
(l) I think that Jerry can't speak Arabic.	Jerry **can't speak** Arabic, **can** he?	**No,** he **can't.**

*COMPARE: ***A yes/no question:***
    A: Do you know Bob Wilson? (*The speaker has no idea. The speaker is simply looking for information.*)
    B: Yes, I do. OR: No, I don't.

A tag question:
    A: You know Bob Wilson, don't you? (*The speaker believes that you know Bob Wilson. The speaker wants to make sure that his/her idea is correct.*)
    B: Yes, I do. (*The speaker expects you to answer **yes**. You can, however, answer **no** if you do not know Bob Wilson.*)

☐ **EXERCISE 35:** Add tag questions and give the expected answers.

1. A: You are a student, _____ ***aren't you?*** _____

    B: _____ ***Yes, I am.*** _____

2. A: Erica lives in the dorm, _____

    B: _____

3. A: You don't live in the dorm, _____

   B: _____

4. A: Ted came to class yesterday, _____

   B: _____

5. A: Kathy will be in class tomorrow, _____

   B: _____

6. A: Mr. Lee is at home now, _____

   B: _____

7. A: Our teacher didn't give us a homework assignment, _____

   B: _____

8. A: You can speak Spanish, _____

   B: _____

9. A: Tim and Brian can't speak Arabic, _____

   B: _____

10. A: You should write a letter to your father, _____

    B: _____

11. A: It snows a lot in Minneapolis, _____

    B: _____

12. A. You weren't at home last night around nine, _____

    B: _____

13. A: This is your pen,* _____

    B: _____

14. A: That is Mike's dictionary, _____

    B: _____

15. A: Those are your gloves, _____

    B: _____

16. A: These are Jean's glasses, _____

    B: _____

---

*When **this** or **that** is used in the first part of the sentence, **it** is used in the tag question:
This is your book, isn't it?
When **these** or **those** is used in the first part of the sentence, **they** is used in the tag
question: *These are your shoes, aren't they?*

17. A: This isn't a hard exercise, _____

    B: _____

18. A: That was an easy test, _____

    B: _____

☐ **EXERCISE 36—ORAL (BOOKS CLOSED):** Ask and answer tag questions.

> *Example:* You think that someone in this room lives in an apartment.
> STUDENT A: (Ali), you live in an apartment, don't you?
> STUDENT B: Yes, I do. OR: No, I don't.

> *Example:* You think that someone in this room lives in an apartment.
> STUDENT A: (Ali), (Maria) lives in an apartment, doesn't she?
> STUDENT B: Yes, she does. OR: No, she doesn't. OR: I don't know.

You think that someone in this room . . . .

1. lives in the dorm
2. doesn't live in an apartment
3. lives in an apartment
4. doesn't live in the dorm
5. was in class yesterday
6. wasn't in class yesterday
7. came to class yesterday
8. didn't come to class yesterday
9. is married
10. isn't married

11. can speak (*language*)
12. is from (*country*)
13. can't speak (*language*)
14. isn't from (*country*)
15. likes to play (*name of a sport*)
16. will be in class tomorrow
17. can whistle
18. knows (*name of a person*)
19. wore blue jeans to class yesterday
20. has brown eyes

☐ **EXERCISE 37—ORAL:** Ask and answer tag questions.

> STUDENT A: Make a statement about a classmate by beginning a sentence
> with *I think that* (name of a classmate) . . . .
> STUDENT B: Change that supposition into a sentence with a tag question.
> STUDENT C: Answer the question.

Example:

STUDENT A: *I think that Juan* is from Venezuela. What do you think?
STUDENT B: I'll ask him. Juan, you're from Venezuela, aren't you?
STUDENT C: Yes, I am./Yes, that's right. OR: No, I'm not./No, what makes
you think that?

NOTE: If a questioner gets an unexpected answer, s/he will often show surprise. Notice the ways STUDENT B expresses surprise:

STUDENT B: You're from Venezuela, aren't you?
STUDENT C: Venezuela? No. I'm from Colombia.
STUDENT B: *Oh?/Really?/You are? Hmm. I wonder why I thought you were from Venezuela.*

Make suppositions about the following topics or any topic of your own choosing. Begin with *I think that* (name of classmate)....

1. hometown
2. place of residence
3. field of study
4. previous English study
5. clothes worn yesterday
6. transportation to school
7. activities before and/or after class
8. contents of a pocket/bookbag/briefcase
9. size and composition of family
10. presence in class yesterday
11. length of time in this city/country
12. etc.

☐ **EXERCISE 38—PREPOSITIONS:** Complete the sentences with prepositions. (See Appendix 1 for a list of preposition combinations.)

1. What's the matter _____ you? What's wrong?

2. We can go out for dinner, or we can eat at home. It doesn't matter _____ me.

3. To make this recipe, you have to separate the egg whites _____ the yolks.

4. I don't know anything _____ astrology.

5. I'm looking forward _____ my vacation next month.

6. Dennis dreamed _____ his friend last night.

7. Right now I'm doing an exercise. I'm looking _____ my book.

8. Jim can't find his book. He's looking _____ it.

9. Jim is searching _____ his book.

10. I asked the waitress _____ another cup of coffee.

11. I asked Rebecca _____ her trip to Japan.

12. Does this pen belong _____ you?

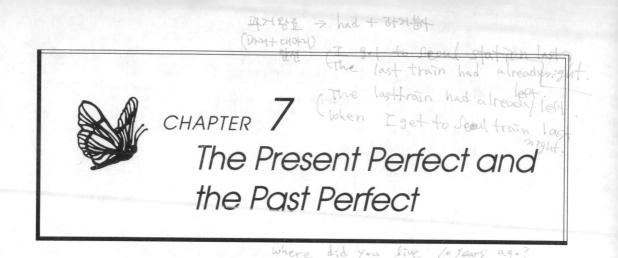

CHAPTER 7

The Present Perfect and the Past Perfect

7-1 THE PAST PARTICIPLE

	SIMPLE FORM	SIMPLE PAST	**PAST PARTICIPLE**	
REGULAR VERBS	finish stop wait	finished stopped waited	**finished** **stopped** **waited**	The **past participle** is one of the principal parts of a verb. (See Chart 2-3.) The past participle is used in the PRESENT PERFECT tense and the PAST PERFECT tense.★
IRREGULAR VERBS	see make put	saw made put	**seen** **made** **put**	The past participle of regular verbs is the same as the simple past form: both end in **-ed**. See Chart 2-4 for a list of irregular verbs.

★The past participle is also used in the passive. See Chapter 11.

□ **EXERCISE 1:** Write the PAST PARTICIPLE.

SIMPLE FORM	SIMPLE PAST	PAST PARTICIPLE
1. finish	finished	_**finished**_
2. see	saw	_**seen**_
3. go	went	_____
4. have	had	_____
5. meet	met	_____
6. call	called	_____
7. fall	fell	_____
8. do	did	_____
9. know	knew	_____

10. fly	flew	_____
11. come	came	_____
12. study	studied	_____
13. stay	stayed	_____
14. begin	began	_____
15. start	started	_____
16. write	wrote	_____
17. eat	ate	_____
18. cut	cut	_____
19. read	read	_____
20. be	was/were	_____

7-2 FORMS OF THE PRESENT PERFECT

STATEMENT: **HAVE/HAS** + **PAST PARTICIPLE** (a) I **have finished** my work. (b) The students **have finished** Chapter 5. (c) Jim **has eaten** lunch.	The basic form of the present perfect: **have or has** + **the past participle**. Use **have** with *I*, *you*, *we*, *they*, or a plural noun (e.g., *students*). Use **has** with *she*, *he*, *it*, or a singular noun (e.g., *Jim*).
(d) **I've/You've/We've/They've** eaten lunch. (e) **She's/He's** eaten lunch. (f) **It's** been cold for the last three days.	With pronouns, **have** is contracted to apostrophe + **ve** ('ve) and **has** to apostrophe + **s** ('s).
NEGATIVE: **HAVE/HAS** + **NOT** + **PAST PARTICIPLE** (g) I **have not** (**haven't**) **finished** my work. (h) Ann **has not** (**hasn't**) **eaten** lunch.	*have* + *not* = *haven't* *has* + *not* = *hasn't*
QUESTION: **HAVE/HAS** + **SUBJECT** + **PAST PARTICIPLE** (i) **Have you finished** your work? (j) **Has Jim eaten** lunch? (k) How long **have you lived** here?	In a question, the helping verb (*have* or *has*) precedes the subject.
(l) A: Have you seen that movie? 　 B: Yes, I **have**. OR: No, I **haven't**. (m) A: Has Jim eaten lunch? 　 B: Yes, he **has**. OR: No, he **hasn't**.	The helping verb (*have* or *has*) is used in a short answer to a yes/no question. The helping verb in the short answer is not contracted with the pronoun.

7-3 MEANINGS OF THE PRESENT PERFECT

(time?)	(a) Jim **has** already **eaten** lunch. (b) Ann **hasn't eaten** lunch yet. (c) **Have** you ever **eaten** at that restaurant? (d) I**'ve** never **eaten** there.	The present perfect expresses activities or situations that occurred (or did not occur) "before now," at some unspecified time in the past.*
××××	(e) Pete **has eaten** at that restaurant many times. (f) I**'ve been** to that theater five or six times. (g) I**'ve had** three tests so far this week.	The present perfect expresses activities that were repeated several or many times in the past. The exact times are unspecified.
	(h) Erica **has lived** in this city *since 1989*. (i) I **have known** Ben *for ten years*. (j) We**'ve been** in class *since ten o'clock this morning*.	When the present perfect is used with *since* or *for*, it expresses situations that began in the past and continue to the present.

*If the exact time is specified, the simple past tense is used. (See Chart 7-4.)

SPECIFIC TIME: Jim *ate* lunch *at 12:00/two hours ago/yesterday.*

UNSPECIFIED TIME: Jim **has** already **eaten** lunch. (*at some unspecified time before now*)

☐ **EXERCISE 2:** Complete the sentences. Use the words in parentheses. Use the PRESENT PERFECT. Discuss the meaning of the present perfect.

(I, meet) _____I've (I have) met_____ Ann's husband. I met him at a

party last week.

2. (I, finish) _____I've finished_____ my work. I finished it two

hours ago.

3. (she, fly) Ms. Parker travels to Washington, D.C., frequently.

_____She has flown_____ there many times.

4. (they, know) Bob and Jane are old friends. _____They 've_____

~~each~~ _____ each other for a long time.

5. (it, be) I don't like this weather. _____It has been_____ cold

and cloudy for the last three days.

6. (you, learn) Your English is getting better. _____You've learned_____

_____ a lot of English since you came here.

7. (we, be) My wife and I came here two months ago. __We've__ __been__ in this city for two months.

8. (he, finish) Rob can go to bed now. __He's been finished__ his homework.

9. (he, be) Matt is at home in bed. __He's been__ 아파서 누워있다 _____ sick for three days.

10. (she, be) Kate is falling behind in her schoolwork. __She's__ __been__ 뒤처지고있다 _____ absent from class a lot lately. 마거부터 지금까지 경석 최근 현재완료

□ **EXERCISE 3:** When speakers use the present perfect, they often contract **have** and **has** with nouns in everyday speech. Listen to your teacher say these sentences in normal contracted speech and practice saying them yourself.

1. Bob has been in Chicago since last Tuesday. (''*Bob's been in . . . .*'')
2. Jane has been out of town for two days.
3. The weather has been terrible lately.
4. My parents have been married for forty years.
5. Mike has already eaten breakfast.
6. My friends have moved into a new apartment.
7. My roommate has been in bed with a cold for the last couple of days.
8. My aunt and uncle have lived in the same house for twenty-five years. = in a long time / for a long time

□ **EXERCISE 4:** Complete the sentences. Use the words in parentheses. Use the PRESENT PERFECT. Discuss the meaning of the present perfect.

1. (I, write, not) __I haven't written__ my sister a letter in a long time. I should write her soon. 거의 보내지 않았다

2. (I, write, never)* __I've never written__ a letter to the President of the United States. 전혀 보낸 적 없다 (경험) ∕ he hasn't

3. (he, finish, not) Greg is working on his composition, but __he's not__ __finished__ it yet. He'll probably finish it in a couple of hours. 2번 축약 안됨!

4. (I, meet, never) __I've met never__ Nancy's parents. I hope I get the chance to meet them soon.

_____

*__Never__ has the same usual position as other frequency adverbs. (See Chart 7-8.) With the present perfect, __never__ comes between the helping verb (*have* or *has*) and the main verb.

5. (*Ron, never, be*) Ron's never been _____ in Hong Kong, but
he would like to go there someday.

6. (*Linda, be, not*) Linda ~~is not~~ hasn't been _____ in class for the last
couple of days. I hope she's okay.

7. (*they, come, not*) The children are late. they ~~are not~~ haven't come _____
home from school yet. I hope nothing's wrong.

8. (*we, finish, not*) we haven't finished _____ this exercise yet.

9. (*Alice, go, never*) Alice's never gone _____ to the Museum of
Science and Industry in Chicago, but she would like to.

10. (*I, call, not*) I haven't call _____ Irene yet. I'll call
her tomorrow.

7-4 USING THE SIMPLE PAST vs. THE PRESENT PERFECT

SIMPLE PAST: (a) I **finished** my work *two hours ago*. PRESENT PERFECT: (b) I **have already* finished** my work.	In (a): I finished my work at a specific time in the past (*two hours ago*). In (b): I finished my work at an unspecified time in the past (sometime before now).
SIMPLE PAST: (c) I **was** in Europe *last year/three years ago/in 1989/in 1985 and 1989/when I was ten years old*. PRESENT PERFECT: (d) I **have been** in Europe *many times/several times/a couple of times/once/*(no mention of time).	The simple past expresses an activity that occurred at a specific time (or times) in the past, as in (a) and (c). The present perfect expresses an activity that occurred at an unspecified time (or times) in the past, as in (b) and (d).

***Already** has the same usual placement as frequency adverbs. (See Chart 7-8.) **Already** means "before." (See Chart 7-9.)

□ **EXERCISE 5:** Complete the sentences with the words in parentheses. Use the PRESENT
PERFECT or the SIMPLE PAST.

1. A: Have you ever been in Europe?

   B: Yes, I _____ **have** _____. I (*be*) _____ **have been** _____ in Europe
   several times. In fact, I (*be*) _____ **was** _____ in Europe last year.

2. A: Have you ever eaten at Al's Steak House?

   B: Yes, I _have_. I (eat) _have eaten_ there many

   times. In fact, my wife and I (eat) ~~had~~ _ate_ there last

   night.

3. A: Have you ever talked to Professor Alston about your grades?

   B: Yes, I _have_. I (talk) _have talked_ to him about

   my grades a couple of times. In fact, I (talk) ~~~~ _talked_ to

   him after class yesterday about the F I got on the last test.

4. A: What European countries (you, visit) _you have visited_?

   B: I (visit) _'ve visited_ Hungary, Germany, and Switzerland. I

   (visit) ~~had~~ _visited_ Hungary in 1988. I (be) _was_

   in Germany and Switzerland in 1990.

5. A: (Bob, have, ever) _Have ∧ ever_ a job?

   B: Yes, he _has_. He (have) _has_ ~~has had~~ lots of

   part-time jobs. Last summer he (have) _____ a job at

   his uncle's waterbed store.

□ **EXERCISE 6:** Complete the sentences with the words in parentheses. Use the PRESENT
   PERFECT or the SIMPLE PAST. Use the present perfect with **already.***

   1. A: Are you going to finish your work before you go to bed?

      B: I (finish, already) **have already finished** it. I (finish)
         finished my work two hours ago.

   2. A: Is Jim going to eat lunch with us today?

      B: No. He (eat, already) _has a eaten already_. He (eat)
         ate lunch an hour ago.

   3. A: Do you and Erica want to go to the movie at the Bijou with us
         tonight?

      B: No thanks. We (see, already) _have already seen_ it. We
         (see) ~~~~ _saw_ it last week.

   *In informal spoken English, the simple past is often used with **already**. Practice using
    the present perfect with **already** in this exercise.

4. A: When are you going to write your paper for Dr. Roth?

B: I (write, already) *have already ~~already~~ written* it. I (write)
~~writedwor~~ it two days ago.

~~wroted~~

5. A: When is Jane going to call her parents and tell them about her engagement?

B: She (call, already) *'s already called* them. She (call)
called them last night.

6. A: This is a good book. Would you like to read it when I'm finished?

B: Thanks, but I (read, already) *have already read* it. I
(read) *read* it a couple of months ago.

☐ **EXERCISE 7—ORAL:** Ask and answer questions using the PRESENT PERFECT.

STUDENT A: Use *ever* in the question. *Ever* comes between the subject (*you*)
and the main verb.*

STUDENT B: Give a short answer first and then a complete sentence answer.

Use {
many times 아주많은
several times (조금. 몇번) 네ㅡ몇번
a couple of times 두세번 in the complete sentence.
once in my lifetime
never 절대해보지 x
ever 이때까지 딱 한번 .
}

Example: be in Florida**

STUDENT A: Have you ever been in Florida?

STUDENT B: Yes, I have. I've been in Florida many times. OR: No, I
haven't. I've never been in Florida.

1. be in Europe
2. be in Africa
3. be in the Middle East
4. be in Asia

5. eat Chinese food
6. eat Italian food
7. eat (*a certain kind of*) food
8. eat at (*name of a restaurant*)

9. ride a horse
10. ride a motorcycle
11. ride an elephant
12. ride in a taxi

13. be in (*name of a city*)
14. be in (*name of a state/province*)
15. be in (*name of a country*)
16. be in love

pool 또켓블

_____

*In these questions, *ever* means *in your lifetime, at any time(s) in your life before now.*

**When using the present perfect, a speaker might also use the idiom *be to* (*a place*): *Have you ever been to Florida?*

17. play soccer	21. walk to (*a place in this city*)
18. play baseball	22. stay up all night
19. play pool	23. go to (*a place in this city*)
20. play a video game	24. use a computer

☐ **EXERCISE 8:** Write the SIMPLE PAST and the PAST PARTICIPLES of these irregular verbs.

1. see	**saw**	**seen**	7. drive	_____	_____
2. eat	_____	_____	8. ride	_____	_____
3. give	_____	_____	9. write	_____	_____
4. fall	_____	_____	10. bite	_____	_____
5. take	_____	_____	11. hide	_____	_____
6. shake	_____	_____			

telegram
전보   전보를

☐ **EXERCISE 9—ORAL:** Ask and answer questions using the PRESENT PERFECT in order to practice using past participles of irregular verbs.

STUDENT A: Ask a question beginning with "Have you ever...?"
STUDENT B: Answer the question.

Example: eat at the student cafeteria
STUDENT A: Have you ever eaten at the student cafeteria?
STUDENT B: Yes, I have. I've eaten there many times. In fact, I ate breakfast there this morning. OR: No, I haven't. I usually eat all my meals at home.

1. ride a horse
2. take a course in chemistry
3. write a poem
4. give the teacher an apple
5. shake hands with (...)
6. bite into an apple that had a worm inside

7. drive a semi (a very large truck)
8. eat raw fish
9. hide money under your mattress
10. fall down stairs
11. see the skeleton of a dinosaur

Have you spent whole day doing nothing?
당신은 아무일도 안하고 하루를 보낸적이 있나요?

The Present Perfect and the Past Perfect ☐ **167**

☐ **EXERCISE 10:** Write the SIMPLE PAST and the PAST PARTICIPLES.

1. break _____ _____   8. throw _____ _____

2. speak _____ _____   9. blow _____ _____

3. steal _____ _____   10. fly _____ _____

4. get _____ _____   11. drink _____ _____

5. wear _____ _____   12. sing _____ _____

6. draw _____ _____   13. swim _____ _____

7. grow _____ _____   14. go _____ _____

☐ **EXERCISE 11—ORAL:** Ask questions beginning with "Have you ever...?" and give answers.

1. fly in a private plane   11. sing (*name of a song*)
2. break your arm   12. drink carrot juice
3. draw a picture of a mountain   13. throw a football
4. swim in the ocean   14. blow a whistle
5. speak to (...) on the phone
6. go to a costume party

7. wear a costume to a party
8. get a package in the mail
9. steal anything
10. grow tomatoes

☐ **EXERCISE 12:** Write the SIMPLE PAST and the PAST PARTICIPLES.

1. have   _____ _____
2. make   _____ _____
3. build   _____ _____
4. lend   _____ _____
5. send   _____ _____
6. spend   _____ _____
7. leave   _____ _____

8. lose   _____ _____
9. sleep   _____ _____
10. feel   _____ _____
11. meet   _____ _____
12. sit   _____ _____
13. win   _____ _____
14. hang* _____ _____

☐ **EXERCISE 13—ORAL:** Ask questions beginning with "Have you ever...?" and give answers.

1. lose the key to your house
2. meet (. . .)
3. have the flu
4. feel terrible about something
5. send a telegram
6. sit on a cactus

10. sleep in a tent

11. make a birthday cake
12. build sand castles

7. leave your sunglasses at a restaurant
8. spend one whole day doing nothing
9. lend (. . .) any money

13. win money at a racetrack
14. hang a picture on the wall

_____

*__Hang__ is a regular verb (*hang, hanged, hanged*) when it means to kill a person by putting a rope around his/her neck. __Hang__ is an irregular verb when it refers to hanging a thing (on the wall, in a closet, on a hook, etc.).

☐ **EXERCISE 14:** Write the SIMPLE PAST and the PAST PARTICIPLES.

1. sell _____ _____
2. tell _____ _____
3. hear _____ _____
4. hold _____ _____
5. feed _____ _____
6. read _____ _____
7. find _____ _____
8. buy _____ _____

9. think _____ _____
10. teach _____ _____
11. catch _____ _____
12. cut _____ _____
13. hit _____ _____
14. quit* _____ _____
15. put _____ _____

☐ **EXERCISE 15—ORAL:** Ask questions beginning with "Have you ever...?" and give answers.

1. teach a child to count to ten
2. hold a newborn baby
3. find any money on the sidewalk
4. cut your own hair
5. think about the meaning of life
6. hear strange noises at night
7. read *Tom Sawyer* by Mark Twain
8. feed pigeons in the park

9. tell a little white lie
10. quit smoking
11. buy a refrigerator
12. sell a car
13. hit another person with your fist
14. put off doing your homework
15. catch a fish

——————
*__Quit__ can be used as a regular verb in British English: *quit, quitted, quitted.*

7-5 USING *SINCE* AND *FOR*

<table>
<tr>
<td rowspan="4">SINCE</td>
<td>(a) I have been here { since eight o'clock.
since Tuesday.
since May.
since 1989.
since January 3, 1988.
since the beginning of the semester.
since yesterday.
since last month.</td>
<td>Since is followed by the mention of a specific point in time: an hour, a day, a month, a year, etc.

Since expresses the idea that an activity began at a specific time in the past and continues to the present. The present perfect also expresses the idea that an activity began in the past and continues to the present.</td>
</tr>
<tr>
<td>(b) INCORRECT: I am living here since May.
(c) INCORRECT: I live here since May.
INCORRECT: I am here since May.
(d) INCORRECT: I lived here since May.
INCORRECT: I was here since May.
(e)   CORRECT: I have lived here since May.*
CORRECT: I have been here since May.</td>
<td>The present perfect is used in sentences with since.
In (b): The present progressive is NOT used.
In (c): The simple present is NOT used.
In (d): The simple past is NOT used.</td>
</tr>
<tr>
<td>MAIN CLAUSE   SINCE CLAUSE
(present perfect)   (simple past)
(f) I have lived here   since I was a child.
(g) Al has met many people   since he came here.</td>
<td>Since may also introduce a time clause (i.e., a subject and verb may follow since).

Notice in the examples: The present perfect is used in the main clause; the simple past is used in the "since clause."</td>
</tr>
</table>

<table>
<tr>
<td rowspan="2">FOR</td>
<td>(h) I have been here { for ten minutes.
for two hours.
for five days.
for about three weeks.
for almost six months.
for many years.
for a long time.</td>
<td>For is followed by the mention of a length of time: two minutes, three hours, four days, five weeks, etc.

Note: If the noun ends in -s (hours, days, weeks, etc.), use for in the time expression, not since.</td>
</tr>
<tr>
<td>(i) I have lived here for two years. I moved here two years ago, and I still live here.
(j) I lived in Chicago for two years. I don't live in Chicago now.</td>
<td>In (i): The use of the present perfect in a sentence with for + a length of time means that the action began in the past and continues to the present.

In (j): The use of the simple past means that the action began and ended in the past.</td>
</tr>
</table>

*ALSO CORRECT: *I have been living* here *since May*. See Chart 7-6 for a discussion of the present perfect progressive.

□ **EXERCISE 16:** Complete the sentence "I have been here . . . ." by using *since* or *for* with the given expressions.

I have been here . . .

1. ___*for*___ two months.
2. ___*since*___ September.
3. _____ 1988.
4. _____ last year.
5. _____ two years.
6. _____ last Friday.
7. _____ 9:30.
8. _____ three days.

9. _____ the first of January.
10. _____ almost four months.
11. _____ the beginning of the term.
12. _____ the semester started.
13. _____ a couple of hours.
14. _____ fifteen minutes.
15. _____ yesterday.
16. _____ about five weeks.

□ **EXERCISE 17:** Complete the sentences.

1. I've been in this building ...... { since ___*nine o'clock this morning.*___
  for ___*27 minutes.*___

2. We've been in class .... { since _____
  for _____

3. I've been in this city .... { since _____
  for _____

4. I've had a driver's license...... { since _____
  for _____

5. I've had this book .... { since _____
  for _____

□ **EXERCISE 18—ORAL (BOOKS CLOSED):** Answer the questions. STUDENT A should use *since* in his/her answer; STUDENT B should use *for*.

Example: How long have you had this book?
STUDENT A: I've had this book **since** (the beginning of the term).
To B: How long has (. . .) had this book?
STUDENT B: S/he has had this book **for** (five weeks).

1. How long have you been in (*this country/city*)?
2. How long have you been at (*this school*)?
3. How long have you been up today?
4. How long have you known (. . .)?

5. Where do you live? How long have you lived there?
6. How long have you had your wristwatch?
7. Who has a car/bicycle? How long have you had it?
8. How long have you been in this room today?
9. Who is wearing new clothes? What? How long have you had it/them?
10. Who is married? How long have you been married?

□ **EXERCISE 19:** Add tag questions to the following and give the expected responses.
   (See Chart 6-14 if necessary.)

1. A: You've already seen that movie, _____*haven't you?*_____
   B: _____*Yes, I have.*_____

2. A: Alex hasn't called, _____*has he?*_____
   B: _____*No, he hasn't.*_____

3. A: You talked to Mike last night, _____*didn't you?*_____
   B: _____*Yes, I did.*_____

4. A: Jessica has already left for Kansas City, _____
   B: _____

5. A: Steve left for Kansas City yesterday, _____
   B: _____

6. A: You've already eaten lunch, _____
   B: _____

7. A: You didn't eat at the cafeteria, _____
   B: _____

8. A: You usually bring a sack lunch to school, _____
   B. _____

9. A: Rita and Philip have been married for five years, _____
   B: _____

10. A: Kathy has already finished her work, _____
    B: _____

11. A: Janet has a car, _____ *

    B: _____

_____
*In American English, a form of *do* is usually used with main verb *have* in questions and negatives: *You have a bike, don't you?*
Principally British: *You have a bike, haven't you?*

12. A: We have to hand in our assignments today, _____

    B: _____

13. A: Jack doesn't have to join the army, _____

    B: _____

14. A: You used to live in Los Angeles, _____

    B: _____

15. A: You studied tag questions in Chapter 6, _____

    B: _____

16. A: You haven't forgotten about them, _____

    B: _____

☐ **EXERCISE 20:** Complete the sentences with the words in parentheses. Use the PRESENT PERFECT or the SIMPLE PAST.

1. Carol and I are old friends. I (*know*) _____ her since I (*be*) _____ a freshman in high school.

2. Maria (*have*) _____ a lot of problems since she (*come*) _____ to this country.

3. I (*have, not*) _____ any problems since I (*come*) _____ here.

4. Since the semester (*begin*) _____, we (*have*) _____ four tests.

5. Mike (*be*) _____ in school since he (*be*) _____ six years old.

6. My mother (*be, not*) _____ in school since she (*graduate*) _____ from college in 1968.

7. Since we (*start*) _____ doing this exercise, we (*complete*) _____ six sentences.

8. My name is Surasuk Jutukanyaprateep. I'm from Thailand. Right now I'm studying English at this school. I (*be*) _____ at this school since the beginning of January. I (*arrive*) _____

here January 2, and my classes (*begin*) _____ January 6.
Since I (*come*) _____ here, I (*do*) _____
many things, and I (*meet*) _____ many people. I (*go*)
_____ to several parties. Last Saturday I (*go*)
_____ to a party at my friend's house. I (*meet*)
_____ some of the other students from Thailand at the
party. Of course, we (*speak*) _____ Thai, so I (*practice,*
not) _____ my English that night. There (*be*)
_____ only people from Thailand at the party. However,
since I (*come*) _____ here, I (*meet*) _____
a lot of other people. I (*meet*) _____ students from
Latin America, Africa, the Middle East, and Asia. I enjoy meeting
people from other countries.

☐ **EXERCISE 21—ORAL (BOOKS CLOSED):** Answer the questions.

(*To the teacher: Ask a question that prompts the use of the present perfect, and then immediately follow up with a related question that prompts the use of the simple past.*)

Example: What countries have you been in?
Response: Well, I've been in England, and I've been in Mexico.
  Teacher: Oh? When were you in England?
Response: I was in England three years ago.
  Teacher: How about you, ( )? What countries have you been in?
    etc.

1. What countries have you been in?

2. What cities (*in the United States, in Florida, etc.*) have you been in?

3. What are some of the things you have done since you came to (*this city*)?

4. Who are some of the people you have met since you came to (*this city*)?

5. What have we studied in this class since (*the beginning of the term*)?

6. What have we done in class today since (*nine o'clock*)?

7-6 THE PRESENT PERFECT PROGRESSIVE

(a) I *have been studying* English at this school since May. (b) Adam *has been sleeping* for two hours.	Form of the present perfect progressive: *have/has* + *been* + *ing* The present perfect progressive expresses how long an activity has been in progress.
(c) How long *have you been studying* English here? (d) How long *has Adam been sleeping*?	Question form: *have/has* + *subject* + *been* + *-ing*
COMPARE (e) and (f). PRESENT PROGRESSIVE: (e) I *am sitting* in class right now.	The present progressive expresses an activity that is in progress (is happening) right now.
PRESENT PERFECT PROGRESSIVE: (f) I *have been sitting* in class { since 9 o'clock. / for 45 minutes.	The present perfect progressive expresses the duration (the length of time) an activity is in progress. Time expressions with *since* and *for* are used with the present perfect progressive.

☐ **EXERCISE 22:** Complete the sentences. Use the PRESENT PROGRESSIVE or the PRESENT PERFECT PROGRESSIVE.

1. Mark isn't studying right now. He (*watch*) _____

   TV. He (*watch*) _____ TV since seven o'clock.

2. Kate is standing at the corner. She (*wait*) _____

   for the bus. She (*wait*) _____ for the bus

   for twenty minutes.

3. Right now we're in class. We (*do*) _____ an

   exercise. We (*do*) _____ this exercise for

   a couple of minutes.

4. Scott and Rebecca (*talk*) _____ on the phone

   right now. They (*talk*) _____ on the

   phone for over an hour.

5. I (*sit*) _____ in class right now. I (*sit*)

   _____ since ten minutes after one.

6. A: You look busy right now. What (*you, do*) _____?

   B: I (*work*) _____ on my physics experiment.

   It's a long and difficult experiment.

A: How long (*you, work*) _____ on it?

B: I started planning it last January. I (*work*) _____

on it since then.

□ **EXERCISE 23—ORAL (BOOKS CLOSED):** Answer the questions. Use *since* or *for* in your answer.

1. How long have you been sitting in class?
2. How long have you been studying English?
3. How long have you been living in (*this city*)?
4. Who lives in an apartment/a dormitory? How long have you been living there?
5. I am standing up/sitting down. How long have I been standing up/sitting down?
6. I began to teach English in (*year*). How long have I been teaching English?
7. I began to work at this school in (*month or year*). How long have I been working here?
8. We're doing an exercise. How long have we been doing this exercise?
9. Who drives? How long have you been driving?
10. Who drinks coffee? How old were you when you started to drink coffee? How long have you been drinking coffee?
11. Who smokes? When did you start? How long have you been smoking?
12. How long have you been wearing glasses?

7-7 THE PRESENT PERFECT vs. THE PRESENT PERFECT PROGRESSIVE

PRESENT PERFECT: (a) Rita **has talked** to Josh on the phone many times.	The present perfect is used to express repeated actions in the past, as in (a).
PRESENT PERFECT PROGRESSIVE: (b) Rita **has been talking** to Josh on the phone for twenty minutes.	The present perfect progressive is used to express the *duration* of an activity that is in progress, i.e., how long something has continued to the present time. In (b): Their conversation began 20 minutes ago and has continued since that time. It has been in progress for 20 minutes. It is still in progress.
PRESENT PERFECT: (c) I **have lived** here for two years. PRESENT PERFECT PROGRESSIVE: (d) I **have been living** here for two years.	With some verbs (e.g., *live, work, teach*), duration can be expressed by either the present perfect or the present perfect progressive. (c) and (d) have essentially the same meaning.

☐ **EXERCISE 24:** Complete the sentences. Use the PRESENT PERFECT or the PRESENT
PERFECT PROGRESSIVE. In some sentences, either form is possible.

1. The post office isn't far from here. I (*walk*) _____

   there many times.

2. I'm tired. We (*walk*) _____ for more

   than an hour. Let's stop and rest for a while.

3. Mr. Alvarez (*work*) __*has been working*__ at the power

   company for fifteen years. He likes his job.

4. I (*read*) __*have read*__ this chapter in my chemistry text

   three times, and I still don't understand it!

5. My eyes are getting tired. I (*read*) __'ve been reading__

   _____ for two hours. I think I'll take a break.

6. Mrs. Jackson (*teach*) __*has been teaching*__ kindergarten

   for twenty years. She's one of the best teachers at the elementary school.

7. Debbie is writing a letter to her boyfriend. She (*write*) __*has been*__

   __*writing*__ it since she got home from class. It's going

   to be a long letter!

8. I (*write*) __'ve written__ my folks at least a dozen letters

   since I left home and came here.

☐ **EXERCISE 25:** Following is a general review of verb tenses. Complete the sentences by
using the proper forms of the words in parentheses.

1. A: (*you, have*) __*Do you have*__ any plans for vacation?

   B: Yes, I do. I (*plan*) __*am planning*__ to go to New Orleans.

   A: (*you, be, ever*) __*Have you ever been*__ there before?

   B: Yes, I have. I (*be*) __*was*__ in New Orleans two

   months ago. My brother (*live*) __*lives/is living*__ there, so I

   (*go*) __*go*__ there often.

2. A: Where's Jessica?

   B: She (*study*) _____ at the library.

   A: When (*she, get*) _____ back home?

   B: In an hour or so. Probably around five o'clock.

A: How long (she, study) _____ at the library?

B: Since two o'clock this afternoon.

A: (she, study) _____ at the library every day?

B: Not every day, but often.

3. A: Shhh. Irene (talk) _____ on the phone long-distance.

B: Who (she, talk) _____ to?

A: Her brother. They (talk) _____ for almost an hour. I think her brother is in some kind of trouble.

B: That's too bad. I hope it's nothing serious.

4. A: (you, know) _____ Don's new address?

B: Not off the top of my head. But I (have) _____ it at home in my address book. When I (get) _____ home this evening, I (call) _____ and (give) _____ you his address.

A: Thanks. I'd appreciate it.

5. A: Where's Juan? He (be) _____ absent from class for the last three days. (anyone, see) _____ him lately?

B: I have. I (see) _____ him yesterday. He has a bad cold, so he (be) _____ home in bed since the weekend. He (be, probably) _____ back in class tomorrow.

6. A: How long (you, have to) _____ wear glasses?

B: Since I (be) _____ ten years old.

A: (you, be) _____ nearsighted or farsighted?

B: Nearsighted.

7. A: Let's go to a restaurant tonight.

B: Okay. Where should we go?

A: (you, like) _____ Thai food?

B: I don't know. I (eat, never) _____ any. What's it like?

A: It's delicious, but it can be pretty hot!

B: That's okay. I (love) _____ really hot food.

A: There (*be*) _____ a Thai restaurant downtown. I (*go*)
_____ there a couple of times. The food is excellent.

B: Sounds good. I (*be, never*) _____ to a Thai
restaurant, so it (*be*) _____ a new experience for me.
After we (*get*) _____ there, can you explain the menu to me?

A: Sure. And if I can't, our waiter or waitress can.

8. A: (*you, smoke*) _____?

B: Yes, I do.

A: How long (*you, smoke*) _____?

B: Well, let me see. I (*smoke*) _____
since I (*be*) _____ seventeen. So I (*smoke*)
_____ for almost four years.

A: Why (*you, start*) _____?

B: Because I (*be*) _____ a dumb, stupid kid.

A: (*you, want*) _____ to quit?

B: Yes. I (*plan*) _____ to quit very soon. In fact, I
(*decide*) _____ to quit on my next birthday. My
twenty-first birthday is two weeks from now. On that day, I (*smoke*)
_____ my last cigarette.

A: That's terrific! You (*feel*) _____ much better
after you (*stop*) _____ smoking.

B: (*you, smoke, ever*) _____?

A: No, I haven't. I (*have, never*) _____ a
cigarette in my life. When I (*be*) _____ ten years old, I
(*smoke*) _____ one of my uncle's cigars. My sister
and I (*sneak*) _____ a couple of his cigars out of the
house and (*go*) _____ behind the garage to smoke
them. Both of us (*get*) _____ sick. I (*have, not*)
_____ anything to smoke since then.

B: That's smart.

7-8 MIDSENTENCE ADVERBS

(a) I **always** get up at 6:30. (b) You **probably** know the right answer.	Some adverbs typically occur in the middle of a sentence, not at the beginning or end of a sentence. These adverbs, such as **always**, are called "midsentence adverbs."

LIST OF COMMON MIDSENTENCE ADVERBS
 	
 FREQUENCY ADVERBS   OTHER MIDSENTENCE ADVERBS
 	
 positive   ever   ~~not ever~~   already*
 always   ~~not always~~   finally
 almost always   just
 usually* ~ ~~not 항상에~~   probably
 often*
 frequently*   usually not
 generally*
 sometimes*
 occasionally*
 	
 negative   seldom
 rarely
 hardly ever
 almost never
 never
 not ever
 	
 ★ 아닌건:
 。 일반동사앞 be 동사
 뒤에 와야함
 	
 ★ : 아무데나 다 됨.
	The adverbs in the list usually occur in the middle of a sentence. When these adverbs occur in the middle of a sentence, they have special positions, as shown in examples (c) through (h) below.
	
	 The adverbs with an asterisk (*) may also occur at the beginning or end of a sentence.
	    I sometimes get up at 6:30.
	    Sometimes I get up at 6:30.
	    I get up at 6:30 sometimes.
	
	 The other adverbs in the list (without asterisks) rarely occur at the beginning or end of a sentence. Their usual position is in the middle of a sentence.

(c) He **always** comes to class. She **finally** finished her work.	In (c): In a STATEMENT, midsentence adverbs come in front of simple present and simple past verbs (except **be**).
(d) They are **always** on time for class. He was **probably** at home last night.	In (d): Midsentence adverbs follow **be** in the simple present (*am, is, are*) and simple past (*was, were*).
(e) I will **always** remember her. She is **probably** sleeping. They have **finally** finished their work.	In (e): Midsentence adverbs come between a helping verb and a main verb.
(f) Do **you always** eat breakfast? Did **Tom finally** finish his work? Is **she usually** on time for class?	In (f): In a QUESTION, the adverbs come directly after the subject.
(g) She **usually doesn't** eat breakfast. I **probably won't** go to the meeting.	In (g): In a NEGATIVE sentence, most adverbs come in front of the negative verb (except *always* and *ever*).
(h) She **doesn't always** eat breakfast. He **isn't ever** on time for class.	In (h): **Always** and **ever** follow a negative helping verb or negative **be**.
(i) CORRECT: She never eats meat. (j) INCORRECT: She doesn't never eat meat.	Negative adverbs (*seldom, rarely, hardly ever, never*) are NOT used with a negative verb.

① I usually don't put on make up. 나는 보통 화장을 안해.
I don't usually put on make up. 나는 보통 화장을 하는건 아냐.

□ **EXERCISE 26:** Add the word in italics to the sentence. Put the word in its usual midsentence position.

always

1. *always*   Tom studies at home in the evening.

2. *always*   Tom is at home in the evening.

3. *always*   You can find Tom at home in the evening.

4. *usually*   The mail comes at noon.

5. *usually*   The mail is here by noon.

6. *probably*   The mail will be here soon.

7. *often*   Ann stays home at night.

8. *often*   Ann is at home at night.

9. *probably*   Ann will stay home tonight.

10. *finally*   Jack wrote me a letter.

11. *finally*   The semester is over.

12. *finally*   I have finished my composition.

13. *always*   Does Tom study at home in the evening?

14. *always*   Is Tom at home in the evening?

15. *always*   Can you find Tom at home in the evening?

16. *usually*   Do you study at the library?

17. *ever*   Is the teacher absent?

18. *just*   What did you say?

19. *usually*   When do you go to bed?

20. *generally*   What time do you eat lunch?

21. *occasionally*   My son stays overnight with a friend.

22. *frequently*   We have company for dinner.

23. *sometimes*   Do you feel homesick?

24. *already*   I have read that book.

25. *already*   The mail is here.

□ **EXERCISE 27—ORAL:** Add the given words to the sentence. Put the adverbs in their usual midsentence position. Make any necessary changes in the sentence.

1. Jack doesn't shave in the morning.
   a. usually → *Jack usually doesn't shave in the morning.*
   b. often → *Jack often doesn't shave in the morning.*

c. frequently	g. always	j. hardly ever
d. generally	h. ever	k. rarely
e. sometimes	i. never	l. seldom
f. occasionally		

2. I don't eat breakfast.

a. generally	d. usually	g. occasionally
b. always	e. never	h. rarely
c. seldom	f. ever	i. hardly ever

3. Jane doesn't come to class on time.

a. never	d. occasionally	f. hardly ever
b. usually	e. always	g. ever
c. seldom		

4. My roommate isn't home in the morning.

a. usually	d. ever	g. frequently
b. generally	e. never	h. hardly ever
c. always	f. seldom	

☐ **EXERCISE 28:** Add the word(s) in italics to the sentence. Put the word in its usual midsentence position. Make any necessary changes.

1. *probably*   Brian knows the answer.

2. *usually*   Is Pat at home in the evening?

3. *finally*   They have finished their work.

4. *seldom*   Jack doesn't write letters.
   Seldom

5. *generally*   I don't stay up late. I go to bed early.

6. *probably*   Susan won't come to the party. She will stay home.

7. *never*   You shouldn't allow children to play with matches.

8. *hardly ever*   Jerry isn't in a bad mood.   never

9. *frequently*   My chemistry lecturer came to class late last semester.

10. *seldom*   The temperature doesn't drop below freezing in Miami.

11. *always*   Rita rides the bus to school.

12. *always*   I don't ride the bus to school.

13. *usually*   Tom doesn't ride the bus to school.

14. *never*   Paul doesn't ride his bike to his office.

15. *often*   Our classroom is too hot.

☐ **EXERCISE 29—ORAL (BOOKS CLOSED):** Respond in complete sentences.

> *Example:* What is something that you always do in the morning?
> *Response:* I always drink a cup of coffee.

What is something that . . .

1. you seldom do?
2. you will probably do tomorrow?
3. you probably won't do tomorrow?
4. you are probably going to do next week?
5. you hardly ever do?
6. you almost always do before you go to bed?
7. you have never done?
8. your roommate/spouse occasionally does?
9. a lazy person seldom does?
10. is always or usually expensive?
11. a polite person usually does?
12. a polite person never does?
13. drivers generally do?
14. your classmates sometimes do?
15. you have already done?
16. you just did?
17. I frequently do in class?
18. I usually don't do in class?
19. you rarely eat?
20. people in your country always or usually do to celebrate the New Year?
21. you usually do, but don't always do?
22. you usually don't do?

7-9 USING *ALREADY, YET, STILL,* AND *ANYMORE*

ALREADY 긍정	(a) The mail came an hour ago. **The mail is *already* here.** be동사뒤 일반동사앞	Idea of *already*: Something happened before now, before this time. *Position: midsentence.**
YET 부정	(b) I expected the mail an hour ago, but **it hasn't come *yet*.** 뒤	Idea of *yet*: Something did not happen before now (up to this time), but it may happen in the future. *Position: end of sentence.*
STILL not앞 긍정부정	(c) It was cold yesterday. **It is *still* cold today.** (d) I could play the piano when I was a child. **I can *still* play the piano.** (e) The mail didn't come an hour ago. **The mail *still* hasn't come.**	Idea of *still*: A situation continues to exist from past to present without change. *Position: midsentence.**
ANYMORE 더이상 안해 부정	(f) I lived in Chicago two years ago, but then I moved to another city. **I don't live in Chicago *anymore*.** 뒤	Idea of *anymore*: A past situation does not continue to exist at present; a past situation has changed. *Anymore* has the same meaning as *any longer*. *Position: end of sentence.*
NOTE: ***Already*** is used in *affirmative* sentences. ***Yet*** and ***anymore*** are used in *negative* sentences. ***Still*** is used in either *affirmative or negative* sentences.		

*See Chart 7-8 for the usual positions of midsentence adverbs.

☐ **EXERCISE 30:** Complete the sentences with *already, yet, still,* or *anymore.*

1. It's 1:00 P.M. I'm hungry. I haven't eaten lunch _____*yet*_____.

2. It's 1:00 P.M. I'm not hungry. I've _____ eaten lunch.

3. Eric was hungry, so he ate a candy bar a few minutes ago. But he's _____ hungry, so he's going to have another candy bar.

4. I used to eat lunch at the cafeteria every day, but now I bring my lunch to school in a paper bag instead. I don't eat at the cafeteria _____.

5. It started raining an hour ago. We can't go for a walk because it's _____ raining. I hope it stops soon.

6. Look! The rain has stopped. It isn't raining _____. Let's go for a walk.

7. I didn't understand this chapter in my biology book when I read it yesterday. Since then, I've read it three times, but I _____ don't understand it!

8. I don't have to study tonight. I've _____ finished all my homework.

9. I started a letter to my parents yesterday, but I haven't finished it _____. I'll finish it later today and put it in the mail.

10. I started a letter to my parents yesterday. I thought about finishing it last night before I went to bed, but I didn't. I _____ haven't finished it.*

☐ **EXERCISE 31:** *Yet* and *still* are frequently used in questions. Complete the following dialogues by using *yet* or *still*.   ⚦ Yet도 의문문에서 긍정으로 쓰인다.

1. A: Is Mary home ___*yet*___?

   B: No, but I'm expecting her soon.

2. A: Is Mary ___*still*___ in class?

   B: Yes, she is. Her class doesn't end until 11:30.

_____

*In negative sentences, *still* and *yet* express similar meanings. The meanings of *I haven't finished it yet* and *I still haven't finished it* are similar.

3. A: Has Dennis graduated __yet__?

   B: No. He's still in school.

4. A: I'm hungry. How about you? Did you eat __yet__?

   B: No. Did you?

   A: Nope. Let's go eat lunch.

5. A: Do you __still__ live on Fifth Street?

   B: Not anymore. I moved.

6. A: Has Karen found a new apartment __yet__?

   B: Not that I know of. She's still living on Elm Street.
   내가 아는 한 아니. 아니.

= Brian knows
as far as I know

7. A: Do you __still__ love me?

   B: Of course I do! I love you very much.

8. A: Is the baby __still__ sleeping?

   B: Yes. Shhh. We don't want to wake him up.

9. A: Is the baby asleep __yet__?

   B: I think so. I don't hear anything from the nursery. I put him down
      for his nap fifteen minutes ago, so I'm pretty sure he's asleep by
      now.

□ **EXERCISE 32:** Complete the dialogues by using *already, yet, still,* or *anymore.*

1. A: Has Rob found a new job __yet__?
   B: No. He __still~~already~~__ works at the bookstore.

2. A: When is your sister going to come to visit you?
   B: She's __still__ here. She got here yesterday.

3. A: Do you __~~already~~ still__ live on Pine Avenue?
   B: No, I don't live there __~~yet~~ anymore__. I moved to another
      apartment closer to school.

4. A: Is Anne home __yet__?
   B: No, she isn't. I'm getting worried. She was supposed to be home at
      eight. It's almost nine and she __still__ isn't here.
   A: Don't worry. She'll probably be here any minute.

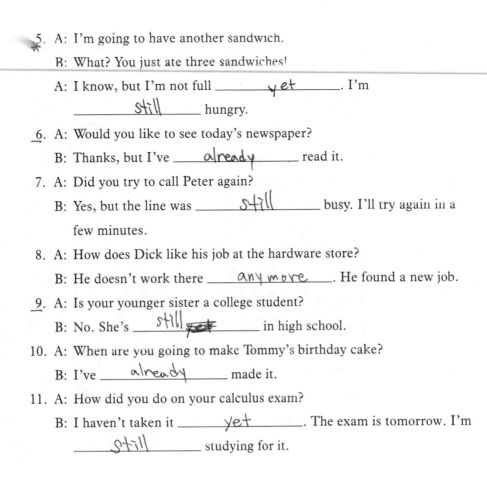

5. A: I'm going to have another sandwich.

   B: What? You just ate three sandwiches!

   A: I know, but I'm not full _____yet_____. I'm
   _____still_____ hungry.

6. A: Would you like to see today's newspaper?

   B: Thanks, but I've _____already_____ read it.

7. A: Did you try to call Peter again?

   B: Yes, but the line was _____still_____ busy. I'll try again in a
   few minutes.

8. A: How does Dick like his job at the hardware store?

   B: He doesn't work there _____anymore_____. He found a new job.

9. A: Is your younger sister a college student?

   B: No. She's _____still ~~yet~~_____ in high school.

10. A: When are you going to make Tommy's birthday cake?

    B: I've _____already_____ made it.

11. A: How did you do on your calculus exam?

    B: I haven't taken it _____yet_____. The exam is tomorrow. I'm
    _____still_____ studying for it.

☐ **EXERCISE 33:** Using the given information, add *already, yet, still,* or *anymore* to the
sentences in italics.

1. I finished my work two hours ago. *In other words, I have finished my*
   work.

   → **In other words, I have already finished my work.**

2. Ann didn't finish her work yesterday. She's doing it now. *In other words,*
   she hasn't finished it.

   → **In other words, she hasn't finished it yet.**

   → **In other words, she still hasn't finished it.***

────────────

*Reminder: In negative sentences, *yet* and *still* often express a similar meaning.

3. I expected Mike to come home an hour ago, but he didn't come. *In other words, he isn't home.*

4. I was hungry an hour ago, but I didn't eat anything. *In other words, I'm hungry.*

5. Erica used to work at the drugstore, but she quit her job. *In other words, she doesn't work there.*

6. Susan has been working at the bookstore for a year. She has tried to find a different job, but she hasn't found one yet. *In other words, she is working at the bookstore.*

7. We're late. The movie started half an hour ago. *In other words, the movie has started.*

8. Greg started smoking four years ago. *In other words, he smokes. He hasn't quit.*

9. We studied Chapter 6 last week. *In other words, we've studied Chapter 6. We haven't studied Chapter 8.*

10. When I was a child, I used to read comic books. But they are for kids. *In other words, I don't read comic books.*

11. We started this exercise ten minutes ago. *In other words, we haven't finished it. We are doing this exercise.*

12. When we were little, my sister and I could speak a little French. I don't remember French, but my sister does. *In other words, I can't speak French. My sister, however, can speak French because she practices using it.*

☐ **EXERCISE 34—WRITTEN:** Write about one (or both) of the following topics.

1. Think of two or three important events that have occurred in your life in the past year or two. In a paragraph for each, briefly tell your reader about these events and give your opinions and/or predictions.

2. Think of two or three important events that have occurred in the world in the past year or two. In a paragraph for each, briefly tell your reader about these events and give your opinions and/or predictions.

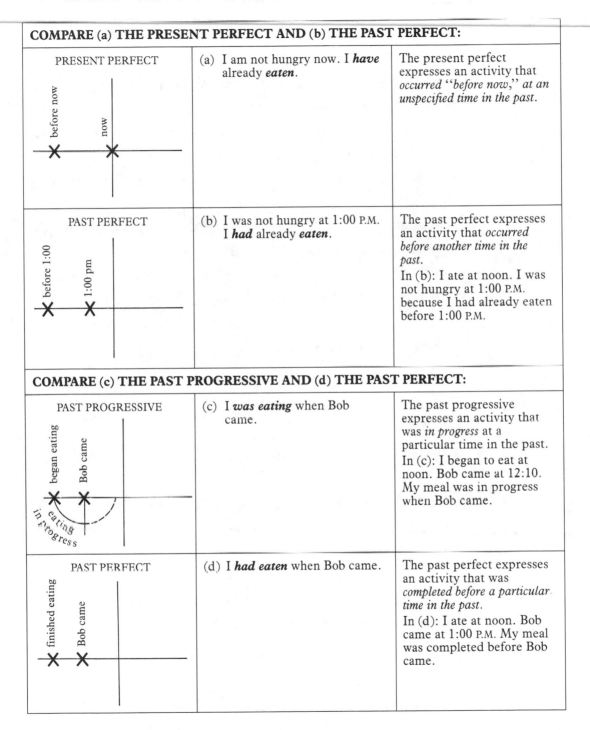

COMPARE (a) THE PRESENT PERFECT AND (b) THE PAST PERFECT:

PRESENT PERFECT	(a) I am not hungry now. I **have** already **eaten**.	The present perfect expresses an activity that *occurred "before now," at an unspecified time in the past.*
PAST PERFECT	(b) I was not hungry at 1:00 P.M. I **had** already **eaten**.	The past perfect expresses an activity that *occurred before another time in the past.* In (b): I ate at noon. I was not hungry at 1:00 P.M. because I had already eaten before 1:00 P.M.

COMPARE (c) THE PAST PROGRESSIVE AND (d) THE PAST PERFECT:

PAST PROGRESSIVE	(c) I **was eating** when Bob came.	The past progressive expresses an activity that was *in progress* at a particular time in the past. In (c): I began to eat at noon. Bob came at 12:10. My meal was in progress when Bob came.
PAST PERFECT	(d) I **had eaten** when Bob came.	The past perfect expresses an activity that was *completed before a particular time in the past.* In (d): I ate at noon. Bob came at 1:00 P.M. My meal was completed before Bob came.

☐ **EXERCISE 35:** Complete the sentences with the words in parentheses. Use the PRESENT PERFECT or the PAST PERFECT.

1. I am not hungry. I (*eat, already*) ___**I have already eaten.**___

2. I was not hungry. I (*eat, already*) ___**I had already eaten.**___

3. It's ten o'clock. I (*finish, already*) 've already finished my homework, so I'm going to go to bed.

4. Last night I went to bed at ten o'clock. I (*finish, already*) 've already finished ___ my homework.

5. By the time* I went to bed last night, I (*finish, already*) had finished ___ my homework.

6. I was late. The party (*start, already*) ~~had~~ had already started by the time I got there.

7. We're late. The party (*start, already*) has already started.

8. Carol missed her plane yesterday because of a traffic jam on her way to the airport. By the time she got to the airport, her plane (*leave, already*) had already left ___. 교통체증

☐ **EXERCISE 36:** Complete the sentences with the words in parentheses. Use the PAST PROGRESSIVE or the PAST PERFECT.

1. When I left for school this morning, it (*rain*) ___**was raining**___, so I used my umbrella.

2. By the time class was over this morning, the rain (*stop*) ___**had stopped**___, so I didn't need my umbrella anymore.

3. Last night I started to study at 7:30. Dick came at 7:35. I (*study*) ___ when Dick came.

4. Last night I started to study at 7:30. I finished studying at 9:00. Dick came at 9:30. By the time Dick came, I (*finish*) ___ my homework.

---

*by the time = *before*

5. When I walked into the kitchen after dinner last night, my wife (wash)
_____ the dishes, so I picked up a dish

   towel to help her.

6. By the time I walked into the kitchen after dinner, my husband (wash,

   already) _____ _____ the dishes and (*put*)

   _____ them away.

☐ **EXERCISE 37:** Complete the sentences with the words in parentheses.

1. A: (*you, enjoy*) _____**Did you enjoy**_____ the concert last night?

   B: Very much. I (*go, not*) _____**hadn't gone**___ to a concert in a long time.

2. A: (*you, see*) _____ John yesterday?

   B: Yes, I did. It (*be*) _____ good to see him again. I (*see,*

   not) _____ him in a long time.

3. A: Hi, Jim! It's good to see you again. I (*see, not*) _____

   _____ you in weeks.

   B: Hi, Sue! It (*be*) _____ good to see you again, too. I

   (*see, not*) _____ you since the end of last

   semester. How's everything going?

4. A: (*you, get*) _____ to class on time yesterday

   morning?

   B: No. By the time I (*get*) _____ there, it (*begin, already*)

   _____.

5. A: (*you, go*) _____ out to eat last night?

   B: No. By the time I (*get*) _____ home, my husband

   (*make, already*) _____ dinner for us.

   A: How (*be*) _____ it?

   B: Terrific. We (*have*) _____ chicken, rice, and a salad.

   While we (*eat*) _____, George Drake (*stop*)

   _____ by to visit us, so we (*invite*) _____

   him to join us for dinner. But he (*eat, already*) _____

   _____ his dinner, so he (*be, not*) _____ hungry.

A: What (*you, do*) _____ after dinner?

B: I wanted to go a movie—*Galaxy Invaders*. But George and my

husband (*see, already*) _____ it, so

we (*go*) _____ to *Ghost Ship* instead. It (*be*)

_____ pretty good.

☐ **EXERCISE 38—PREPOSITIONS:** Complete the sentences with prepositions.
(See Appendix 1 for a list of preposition combinations.)

1. I apologized _____ Ann _____ stepping on her toe.

2. I thanked Sam _____ helping me fix my car.

3. My grandfather doesn't approve _____ gambling.

4. Please forgive me _____ forgetting your birthday.

5. My friend insisted _____ taking me to the airport.

6. Please excuse me _____ being late.

7. Children depend _____ their parents for love and support.

8. In my composition, I compared this city _____ my hometown.

9. Umbrellas protect people _____ rain.

10. We're relying _____ Jason to help us move into our new apartment.

11. We had mice in the house, so we set some traps to get rid _____

them.

12. What happened _____ your finger? Did you cut it?

CHAPTER 8
Count/Noncount Nouns and Articles

8-1 COUNT AND NONCOUNT NOUNS

	SINGULAR	PLURAL	Some nouns are called COUNT NOUNS:
COUNT NOUN	*a* chair *one* chair	chairs *two* chairs *three* chairs *some* chairs *several* chairs *a lot of* chairs *many* chairs *a few* chairs	(1) In the singular, they can be preceded by *a/an* or *one*. (2) They have a plural form: *-s* or *-es*.*
NONCOUNT NOUN	furniture *some* furniture *a lot of* furniture *much* furniture *a little* furniture	Ø	Some nouns are called NONCOUNT NOUNS: (1) They are NOT immediately preceded by *a/an* or *one*. (2) They do NOT have a plural form (no final *-s* is added).

*See Chart 4-1.

☐ **EXERCISE 1:** Notice the expressions of quantity (*two, some, a lot of*, etc.) that are used with count nouns and noncount nouns in Chart 8-1. Draw a line through the expressions of quantity that **cannot** be used to complete the sentences.

NONCOUNT NOUNS: *fruit . . . . mail . . . . . . traffic*
COUNT NOUNS: *apples . . . . . letters . . . . . cars*

1. I ate _____ **fruit.**
   a. some   ~~e. too many~~
   ~~b. several~~   f. too much
   c. a little   g. a lot of
   ~~d. a few~~   ~~h. two~~

2. I ate _____ **apples.**
   a. some   e. too many
   b. several   f. too much
   c. a little   g. a lot of
   d. a few   h. two

3. I get _____ **mail** every day.
   - a. a lot of
   - b. some
   - c. a little
   - d. a few
   - e. too much
   - f. too many
   - g. several
   - h. three

4. I get _____ **letters** every day.
   - a. a lot of
   - b. some
   - c. a little
   - d. a few
   - e. too much
   - f. too many
   - g. several
   - h. three

5. There is _____ **traffic** in the street.
   - a. several
   - b. some
   - c. too many
   - d. a little
   - e. a lot of
   - f. a few
   - g. too much
   - h. five

6. There are _____ **cars** in the street.
   - a. several
   - b. some
   - c. too many
   - d. a little
   - e. a lot of
   - f. a few
   - g. too much
   - h. five

8-2 NONCOUNT NOUNS

(a) I bought *some furniture*.
(b) I got *some mail* yesterday.
	A noncount noun* is NOT preceded by *a/an*, *one*, *two*, *three*, etc.
	    INCORRECT: *I bought a furniture.*
	A noncount noun does NOT have a plural form.
	    INCORRECT: *I bought some furnitures.*

INDIVIDUAL PARTS (COUNT NOUNS)	THE WHOLE (A NONCOUNT NOUN)	
(c) chairs / tables / beds / etc.	furniture	Noncount nouns usually refer to a whole group of things that is made up of many individual parts, a whole category made up of different varieties. For example, some common noncount nouns are *furniture*, *mail*, *money*, *fruit*, and *jewelry*.

(d) letters / postcards / bills / etc.	mail	A language is not always logical. For instance:
		    I had some corn for dinner. (noncount)
		    I had some peas for dinner. (count)
		Both *corn* and *peas* express a larger whole made up of smaller parts, but *corn* is a noncount noun and *pea* is a count noun.
		    Vegetables are good for you. (count)
		    Fruit is good for you. (noncount)
		Both *vegetables* and *fruit* describe whole categories of food, but one is count and the other noncount.

(e) pennies / nickels / dollars / etc.	money	

(f) apples / bananas / oranges / etc.	fruit	Logically, you can count furniture. But in grammar, you cannot count furniture. For example: *I see a table and a bed.*
		    CORRECT: *I see some furniture.*
		    INCORRECT: *I see two furnitures.*

(g) rings / bracelets / necklaces / etc.	jewelry	

*A noncount noun is also sometimes called a *mass noun*.

SOME COMMON NONCOUNT NOUNS: WHOLE GROUPS MADE UP OF INDIVIDUAL PARTS		

A. *clothing*
   equipment
   food
   fruit
   furniture
   garbage
   hardware
   jewelry
   machinery
   mail
   makeup
   money
    cash
    change
   postage
   scenery
   stuff
   traffic
	B. *homework*
	   housework
	   work
	
	C. *advice*
	   information
	   news
	
	D. *history*
	   literature
	   music
	   poetry
	
	E. *English, Arabic, Chinese,* etc.
	   (names of languages)
		F. *grammar*
		   slang
		   vocabulary
		
		G. *corn*
		   dirt
		   dust
		   flour
		   grass
		   hair
		   pepper
		   rice
		   salt
		   sand
		   sugar
		   wheat

☐ **EXERCISE 2:** Complete the sentences with the correct form, **singular or plural**, of the given nouns. When necessary, choose the correct word in parentheses in some of the sentences.

1. *chair*   I bought some _____ **chairs** _____.

2. *furniture*   I bought some _____ **furniture** _____.

3. *fruit*   There (is, are) a lot of _____ **fruit** _____ on the table.

4. *vegetable*   There (is, are) a lot of _____ **vegetables** _____ on the table.

5. *clothing*   I have a lot of _____ in my closet.

6. *dress*   Mary has a lot of _____ in her closet.

7. *information*   There (is, are) a lot of _____ in an encyclopedia.

8. *fact*   There (is, are) a lot of _____ in an encyclopedia.

9. *grammar*   I know a lot of _____.

10. *vocabulary*   I'm learning a lot of new _____.

11. *word*   I'm learning a lot of new _____.

12. *slang*   I want to learn some American _____.

13. *idiom*   I know a lot of English _____.

14. *traffic*   There (is, are) a lot of _____ in the street.

15. *car*   There (is, are) a lot of _____ on the road.

16. *literature*   I like to read good _____.

17. *novel*   I like to read good _____.

18. *poem*   I like to read _____.

19. *poetry*   I like to read _____.

20. *mail*   Did you get any _____ today?

21. *letter*   Did you get any _____ today?

22. *sand*   I got some _____ in my shoes at the beach.

23. *dust*   There (is, are) a lot of _____ under the bed.

24. *homework*   I have a lot of _____ to do tonight.

25. *assignment*   The teacher gives us a lot of _____.

26. *penny*   Tommy had four _____ in his pocket.

27. *money*   He has some _____ in his pocket.

28. *coin*   I need some _____ for the vending machine.

I want to get a can of soda pop.

29. *change*   I need some _____ for the vending machine.

30. *garbage*   The street is very dirty. There (is, are) some

_____ in the street.

☐ **EXERCISE 3:** Complete the sentences with the **singular or plural** form of the given nouns. When necessary, choose the correct word in parentheses in some of the sentences.

1. *machinery*   It takes a lot of _____ to build a road.

2. *machine*   There (is, are) a lot of washing _____ in a laundromat.

3. *equipment*   There (is, are) a lot of _____ in the chemistry lab.

4. *tool*   There (is, are) a lot of _____ in the garage.

5. *hardware*   That store sells a lot of _____.

6. *ring*

   bracelet

   Marie wears a lot of _____ and

   _____.

7. *jewelry*

   Marie wears a lot of _____.

8. *jewel*

   A crown has a lot of _____.

9. *suggestion*

   Can you give me some ___ _____?

10. *advice*

    Can you give me some _____?

11. *information*

    I need some _____.

12. *news*

    There (isn't, aren't) any interesting _____

    in today's paper.

13. *lake*

    mountain

    We saw a lot of _____ and

    _____ on our vacation.

14. *scenery*

    We saw a lot of beautiful _____ on our

    vacation.

15. *plant*

    Ann has a lot of _____ in her apartment.

16. *grass*

    When we went on a picnic, we sat on the

    _____.

17. *rice*

    People in my country eat a lot of _____.

18. *English*

    Ahmed's children know a lot of _____.

19. *song*

    The children learned a lot of new _____

    in nursery school.

20. *music*

    I enjoy listening to _____.

21. *thing*

    Whose _____ (is, are) (this, these)?

22. *stuff*

    Whose _____ (is, are) (this, these)?

23. *corn*

    Rebecca had some _____ for dinner.

24. *pea*

    Jack had some _____ with his dinner.

25. *makeup*

    My aunt has a drawer full of _____.

26. *bread*

    My uncle always has _____ with his dinner.

27. *sandwich*

    People in Canada often have _____ for lunch.

28. *toast*

    We had eggs and _____ for breakfast.

8-3 MORE NONCOUNT NOUNS

(a) LIQUIDS		SOLIDS and SEMI-SOLIDS				GASES
beer	milk	bread	meat	chalk	rubber	air
blood	oil	butter	beef	copper	silver	fog
coffee	shampoo	cheese	chicken	cotton	soap	oxygen
cream	soup	ice	fish	glass	tin	pollution
gasoline	tea	ice cream	ham	gold	toothpaste	smog
honey	water	lettuce	lamb	iron	wood	smoke
juice	wine	toast	pork	paper	wool	steam

(b) NATURAL PHENOMENA (things that occur in nature)

weather	lightning	darkness
rain	thunder	light
snow	humidity	sunshine

(c) ABSTRACTIONS (An abstraction is something that has no physical form. A person cannot touch it.)

anger	enjoyment	happiness	ignorance	luck	recreation
beauty	entertainment	hate	intelligence	patience	research
confidence	experience	health	justice	peace	stupidity
courage	fun	help	knowledge	poverty	time
cowardice	generosity	honesty	laughter	pride	violence
education	greed	hospitality	love	progress	wealth

☐ **EXERCISE 4:** Complete the sentences with the correct form, **singular or plural**, of the given nouns. Choose the correct word in parentheses as necessary.

1. *snow*   It's winter. There (is, are) a lot of _____**snow**_____
   on the ground.

2. *weather*   There (is, are) a lot of cold _____ in Alaska.

3. *sunshine*   _____ (is, are) a source of vitamin D.

4. *knowledge*   Prof. Nash has a lot of _____ about that
   subject.

5. *fun*   We had a lot of _____ on the picnic.

6. *luck*   I want to wish you good _____.

7. *idea*   Emily has a lot of good _____.

8. *intelligence* I admire Emily for her _____.

9. *gold*   _____ (is, are) expensive.

10. *diamond*   _____ (is, are) expensive, too.

11. *movie*   I like to go to _____.

12. *entertainment*   What do you do for _____ on weekends?

13. *game*   Children like to play _____.

14. *generosity*   Thank you for your _____.

15. *help*   Could you give me some _____ with this?

16. *patience*   Teaching children to read requires _____.

17. *patient*   Doctors take care of _____.

18. *confidence*   You can do it! I have _____ in you.

19. *progress*   Mr. Fernandez's English is improving. He's making a lot of _____.

20. *courage*   Be brave. You must have _____.

21. *pollution*   Automobiles are the biggest source of _____ in most cities.

22. *forest*   The destruction of rain _____ throughout much of the world is harming the earth's environment.

23. *peace*   There have been many conflicts and wars throughout the history of the world, but almost all people prefer _____.

24. *hospitality*   Thank you for your _____.

25. *beef*   The _____ we had for dinner last night (was, were) very good.

26. *fog*   During the winter months along the coast, there (is, are) usually a lot of _____ in the morning.

☐ **EXERCISE 5:** Complete the sentences with *much* or *many* and the **singular or plural** form of the noun. Choose the correct word in parentheses as necessary.

REMINDER: Use *many* with count nouns: *many apples*.
            Use *much* with noncount nouns: *much fruit*.

1. *apple*   How ___***many apples***___ did you buy?

2. *fruit*   How ___***much fruit***___ did you buy?

3. *mail*   How _____ did you get yesterday?

4. *letter*   How _____ did you get yesterday?

5. *postage*   How _____ do I need for this
package?

6. *stamp*   How _____ did you buy?

7. *English*   Anna's husband doesn't know _____.

8. *slang*   Sometimes I can't understand my roommate because he
uses too _____.

9. *word*   How _____ (is, are) there in your dictionary?

10. *coffee*   Louise drinks too _____.

11. *sandwich* Billy has a stomach ache. He ate too

_____.

12. *sugar*   You shouldn't eat too _____.

13. *course*   How _____ are you taking this semester?

14. *homework* How _____ do you have to do tonight?

15. *news*   There (isn't, aren't) _____ in the paper today.

16. *article*   How _____ (is, are) there on
the front page of today's paper?

17. *fun*   I didn't have _____ at the party. It
was boring.

18. *star*   How _____ (is, are) there in the universe?

19. *sunshine* There (isn't, aren't) _____ in Seattle
in winter.

20. *pollution* (Is, Are) there _____ in Miami?

21. *luck*   We didn't have _____ when we went fishing.

22. *kind*   There (is, are) _____ of flowers.

23. *violence* I think there (is, are) too _____
on television.

24. *makeup*   I think that Mary wears too _____.

25. *car*   How _____ pass in front of this
building in 30 seconds?

26. *traffic*   (Is, Are) there _____ in front of
your apartment building?

□ **EXERCISE 6:** Complete the sentences by using *a few* or *a little* and the given noun. Use the plural form of the noun when necessary.

REMINDER: Use *a few* with a count noun: *a few songs*.
Use *a little* with a noncount noun: *a little music*.

1. *music*   I feel like listening to _____ ***a little music*** _____ tonight.

2. *song*   We sang _____ ***a few songs*** _____ at the party.

3. *time*   I'm not finished with my work. I need _____ ***a little*** _____ more _____ ***time*** _____.

4. *desk*   We need _____ more _____ in our classroom.

5. *help*   Do you need _____ with that?

6. *apple*   I bought _____ at the market.*

7. *fruit*   I bought _____ at the market.

8. *advice*   I need _____.

9. *money*   If I accept that job, I'll make _____ more _____.

10. *coin*   Annie put _____ in her pocket.

11. *information*   Could you give me _____?

12. *hour*   Don's plane will arrive in _____ more _____.

13. *toothpaste*   Tommy, put just _____ on your toothbrush, not half the tube!

14. *laughter*   We need to be able to see the humor in a situation even when we're unhappy. _____ never hurts.

15. *laugh*   Greg's joke produced _____ in the audience, but most of the people didn't think it was funny.

16. *grammar*   Pedro already knew _____ English _____ before he took this course.

17. *flower*   I picked _____ from my garden.

18. *progress*   I've made _____ in the last couple of weeks.

*I bought a few apples. = I bought a small number of apples.
I bought a little apple. = I bought one apple and it was small, not large.

19. *chicken* I'm still hungry. I think I'll have _____ more

_____.

20. *chicken* When I was a child, we raised _____

in our back yard.

8-4 NOUNS THAT CAN BE COUNT OR NONCOUNT

Quite a few nouns can be used as either noncount or count nouns. Examples of both noncount and count usages for some common nouns follow:

NOUN	USED AS **NONCOUNT** NOUN	USED AS A **COUNT** NOUN
glass	(a) Windows are made of *glass*.	(b) I drank *a glass* of water.
		(c) Janet wears *glasses* when she reads.
hair	(d) Rita has brown *hair*.	(e) There's *a hair* on my jacket.
iron	(f) *Iron* is a metal.	(g) I pressed my shirt with *an iron*.
light	(h) I opened the curtain to let in *some light*.	(i) Please turn off *the lights* (*lamps*).
paper	(j) I need *some paper* to write a letter.	(k) I wrote *a paper* for Prof. Lee.
		(l) I bought *a paper* (*a newspaper*).
time	(m) How *much time* do you need to finish your work?	(n) How *many times* have you been in Mexico?
work	(o) I have *some work* to do tonight.	(p) That painting is *a work* of art.
coffee	(q) I had *some coffee* after dinner.	(r) *Two coffees*, please.
chicken fish lamb	(s) I had *some chicken/some fish/some lamb* for dinner.	(t) She drew a picture of *a chicken/a fish/a lamb*.

☐ **EXERCISE 7:** Complete the sentences with the given words. Choose words in parentheses as necessary.

1. *lamb*   Joe, would you like (a, some) _____ for dinner

   tonight?

2. *lamb*   _____ (is, are) born in the springtime.

3. *time*   It took a lot of _____ to write my composition.

4. *time*   I really like that movie. I saw it three _____.

5. *paper*   Students in Prof. Young's literature class have to write a lot of

   _____.

6. *paper*   Students who take thorough lecture notes

   use a lot of _____.

7. *paper*   *The New York Times* is (a, some)

   famous _____.

8. *work*   Rodin's statue of "The Thinker" is

   one of my favorite _____

   of art.

9. *work*   I have a lot of _____ to do tomorrow.

10. *light*   If _____ accidentally (gets, get) in a darkroom,

    (it, they) can ruin photographic negatives.

11. *light*   There (is, are) a lot of fluorescent _____ on the

    ceilings of the school building.

12. *hair*   Erin has straight _____, and Sara has curly

    _____.

13. *hair*   Brian has a white cat. When I stood up from Brian's sofa, my

    black slacks were covered with short, white _____.

14. *coffee*   We'd like two cheese sandwiches and two _____,

    please.

15. *coffee*   I don't drink a lot of _____. I prefer tea.

16. *glass*   I wear _____ because I'm nearsighted.

17. *glass*   In some countries, people use _____ for their

    tea; in other countries, they use cups.

18. *glass*   Framed paintings are usually covered with _____

to protect them.

19. *iron*   _____ (is, are) necessary to animal and plant life.

20. *iron*   _____ (is, are) used to make clothes look neat.

8-5 USING UNITS OF MEASURE WITH NONCOUNT NOUNS

(a) I had some tea. (b) I had **two cups of** tea. (c) I ate some toast. (d) I ate **one piece of** toast.	To mention a specific quantity of a noncount noun, speakers use units of measure such as *two cups of* or *one piece of*. A unit of measure usually describes the container (e.g., *a cup of, a bowl of*) the amount (*a pound of, a quart of*),* or the shape (*a bar of soap, a sheet of paper*).

*Weight measure: *one pound = 0.45 kilograms/kilos*   Liquid measure: *one quart = 0.95 litres/liters*
    four quarts = one gallon = 3.8 litres/liters

☐ **EXERCISE 8:** Use the words in the list to complete the sentences. Use the plural form if necessary. Some sentences have more than one possible completion.

bar	*gallon*	*piece*	*sheet*
bottle	*glass*	*pound*	*spoonful*
bowl	*loaf*	*quart*	*tube*
cup			

1. I drank a _____*cup*_____ of coffee.

2. I bought two _____*pounds*_____ of cheese.

3. I bought a _____ of milk at the supermarket.

4. I drank a _____ of orange juice.

5. I had a _____ of toast and an egg for breakfast.

6. I put ten _____ of gas in my car.

7. I had a _____ of soup for lunch.

8. I need a _____ of chalk.

9. I drank a _____ of beer.

10. I bought a _____ of margarine.

11. There are 200 _____ of lined paper in my notebook.

12. There is a _____ of fruit on the table.

13. I used two _____ of bread to make a sandwich.

14. I bought one _____ of bread at the store.

15. I put a _____ of honey in my tea.

16. I need to buy a new _____ of toothpaste.

17. There is a _____ of soap in the bathroom.

18. Let me give you a _____ of advice.

19. I just learned an interesting _____ of information.

20. There were a dozen* _____ of mail for me in my mailbox today.

21. A three-piece suit is made up of three _____ of clothing: slacks, a jacket, and a vest.

☐ **EXERCISE 9—ORAL (BOOKS CLOSED):** Ask and answer questions with *how much* and *how many.*

> *Example:* (. . .) has two children.
> STUDENT A: How many children does (. . .) have?
> STUDENT B: Two.

1. There are (25) students in this class.
2. (. . .) gets a lot of mail every day.
3. There are 50 states in the United States.
4. I drink (two) cups of coffee every day.**
5. I bought one pound of butter.
6. There are ten provinces in Canada.
7. There are 256 pages in this book.
8. I have (twenty dollars).
9. (. . .) cooked two cups of rice.
10. There are (around 25) desks in this room.
11. I use very little salt on my food.
12. (. . .) knows very few students in his/her (chemistry) class.
13. A round-trip ticket from here to (Chicago) costs ($430).
14. There are approximately 22,000 different kinds of fish in the world.
15. I know a lot of English vocabulary.
16. (. . .) invited ten people to his/her house for dinner.
17. There are (about five) pieces of chalk in the chalk tray.
18. (. . .) bought ten gallons of gas(oline)/petrol.

---

*A *dozen* = *twelve*. It is followed by a plural noun: *a dozen eggs.*
**There are two possible questions:
> *How much coffee do you drink every day?*
> *How many cups of coffee do you drink every day?*

8-6 GUIDELINES FOR ARTICLE USAGE

	USING *A* OR Ø (NO ARTICLE)		USING *A* OR *SOME*
SINGULAR COUNT NOUNS	(a) *A dog* makes a good pet. (b) *A banana* is yellow. (c) *A pencil* contains lead.	A speaker uses *a* with a singular count noun when s/he is making a generalization. In (a): The speaker is talking about any dog, all dogs, dogs in general.	(j) I saw *a dog* in my yard. (k) Mary ate *a banana*. (l) I need *a pencil*.
PLURAL COUNT NOUNS	(d) Ø *Dogs* make good pets. (e) Ø *Bananas* are yellow. (f) Ø *Pencils* contain lead.	A speaker uses no article (Ø) with a plural count noun when s/he is making a generalization.* In (d): The speaker is talking about any dog, all dogs, dogs in general. Note: (a) and (d) have the same meaning.	(m) I saw *some dogs* in my yard. (n) Mary bought *some bananas*. (o) Bob has *some pencils* in his pocket.
NONCOUNT NOUNS	(g) Ø *Fruit* is good for you. (h) Ø *Coffee* contains caffeine. (i) I like Ø *music*.	A speaker uses no article (Ø) with a noncount noun when s/he is making a generalization.* In (g): The speaker is talking about any fruit, all fruit, fruit in general.	(p) I bought *some fruit*. (q) Bob drank *some coffee*. (r) Would you like to listen to *some music*?

*Sometimes a speaker uses an expression of quantity (e.g., ***almost all, most, some***) when s/he makes a generalization: *Almost all dogs make good pets. Most dogs are friendly. Some dogs have short hair.*

	USING *THE*	

A speaker uses *a* with a singular count noun when s/he is talking about one thing (or person) that is not specific.
 	
In (j): The speaker is saying, "I saw one dog (not two dogs, some dogs, many dogs). It wasn't a specific dog (e.g., your dog, the neighbor's dog, that dog). It was only one dog out of the whole group of animals called dogs."
	(s) Did you feed *the dog*?
	(t) I had a banana and an apple. I gave *the banana* to Mary.
	(u) *The pencil* on that desk is Jim's.
	(v) *The sun* is shining.
	(w) Please close *the door*.
	(x) Mary is in *the kitchen*.
		The is used in front of:
		   singular count nouns: *the dog*
		   plural count nouns: *the dogs*
		   noncount nouns: *the fruit*
		
		A speaker uses *the* (not *a*, Ø, or *some*) when the speaker and the listener are thinking about the same specific thing(s) or person(s).
		
		In (s): The speaker and the listener are thinking about the same specific dog. The listener knows which dog the speaker is talking about: the dog that they own, the dog that they feed every day. There is only one dog that the speaker could possibly be talking about.

A speaker often uses *some*** with a plural count noun when s/he is talking about things (or people) that are not specific. In (m): The speaker is saying, "I saw more than one dog. They weren't specific dogs (e.g., your dogs, the neighbor's dogs, those dogs). The exact number of dogs isn't important (two dogs, five dogs); I'm simply saying that I saw an indefinite number of dogs."	(y) Did you feed *the dogs*? (z) I had some bananas and some apples. I gave *the bananas* to Mary. (aa) *The pencils* on that desk are Jim's. (bb) Please turn off *the lights*.	In (t): A speaker uses *the* when s/he mentions a noun the second time. First mention: *I had **a banana** . . .* Second mention: *I gave **the banana** . . .* In the second mention, the listener now knows which banana the speaker is talking about: the banana the speaker had (not the banana John had, not the banana in that bowl).
A speaker often uses *some*** with a noncount noun when s/he is talking about something that is not specific. In (p): The speaker is saying, "I bought an indefinite amount of fruit. The exact amount isn't important information (e.g., two pounds of fruit, four bananas and two apples). And I'm not talking about specific fruit (e.g., that fruit, the fruit in that bowl.)"	(cc) *The fruit* in this bowl is ripe. (dd) I drank some coffee and some milk. *The coffee* was hot. (ee) I can't hear you. *The music* is too loud. (ff) *The air* is cold today.	

**In addition to *some*, a speaker might use *several, a few, a lot of,* etc. with a plural count noun, or *a little, a lot of,* etc. with a noncount noun. (See Chart 8-1.)

DIALOGUE 1:

A: ***A dog*** makes a good pet.   B: I agree.

DIALOGUE 2:

A: I saw ***a dog*** in my yard.

DIALOGUE 4:

A: ***Dogs*** make good pets.   B: I agree.

DIALOGUE 5:

A: I saw ***some dogs*** in my yard.

DIALOGUE 7:

A: ***Fruit*** is good for you.   B: I agree.

DIALOGUE 8:

A: I ate ***some fruit***.

DIALOGUE 3:

B: Oh?　　A: Did you feed *the dog*?　　B: Yes.

DIALOGUE 6:

B: Oh?　　A: Did you feed *the dogs*?　　B: Yes.

DIALOGUE 9:

B: Oh?　　A: *The fruit* in this bowl is ripe.　　B: Good.

☐ **EXERCISE 11:** Here are some conversations. Try to decide whether the speakers probably use *the* or *a/an.** Are the speakers thinking about the same objects or persons?

1. A: Do you have _____*a*_____ car?

   B: No. But I have _____*a*_____ bicycle.

2. A: Do you need _____*the*_____ car today, honey?

   B: Yes. I have a lot of errands to do. Why don't I drive you to work today?

   A: Okay. But be sure to fill _____*the*_____ car up with gas sometime today.

3. A: Did you have a good time at _____ party last night?

   B: Yes.

   A: So did I. I'm glad that you decided to go with me.

4. A: What did you do last night?

   B: I went to _____ party.

   A: Oh? Where was it?

5. A: I bought _____ table yesterday.

   B: Oh? I didn't know you went shopping for furniture.

6. A: Have you seen my keys?

   B: Yes. They're on _____ table next to _____ front door.

7. A: Is Mr. Jones _____ graduate student?

   B: No. He's _____ professor.

8. A: Where's _____ professor?

   B: She's absent today.

9. A: Would you like to go to _____ zoo this afternoon?

   B: Sure. Why not?

10. A: Does San Diego have _____ zoo?

    B: Yes. It's world famous.

11. A: Where do you live?

    B: We live on _____ quiet street in the suburbs.

A is used in front of nouns that begin with a consonant sound: a book, a dog, a pencil. **An is used in front of nouns that begin with a vowel sound: an apple, an elephant, an idea, an opinion, an uncle, an hour.*

12. A: I'm hungry and I'm tired of walking. How much farther is it to

_____ restaurant?

B: Just a couple of blocks. Let's cross _____ street here.

A: Are you sure you know where you're going?

13. A: Did Bob find _____ job?

B: Yes. He's working at _____ restaurant.

A: Oh? Which one?

14. A: Did you feed _____ cat?

B: Yes. I fed him a couple of hours ago.

15. A: Does Jane have _____ cat?

B: No, she has _____ dog. She doesn't like cats.

16. A: Where's Dennis?

B: He's in _____ kitchen.

17. A: Do you like your new apartment?

B: Yes. It has _____ big kitchen.

☐ **EXERCISE 12:** Complete the sentences with the given nouns. Use *the* for specific statements. Do not use *the* for general statements.

1. *flowers*   a. _____ **The flowers** _____ in that vase are beautiful.

      b. _____ **Flowers** _____ are beautiful.

2. *mountains*   a. _____ are beautiful.

      b. _____ in Colorado are beautiful.

3. *water*   a. _____ consists of hydrogen and

oxygen.

      b. I don't want to go swimming today. _____

is too cold.

4. *information*   a. _____ in that book is inaccurate.

      b. An encyclopedia is a source of _____.

5. *health*   a. _____ is more important than

money.

      b. Doctors are concerned with _____

of their patients.

6. *men*   a. _____ generally have stronger

   women   muscles than _____.

                b. At the party last night, _____ sat

                on one side of the room and _____

                sat on the other.

7. *problems*   a. Everyone has _____.

                b. Irene told me about _____ she

                had with her car yesterday.

8. *happiness* a. I can't express _____ I felt when

                I heard the good news.

                b. Everyone seeks _____.

9. *vegetables* a. _____ are good for you.

                b. _____ we had for dinner last

                night were overcooked.

10. *gold*   a. _____ is a precious metal.

                b. _____ in Mary's ring is 24

                karats.

☐ **EXERCISE 13:** Add *the* if necessary. Otherwise, make the symbol Ø to show that no article
is necessary.

1. Please pass me ___*the*___ butter.

2. ___Ø___ butter is a dairy product.

3. John, where's _____ milk? Is it in _____ refrigerator or on

   _____ table?

4. _____ milk comes from cows and goats.

5. Tom usually has _____ wine with dinner.

6. Dinner's ready. Shall I pour _____ wine?

7. I'm studying _____ English. I'm studying _____ grammar.

8. _____ grammar in this chapter isn't easy.

9. _____ chemistry is my favorite subject.

10. Do you like _____ weather in this city?

11. _____ copper is used in electrical wiring.

12. _____ air is free.

13. _____ air is humid today.

14. _____ windows are closed. Please open them.

15. _____ windows are made of _____ glass.

16. We usually have _____ meat for dinner.

17. _____ meat we had for dinner last night was tough.

18. People used to use _____ candles for _____ light, but now they use _____ electricity.

☐ **EXERCISE 14:** Use *a/an/some* or *the* in the following. REMINDER: Use *the* when a noun is mentioned for the second time.

1. Yesterday I saw _____*a*_____ dog and _____*a*_____ cat. _____*The*_____ dog was chasing _____*the*_____ cat. _____ cat was chasing _____ mouse. _____ mouse ran into _____ hole, but _____ hole was very small. _____ cat couldn't get into _____ hole, so it ran up _____ tree. _____ dog tried to climb _____ tree too, but it couldn't.

2. Yesterday I bought _____ clothes. I bought _____ suit, _____ shirt, and _____ tie. _____ suit is gray and comes with a vest. _____ shirt is pale blue, and _____ tie has black and gray stripes.

3. Yesterday I saw _____ man and _____ woman. They were having _____ argument. _____ man was yelling at _____ woman, and _____ woman was shouting at _____ man. I don't know what _____ argument was about.

4. I had _____ soup and _____ sandwich for lunch. _____ soup was too salty, but _____ sandwich was pretty good.

5. A: I saw _____ accident yesterday.

   B: Oh? Where?

   A: On Grand Avenue. _____ man in _____ Volkswagen drove
   through a stop sign and hit _____ bus.

   B: Was anyone hurt in _____ accident?

   A: I don't think so. _____ man who was driving _____
   Volkswagen got out of his car and seemed to be okay. His car was
   only slightly damaged. No one in _____ bus was hurt.

6. A: What did you do last weekend?

   B: I went on _____ picnic Saturday and saw _____ movie
   Sunday.

   A: Did you have fun?

   B: _____ picnic was fun, but _____ movie was boring.

□ **EXERCISE 15:** Complete the sentences with *a*, *an*, *some*, *the*, or *Ø*.

1. A: Do you like ____*Ø*____ fruit?

   B: Very much.

2. A: I'm hungry.

   B: Would you like _____ fruit? How about _____ apple?

3. A: _____ fruit we bought at the market was fresh.

   B: That's the best place to buy _____ fruit.

4. _____ gas is expensive nowadays.

5. _____ gas at Mack's Service Station is cheaper than _____ gas
   at the Shell Station.

6. I need _____ gas. Let's stop at the next service station.

7. Kathy bought _____ radio. She likes to listen to _____ music
   when she studies.

8. A: Would you please turn _____ radio down? _____ music is
   too loud.

   B: No problem.

9. A: Do you see _____ man who is standing next to Janet?

   B: Yes. Who is he?

   A: He's _____ president of this university.

10. A one-dollar bill has the picture of _____ president of the United States. It's the picture of George Washington.

11. A: What did you buy when you went shopping?

    B: I bought _____ blouse and _____ jewelry.

    A: What color is _____ blouse?

    B: Red.

12. A: Where's my bookbag?

    B: It's on _____ floor over there, in _____ corner next to _____ sofa.

13. We need to buy _____ furniture. I'd like to get _____ sofa and _____ easy chair.

14. _____ furniture is expensive these days.

15. _____vegetarian doesn't eat _____ meat.

16. Last week I read _____ book about _____ life of Gandhi.

17. I enjoy _____ life.

18. A: Let's go swimming in _____ lake today.

    B: That sounds like _____ good idea.

19. _____ lake is a body of _____ water that is smaller than _____ sea but larger than _____ pond. _____ ocean is larger than _____ sea.

20. During our vacation in Florida, we walked along _____ beach in front of our hotel and looked at _____ ocean.

21. People can drink _____ fresh water. They can't drink _____ seawater because it contains _____ salt.

22. I had _____ interesting experience yesterday. _____ man in _____ blue suit came into my office and handed me _____ bouquet of _____ flowers. I had never seen _____ man before in my life, but I thanked him for _____ flowers. Then he walked out _____ door.

8-7 USING EXPRESSIONS OF QUANTITY AS PRONOUNS

Expressions of quantity are words that describe the number or amount of a noun. Examples of common expressions of quantity: *some, any, many, much, a lot (of), a few, a little, two, a couple (of), three, several, etc.* Expressions of quantity are usually used in front of a noun (e.g., *some paper, a lot of fruit*). They can also be used alone—without a noun—when the meaning is clear, i.e., when both speaker and listener know what the expression of quantity refers to. These expressions function as pronouns.	

(a) A: I need some yellow paper.
    B: I don't have **any**. Ask Matt. I think he has **some**.
	In (a): **any** and **some** are used without a noun. It is clearly understood that:
	    any = any yellow paper
	    some = some yellow paper★

(b) A: I understand you're a baseball fan. Have you gone to a lot of baseball games?
    B: Yes. I've gone to **many**. I saw **three** just last week.
	In (b): *many= many baseball games*
	            three = three baseball games

★In general, *any* is used in negative sentences; *some* is used in affirmative sentences.

☐ **EXERCISE 16—ORAL:** What do the italicized expressions of quantity refer to?

1. There are 25 desks in room 204. How *many* are there in room 207?
   many = many desks

2. A: I'm hungry. Do we have any apples?
   B: I think there are *some* in the refrigerator.

3. A: I'm hungry. Do we have any bread?
   B: I think there is *some* in the refrigerator.

4. A: Do you have any envelopes?
   B: I think there are *some* in the upper right-hand drawer of my desk. If you can't find *any* there, look on the bookcase next to my desk.

5. A: Do you take sugar in your coffee?
   B: No, but I usually add *a little* to my tea.

6. A: Amy, do you have any lined paper for a three-ring notebook?
   B: How *much* do you need?
   A: I don't really need *a lot*.★ *A little* will do. I need just a few sheets.

7. A: There aren't any erasers for the chalkboard in this room.
   B: I can borrow *a couple* from the classroom next door.★

★Note: *of* is not included when **a lot** and **a couple** function alone as pronouns. **Of** is included if **a lot** or **a couple** is followed by a noun/pronoun:
        *Eric has **a lot of friends**. I have met **a lot of them**.*
        *I don't have many friends, but Eric has **a lot**. (no **of**)*

8. A: I need some blank floppy disks. Do you have *any*?

   B: Only *two*. How *many* do you need?

   A: Maybe *four* or *five*.

   B: Ask Janet. She usually keeps *a few* in the supply cabinet.

   A: Would Janet also know where to find some blank cassette tapes?

   B: I'm sure there are *some* in the supply cabinet. How *many* do you need?

   A: Just *a couple*.

8-8 NONSPECIFIC OBJECT PRONOUNS: *SOME, ANY,* AND *ONE*

(a) A: I need *some blank tapes*. (nonspecific) B: I don't have **any**, but Jack has **some**. (b) A: Where are *the blank tapes* that were on my desk? (specific) B: Rita has **them**.	Object pronouns for PLURAL COUNT NOUNS: nonspecific → **some** or **any** specific → **them** In (a): The speakers are not talking about specific tapes. In (b): The speakers are talking about specific tapes, the tapes SPEAKER A left on her desk.
(c) A: I need *a blank tape*. (nonspecific) B: I think you can get **one** from Jack. (d) A: Where's **the blank tape** that was on my desk? (specific) B: Rita has **it**.	Object pronouns for SINGULAR COUNT NOUNS: nonspecific → **one** specific → **it**, **her**, **him**
(e) A: Would you like *some coffee*? (nonspecific) B: No thanks, I just had **some**. I don't want **any** right now. (f) A: Your cup is empty. What happened to *your coffee*? (specific) B: I drank **it**.	Object pronouns for NONCOUNT COUNT NOUNS: nonspecific → **some** or **any** specific → **it**

□ **EXERCISE 17:** Complete the sentences by choosing the correct words in italics.

1. A: I need a red pen. Do you have   *one,* *it*   that I could borrow?

   B: No. See if Joy has   *one,* *it*.

2. A: Where's my grammar book? I need   *one, it*.

   B: I don't know. Did you lend   *one, it*   to someone? Ask Joy if she has   *one, it*.

3. A: I need a Korean–English dictionary. Where can I get   *one, it*?

   B: At the university bookstore.

4. A: I see you have a Korean–English dictionary. May I borrow   *one, it*?

   B: Sure. Here. I'm not using it right now.

5. A: Where can I get some new running shoes at a good price?

   B: You can probably find   *some, them*   at Sam's Sport Shop.

6. A: Where'd you get those new running shoes? They look comfortable.

   B: I found   *some, them*   at Sam's Sport Shop.

7. A: Where did you get this photograph of a tiger?

   B: I took   *one, it*   myself when I was in Nepal.

8. A: Have you ever seen a tiger in the wild?

   B: Yes. I saw   *one, it*   when I visited the national park in southern Nepal.

9. A: The cafeteria has a different hot soup every day.

   B: That sounds good on a cold day like today. I think I'll have   *some, it*   for lunch.

10. A: This soup is delicious! Is it homemade?

    B: Yes. I made   *some, it*   yesterday.

    A: Do you make soup often?

    B: I made   *some, it*   last week and the week before that, too. About once a week, I guess.

11. A: Did you look over your paper carefully for mistakes?

    B: Yes, but I didn't find   *any, them.*   Maybe you can find   *some, them.*

    A: Maybe you didn't make   *any, them.*

12. A: The mistakes on your paper are marked in red ink.

    B: I'll correct   *some, them*   right away.

13. A: Do you have a bicycle?

    B: Not yet, but I've been planning to get   *one, it*   for quite a while.

14. A: Did you ride your bicycle to school today?

    B: Yes. I parked   *one, it*   in the bike racks by the library.

All of the following sentences contain mistakes. Can you find the mistakes and correct them?

1. There are a lot of informations in that book.
2. The oil is a natural resource.
3. Lions are wild animal.
4. I was late because there were too many traffics.
5. I drank two waters.
6. Our teacher gives us too many homeworks.
7. Ann knows a lot of vocabularies.
8. I had a egg for breakfast.
9. There is many kind of trees in the world.
10. I'm studying the English.
11. I'm living in United State.
12. Only twelve student were in class yesterday.
13. I need some advices.
14. We all have a few problem in the life.

☐ **EXERCISE 19—WRITTEN:** Write about one (or both) of the following topics.

1. Look around your room, apartment, house. Tell your reader what you see. Indicate quantity (*some, a lot of, two, etc.*) and position (*in the corner, next to the bed, etc.*).
2. Think of someone you admire. Tell your reader why you admire this person.

☐ **EXERCISE 20—PREPOSITIONS:** Complete the sentences with prepositions. (See Appendix 1 for a list of preposition combinations.)

1. Shhh. I'm trying to concentrate _____ this math problem.
2. My opinion is different _____ yours. I disagree _____ you.
3. How did the bank robbers escape _____ jail?
4. What did you tell your parents _____ the dent in their new car? Did you tell them that you hit a parking meter when you were trying to parallel park?

5. The Jordans lost everything when their house burned down. I feel very sorry _____ them. I'm sorry _____ the fire.

6. We're hoping _____ good weather tomorrow so we can go sailing.

7. Did you hear _____ the earthquake in Turkey?

8. I heard _____ my sister last week. She wrote me a letter.

9. I spoke _____ Dr. Rice _____ my problem.

10. I'm not accustomed _____ cold weather.

11. When you divide 2 _____ 6, the answer is 3.

12. When you subtract 1 _____ 6, the answer is 5.

13. When you multiply 6 _____ 3, the answer is 18.*

14. When you add 6 _____ 4, the answer is 10.**

---

*Also possible: *multiply 6 **times** 3*.
Also possible: *add 6 **and 4*; *add 6 **plus** 4*.

APPENDIX *1*

Preposition Combinations

A *be* absent from
be accustomed to
    add *(this)* to *(that)*
be acquainted with
    admire *(someone)* for *(something)*
be afraid of
    agree with *(someone)* about/on *(something)*
be angry at/with
    apologize to *(someone)* for *(something)*
    apply to *(a place)* for *(something)*
    approve of
    argue with *(someone)* about *(something)*
    arrive at *(a building, a room)*
    arrive in *(a city, a country)*
    ask *(someone)* about *(something)*
    ask *(someone)* for *(something)*
be aware of

B *be* bad for
    believe in
    belong to
be bored with/by
    borrow *(something)* from *(someone)*

C *be* clear to
    compare *(this)* to/with *(that)*
    complain to *(someone)* about *(something)*
be composed of
    concentrate on
    consist of
be crazy about
be crowded with

D depend on/upon *(someone)* for *(something)*
be dependent on/upon *(someone)* for *(something)*
be devoted to

be different from
disagree with *(someone)* about *(something)*
be disappointed in
discuss *(something)* with *(someone)*
divide *(this)* into *(that)*
be divorced from
be done with
dream about/of

E *be* engaged to
be equal to
escape from
be excited about
excuse *(someone)* for *(something)*
be exhausted from

F *be* familiar with
be famous for
be finished with
forgive *(someone)* for *(something)*
be friendly to/with
be frightened of/by
be full of

G get rid of
be gone from
be good for
graduate from

H happen to
hear about/of
hear from
help *(someone)* with *(something)*
hide *(something)* from *(someone)*
hope for
be hungry for

I insist on
be interested in
introduce *(someone)* to *(someone)*
invite *(someone)* to *(something)*
be involved in

K *be* kind to
know about

L laugh at
listen to
look at
look for
look forward to

M *be* mad at
be made of
be married to
matter to
be the matter with
multiply *(this)* by *(that)*

N *be* nice to

O *be* opposed to

P pay for
be patient with
be pleased with
point at
be polite to
be prepared for
protect *(this)* from *(that)*
be proud of

Q *be* qualified for

R *be* ready for
be related to
rely on/upon
be responsible for

S *be* satisfied with
be scared of/by
search for
separate *(this)* from *(that)*
be similar to
be sorry about *(something)*
be sorry for *(someone)*
speak to/with *(someone)* about *(something)*
stare at
subtract *(this)* from *(that)*
be sure of

T take care of
talk to/with *(someone)* about *(something)*
tell *(someone)* about *(something)*
be terrified of/by
thank *(someone)* for *(something)*
be thirsty for
be tired from
be tired of
travel to

W wait for
wait on
be worried about

APPENDIX 2
Guide for Correcting Writing Errors

To the student: Each number represents an area of usage. Your teacher will use these numbers when marking your writing to indicate that you have made an error. Refer to this list to find out what kind of error you have made and then make the necessary correction.

① SINGULAR-PLURAL	① He have been here for six month. ① *He has been here for six months.*	
② WORD FORM	② I saw a beauty picture. *I saw a beautiful picture.*	
③ WORD CHOICE	③ She got on the taxi. *She got into the taxi.*	
④ VERB TENSE	④ He is here since June. *He has been here since June.*	
⑤+ ADD A WORD	⑤+ I want ∧ go to the zoo. *I want to go to the zoo.*	
⑤− OMIT A WORD	⑤− She entered to the university. *She entered the university.*	
⑥ WORD ORDER	⑥ I saw five times that movie. *I saw that movie five times.*	

⑦   INCOMPLETE SENTENCE

             ⑦

I went to bed. Because I was tired.

I went to bed because I was tired.

⑧   SPELLING

             ⑧

An accident occured.

An accident occurred.

⑨   PUNCTUATION

             ⑨

What did he say.

What did he say?

⑩   CAPITALIZATION

             ⑩

I am studying english.

I am studying English.

⑪   ARTICLE

             ⑪

I had a accident.

I had an accident.

⑫?   MEANING NOT CLEAR

             ⑫?

He borrowed some smoke.

(? ? ?)

⑬   RUN-ON SENTENCE*

             ⑬

My roommate was sleeping, we didn't
want to wake her up.

*My roommate was sleeping. We didn't
want to wake her up.*

---

*A run-on sentence occurs when two sentences are incorrectly connected: the end of one sentence and the beginning of the next sentence are not properly marked by a period and a capital letter. (See Chart 9-1.)

APPENDIX *3*
Basic Vocabulary List

The following list contains approximately 750 of the most commonly used words in English. *Fundamentals of English Grammar* assumes that students using this book are familiar with most of the words on the list.

The text uses many other words that are not on the list. Students may wish to add new vocabulary to this list.

The list is divided into two groups. Group One contains the most frequently used words. Group Two has other common words that the students will encounter in the text.

The words are listed according to their usual usage: NOUN, VERB, ADJECTIVE, or ADVERB.

BASIC VOCABULARY LIST: GROUP ONE

NOUNS (Group One)

accident	body	country
address	book	cup
afternoon	boy	date
age	box	daughter
air	bread	day
airplane	breakfast	desk
animal	brother	dictionary
apartment	building	dinner
arm	bus	direction
aunt	car	doctor
baby	chair	door
back	child	ear
bank	circle	earth
bed	city	end
beginning	class	evening
bicycle	clothes	eye
bird	coat	face
birthday	color*	family
boat	corner	father

*British English = colour

finger	movie	trouble
fire	music	uncle
fish	name	university
floor	night	vacation
food	noon	vegetable
foot	nose	vocabulary
friend	notebook	voice
front	number	wall
fruit	office	water
future	page	way
garden	parents	weather
glass	park	week
girl	part	wife
hair	party	window
half	past	woman
hand	pen	word
hat	pencil	work
head	people	world
holiday	pepper	year
home	person	zoo
homework	picture	
hospital	place	VERBS (Group One)
hotel	plant	
hour	present	answer
house	price	arrive
human being	problem	ask
husband	question	be
idea	reason	become
information	restaurant	begin
insect	rice	believe
job	river	break
juice	room	bring
land	roommate	build
language	school	buy
leg	shoe	call
letter	side	carry
library	sister	catch
life	sky	change
light	smile	close
line	son	come
lunch	sound	continue
man	street	cost
meat	student	cry
mile	sun	cut
minute	table	die
mistake	teacher	do
money	test	drink
month	thing	eat
moon	time	end
morning	town	enter
mother	tree	explain

		ADJECTIVES (Group One): Opposites

fall
feel
fight
find
finish
fix
get
give
go
grow
happen
have
hear
help
hold
hope
hurt
interest
keep
know
laugh
learn
leave
let
like
listen
live
look
lose
love
make
mean
meet
move
need
open
pay
plan
put
rain
read
ride
run
say
see
sell
send
sit
sleep
speak
stand

start
stay
stop
study
take
talk
teach
tell
think
touch
try
turn
use
wait
walk
want
wash
watch
work
write
understand
visit

ADJECTIVES (Group One): Opposites

bad	good
beautiful	ugly
big	little
big	small
cheap	expensive
clean	dirty
cold	hot
cool	warm
dangerous	safe
dark	light
deep	shallow
different	same
difficult	simple
dry	wet
early	late
east	west
empty	full
fast	slow
fat	thin
first	last
happy	sad
hard	easy
hard	soft
healthy	ill
healthy	sick
heavy	light
high	low
intelligent	stupid
large	little
large	small
left	right
long	short
messy	neat
modern	old-fashioned
narrow	wide
noisy	quiet
north	south
old	new
old	young
poor	rich
private	public
right	wrong
rough	smooth
short	tall
sour	sweet
strong	weak

ADVERBS (Group One)

again
ago
also
always
early
ever
fast
finally
generally
hard
here
immediately
late
maybe
never
now
occasionally
often
once
only
probably
quickly
really
slowly
sometimes
soon
suddenly
then
there
today
tomorrow
tonight
usually
very
yesterday

NOUNS (Group Two)

amount
army
art
bag
ball
beach
bill
blood
bottom
bridge
business
cat
ceiling
center*
century
chance
clock
cloud
coffee
college
computer
concert
condition
conversation
course
crowd
definition
difference
distance
dog
dress
earthquake
egg
enemy
example
experience
fact
fall/autumn
fear
field
flower
forest
form
furniture

game
gas(oline)**
gold
government
grass
group
hall
health
heart
heat
hill
history
hole
horse
hundred
ice
individual
industry
island
key
kitchen
knife
lake
law
list
luck
magazine
mail
market
math(ematics)
meaning
member
middle
midnight
milk
million
mind
mountain
mouth
nation
nature
neck
neighbor
newspaper

*British English = centre

**British English = petrol

noise
object
ocean
office
opinion
pain
paint
pair
pants
peace
period
picnic
pleasure
pocket
position
power
pronunciation
purpose
radio
result
ring
rule
salt
sandwich
science
sea
season
seat
shape
shirt
shoulder
situation
size
skin
snow
song
space
spelling
spring
stamp
star
store
subject
success
sugar
storm
suit
summer
tape recorder
tea

telephone
television
theater*
thousand
top
toy
train
trip
trouble
umbrella
universe
valley
value
war
wind
wing
winter
wood

VERBS (Group Two)

accept
act
add
agree
allow
appear
attempt
attend
beat
blow
borrow
burn
cause
choose
collect
complete
consider
contain
control
cook
cross
count
cover
dance
decide
disappear
discover
divide
doubt

draw
dream
dress
drive
drop
enjoy
exist
expect
fail
fill
fit
flow
fly
forget
guess
hang
hate
hit
hurry
improve
include
introduce
invite
join
kill
kiss
lead
lend
lift
marry
notice
obtain
offer
order
own
pass
permit
pick
point
pour
practice
prepare
promise
prove
provide
pull
push
reach
realize
receive

*British English = theatre (This spelling is also frequently used in American English.)

	ADJECTIVES (Group Two)	ADJECTIVE OPPOSITES	
recognize	absent	accurate	inaccurate
refuse	angry	certain	uncertain
remember	bald	clear	unclear
repeat	bright	comfortable	uncomfortable
reply	busy	common	uncommon
report	calm	complete	incomplete
require	dead	convenient	inconvenient
return	delicious	dependent	independent
rise	delightful	direct	indirect
save	dizzy	fair	unfair
search	essential	familiar	unfamiliar
seem	famous	happy	unhappy
separate	flat	healthy	unhealthy
serve	foolish	important	unimportant
share	foreign	interesting	uninteresting
shout	free	kind	unkind
show	fresh	lawful	unlawful
sign	funny	legal	illegal
sing	glad	logical	illogical
smell	great	necessary	unnecessary
spell	handsome	normal	abnormal
spend	humid	pleasant	unpleasant
spread	hungry	polite	impolite
succeed	lazy	possible	impossible
suggest	mad	proper	improper
supply	native	rational	irrational
surprise	nervous	real	unreal
surround	nice	regular	irregular
taste	pretty	responsible	irresponsible
tear	proud	sure	unsure
thank	rapid	true	untrue
tie	ripe	usual	unusual
travel	round	visible	invisible
wave	serious		
wear	sharp		
win	sorry		
wish	special		
wonder	strange		
worry	terrific		
	tough		
	unique		
	various		
	whole		
	wild		
	wise		
	wonderful		

ADVERBS (Group Two)

actually
afterward(s)
almost
already
anymore
anywhere
apparently
carefully
certainly
completely
constantly
downtown
easily
enough
entirely
especially
everywhere
extremely
fortunately
just
later
next
obviously
perhaps
quietly
rarely
regularly
seldom
seriously
somewhere
still
surely
together
too
well
yet

Differences between American English and British English

DIFFERENCES IN VOCABULARY

Speakers of American English and speakers of British English have no trouble understanding each other. The differences are small and do not interfere with communication. Some differences in the usage of common vocabulary are listed below.

American English	British English
attorney, lawyer	barrister, solicitor
bathrobe	dressing gown
can (of beans)	tin (of beans)
cookie	biscuit
corn	maize
diaper	nappy
driver's license	driving license
drug store	chemist's
elevator	lift
eraser	rubber
flashlight	torch
gas, gasoline	petrol
hood of a car	bonnet of a car
living room	sitting room, drawing room
raise in salary	rise in salary
rest room	public toilet, WC (water closet)
schedule	timetable
sidewalk	pavement, footpath
sink	basin
soccer	football
stove	cooker
truck	lorry, van
trunk of a car	boot of a car
be on vacation	be on holiday

DIFFERENCES IN SPELLING

American English and British English have a few differences in spelling. The list below shows the spelling differences in some common words.

American English spelling	British English spelling
theater, center, liter	theatre, centre, litre
color, honor, labor, odor	colour, honour, labour, odour
jewelry, traveler, woolen	jewellry, traveller, woollen
skillful, fulfill	skilful, fulfil
check	cheque (bank note)
curb	kerb
forever	for ever/forever
jail	gaol
program	programme
specialty	speciality
story	storey (of a building)
tire	tyre (of a car)
realize, analyze, apologize	realise, analyse, apologise
defense, offense, license	defence, offence, licence (n.)
burned	burnt (*or* burned)
dreamed	dreamt (*or* dreamed)
smelled	smelt (*or* smelled)
spelled	spelt (*or* spelled)
spoiled	spoilt (*or* spoiled)

Index—Volume A

A/an, 193, 206–207 *(Look on pages 193 and pages 206 through 207.)*	The numbers following the words listed in the index refer to page numbers in the main text.
Adjectives, vocabulary list, A8 *(Look in the back part of this book on the eighth page of the Appendixes.)*	Numbers in the index that are preceded by the letter "A" refer to pages in the Appendixes, which are found in the last part of the text. The main text ends on page 220, and the Appendixes immediately follow. Page 220 is followed by page A1.
Consonants, 8*fn*. *(Look at the footnote on page 8.)*	The letters "*fn*." mean "footnote." Footnotes are at the bottom of a page or the bottom of a chart.

A

A/an, 193, 206–207
Adjectives, defined, 72
 with *be*, 72
 nouns used as, 73
 possessive (*my, our*), 79
 vocabulary list, A8, A11
Adverb clauses:
 if-clauses, 53
 time clauses, 37, 53, 171
Adverbs:
 frequency, 6, 181
 midsentence, 181
 vocabulary list, A9, A12
A few/a little, 193
After, 37, 53, 71
Already, 181, 184
Always, etc. (midsentence adverbs), 181
And, 58
Another, 84, 88
Any, 217

Anymore, 184
Apostrophe, 77
Articles, 206–207
As soon as, 53
At as time preposition, 45
Auxiliary verbs:
 modal, 94
 in questions, 128
 in short responses to yes/no questions, 124
 in tag questions, 156

B

Be, 3
Be about to, 65
Before, 37, 53, 71
Be going to, 47
 vs. *will*, 51
British English, 45*fn*., 170*fn*., 173*fn*.
 spelling differences vs. American English, A14
 vocabulary differences vs. American English, A13

By, with reflexive pronoun (*by myself*), 81

C

Can, 94
  ability, 95
  permission, 98
  polite question, 100
Capitalization, 91
Clauses, main, 37 (SEE ALSO *If*-clauses, Time
  clauses)
Commas, with time clauses, 37
Consonants, 8*fn.*
Continuous verbs (SEE Progressive verbs)
Contractions of verbs:
  be, 3*fn.*
  had, 105
  have, 161
  with *not,* 3*fn.*
  with nouns, 49
  with question words, 134
  will, 49
  would, 119
Could, 94
  past ability, 95
  in polite questions, 100
  possibility, present/future, 100
Count/noncount nouns, 193–207
  noncount nouns, 193–195, 198, 202

D

Does, do, did:
  in negative, 3, 19
  in questions, 3, 19, 128
  in short answers, 12, 19
Do, as main verb in *what*-questions, 135

E

-Ed, 18, 21
  spelling, 29
Expressions of quantity, 216

F

A few, 193
For and **since** (time), 171, 176
Frequency adverbs, 6, 181
Future time, 47–65
  be going to and *will,* 47, 49, 51
  in *if*-clauses, 53
  immediate (*be about to*), 65
  using present tenses to express, 61–63
  in time clauses, 53

H

Habitual past, 42
Had:
  contracted with pronouns, 105
  in past perfect, 189

Had better, 94, 105
Hanged vs. **hung,** 169*fn.*
Have, auxiliary in present perfect, 161
  progressive vs. nonprogressive, 9*fn.*
  in questions, main verb, 126*fn.*
Have got to, 94, 108
Have to, 94, 108
  do not have to, 109
  form in questions, 129*fn.*
Helping verbs (SEE Auxiliary verbs, Negatives,
  Questions, and individual items)
How, 144, 152
  how about, 154
  how far, 146
  how long, 148
  how many/much, 199
  how often, 145

I

If-clauses, 53
Immediate future (*be about to*), 65
Imperative sentences, 114
In as time preposition, 45
Infinitives, form, 94
  with *it,* to express length of time, 147
  with modals, 94
Information questions, 128
-Ing, present participle, 21
  spelling, 29
  in tenses, 3, 32, 176–177
Intend, plan, hope, 64
Irregular noun plurals, 68–69, 77
Irregular verbs, list, 22
Its vs. **it's,** 79*fn.*
It takes (length of time), 147

L

Let's, 116
Lied vs. **lay, lain,** 31*fn.*
Like . . . better, 119
A little, 193

M

Main clause, 37
Many/much, 193
Mass noun, 194*fn.*
May, 94, 98, 100
Maybe vs. **may be,** 98
Measure, units of (*a cup of, a piece of*), 204
Midsentence adverbs, 181
Might, 94, 98
Modal auxiliaries, 94–113 (SEE ALSO individual
  items)
Must, 94
  logical conclusion, 112
  necessity, 108
Must not, 109, 112